The Revels Plays

COMPANION LIBRARY

E. A. J. HONIGMANN, J. R. MULRYNE
and R. L. SMALLWOOD
general editors

Shakespeare
and his contemporaries

Essays in comparison

THE REVELS PLAYS COMPANION LIBRARY

Shakespeare and his contemporaries

ESSAYS IN COMPARISON

edited by E. A. J. HONIGMANN

Manchester University Press

published by

MANCHESTER UNIVERSITY PRESS
Oxford Road, Manchester M13 9PL, UK
and 51 Washington Street, Dover,
New Hampshire 03820, USA

BRITISH LIBRARY CATALOGUING IN PUBLICATION DATA

Shakespeare and his contemporaries: essays in comparison.—(The Revels plays companion library)
  1. English drama—Early modern and Elizabethan, 1500–1600—History and criticism 2. English drama—17th century—History and criticism
  I. Honigmann, E. A. J. II. Series
  822'.3'09   PR651

LIBRARY OF CONGRESS CATALOGING IN PUBLICATION DATA

Shakespeare and his contemporaries. (The Revels plays companion library)
  Includes index.
  1. Shakespeare, William, 1564–1616—Criticism and interpretation—Addresses, essays, lectures. 2. English drama—17th century—History and criticism—Addresses, essays, lectures. 3. English drama—Early modern and Elizabethan, 1500–1600—History and criticism—Addresses, essays, lectures.
  I. Honigmann, E. A. J. II. Title. III. Series.
  PR2976.S335   11986   822.3'3   85–13581

ISBN 0–7190–1812–9 *cased only*

Photoset in Linotron Sabon by
Northern Phototypesetting Co., Bolton

Printed and bound in Great Britain by
Biddles Ltd, Guildford and King's Lynn

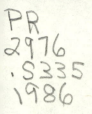
CONTENTS

LIST OF CONTRIBUTORS

BERNARD BECKERMAN

is Professor of Dramatic Literature at Columbia University in the City of New York. He is the author of *Shakespeare at the Globe* (1962) and *Dynamics of Drama* (1970), and has contributed articles in many books and journals.

NEVILLE DAVIES

is a Fellow of The Shakespeare Institute, University of Birmingham. His contributions to books and journals are mostly on English Literature of the sixteenth and seventeenth centuries. He is editing *Pericles* for the New Cambridge Shakespeare.

PHILIP EDWARDS

is Professor of English at the University of Liverpool. He has edited *The Spanish Tragedy* for The Revels Plays (1959), *Pericles* (New Penguin Shakespeare, 1976) and (with C. Gibson) Massinger's *Plays and Poems*. His other books include *Sir Walter Raleigh* (1953), *Shakespeare and the Confines of Art* (1968) and *Threshold of a Nation* (1979).

R. A. FOAKES

is Professor of English at the University of California, Los Angeles. He has edited *The Revenger's Tragedy* for The Revels Plays (1966), and also Shakespeare's *Henry VIII* (1957), *The Comedy of Errors* (1962), *Macbeth* and *Much Ado* (1968). His other books include *Coleridge on Shakespeare* (1971) and *Shakespeare, the Dark Comedies to the Last Plays* (1971).

GEORGE K. HUNTER

is Professor of English at Yale University. He has edited *The Malcontent* for The Revels Plays (1975), and also Shakespeare's *All's Well* (1959) and other Elizabethan plays. He is the author of *John Lyly: the humanist as courtier* (1962), *Dramatic Identities and Cultural Tradition: Studies in Shakespeare and His Contemporaries* (1978) and of a critical study of *Paradise Lost* (1980).

ALEXANDER LEGGATT

is Professor of English at University College, University of Toronto. His publications include *Citizen Comedy in the Age of Shakespeare* (1973), *Shakespeare's Comedy of Love* (1974) and *Ben Jonson: His Vision and his Art* (1981).

DIETER MEHL

is Professor of English at the University of Bonn. His books include *The Elizabethan Dumb Show* (1965) and *The Middle English Romances of the Thirteenth and Fourteenth Centuries* (1969).

EDWARD PECHTER

is Associate Professor of English at Concordia University, Montreal. He is the author of *Dryden's Classical Theory of Literature* (1975), and also teaches courses on Shakespeare and Elizabethan drama.

KURT TETZELI VON ROSADOR

is Professor of English at the Westfälische Wilhelms-Universität, Münster. He teaches courses on Dickens, the Victorian novel, Shakespeare, etc., and is the author of *Magie im elisabethanischen Drama* (1970).

GENERAL EDITORS' PREFACE

Since the late 1950s the series known as the Revels Plays has provided for students of the English Renaissance drama carefully edited texts of the major Elizabethan and Jacobean plays. The series now includes some of the best known drama of the period and has continued to expand, both within its original field and, to a lesser extent, beyond it, to include some important plays from the earlier Tudor and from the Restoration periods. The Revels Plays Companion Library is intended to further this expansion and to allow for new developments.

The aim of the Companion Library is to provide students of the Elizabethan and Jacobean drama with a fuller sense of its background and context. The series includes volumes of a variety of kinds. Small collections of plays, by a single author or concerned with a single theme and edited in accordance with the principles of textual modernisation of the Revels Plays, offer a wider range of drama than the main series can include. Together with editions of masques, pageants, and the non-dramatic work of Elizabethan and Jacobean playwrights, these volumes make it possible, within the over-all Revels enterprise, to examine the achievement of the major dramatists from a broader perspective. Other volumes provide a fuller context for the plays of the period by offering new collections of documentary evidence on Elizabethan theatrical conditions and on the performance of plays during that period and later. A third aim of the series is to offer modern critical interpretation, in the form of collections of essays or of monographs, of the dramatic achievement of the English Renaissance.

So wide a range of material necessarily precludes the standard format and uniform general editorial control which is possible in the original series of Revels Plays. To a considerable extent, therefore, treatment and approach is determined by the needs and intentions of individual volume editors. Within this rather ampler area, however, we hope that the Companion Library maintains the standards of scholarship which have for so long characterised the Revels Plays, and that it offers a useful enlargement of the work of the series in preserving, illuminating, and celebrating the drama of Elizabethan and Jacobean England.

E. A. J. Honigmann
J. R. Mulryne
R. L. Smallwood

PREFACE

The first volume of The Revels Plays, a series planned by Clifford Leech thirty years ago, appeared in 1958. More than three dozen volumes have now been published, and many more are in progress. The editors, who include specialists from many parts of the world, have given the series an international reputation: it is therefore fitting that, with the inauguration of The Revels Plays Companion Library, we should celebrate their achievement and dedicate this volume to Clifford Leech and David Hoeniger.

When I proposed this collection of essays to my colleagues, J. R. Mulryne and R. L. Smallwood, we decided that we would invite contributors to re-examine the technical inventiveness of 'Elizabethan' dramatists. And since we all judge the originality of the Elizabethans, consciously or unconsciously, by comparison with their greatest contemporary, we suggested that each contributor should select two plays that appear to be connected in their handling of technical problems:

> As far as possible the connection between each pair of plays will be different, but will point to the central concerns of the plays: we hope that it will bring a new focus to the discussion of familiar texts, making us ask more sharply 'how does it work?' and 'what's special here?' Contributors are invited to compare scenes or themes or speeches or characters, etc., that is, whatever seems most original in the two plays; we hope that, comparing two scenes, or the like, that are not normally explored together in depth, contributors will be able to explain (i) the uniqueness of one or both plays, and (ii) the technical inventiveness of the dramatists.

It must be stressed that contributors were encouraged to go where they were prompted by their own enthusiasm, and that their essays can therefore be read in any order. I have, however, so arranged them that those dealing with related matters may be read consecutively – for example, the essays by Philip Edwards and Neville Davies (on narrative technique), or those by Bernard Beckerman and Kurt Tetzeli von Rosador (both on *Doctor Faustus*). The thread that holds the book together is our conviction that the innovative skills of the Elizabethans – and of Shakespeare – were much more diversified than is commonly assumed.

I am responsible for the suggestion that we would ask for 'essays in comparison.' Too many of the books of recent years – including some of the very best – deal with either Shakespeare or his contemporaries, perhaps because it is thought that this is what teachers or publishers demand. Much can be gained by *not* dividing Shakespeare from the others, as the present volume amply demonstrates. Our method is to shake them up in cocktails, as it were, instead of consuming them in separate gulps. How many of those who have discussed the motivation of Iago, to give one example, have recognised the importance of Macilente? I would go even further than R. A.

Foakes, arguing that some of Jonson's explanatory comments on Macilente are so subtle, and so relevant to Iago's supposedly 'motiveless' malignity, that one can imagine them catching a rival dramatist's attention. Macilente, said Jonson, is a man 'who, wanting that place in the world's account which he thinks his merit capable of, falls into such an envious apoplexy, with which his judgement is so dazzled and distasted, that he grows violently impatient of any opposite happiness in another.' This could have prompted Iago's almost editorial self-explanation that

> If Cassio do remain,
> He hath a daily beauty in his life
> That makes me ugly. (V.1. 18–20)

Foakes, of course, is not merely concerned with characterisation but with the dramatist's strategies – his use of the satirist in drama, the satirist's function in guiding our perception of the heroic, and so on. One problem leads to another, for Shakespeare as for Jonson; their solutions differ, but we understand the dramatists' technical decisions much more clearly when we are made aware of rejected alternatives – when, in short, we follow 'The descent of Iago'. Edward Pechter writes just as rewardingly about Shakespeare and Jonson, their similar problems and their very different solutions; and – a sign of the times – he is particularly interested in the build-up of expectation, in 'what sits in our mind', at special moments in their plays.

All of the essays have been influenced, directly or indirectly, by recent criticism. Alexander Leggatt's seems to me to grow out of thirty years of increasing unease about E. M. W. Tillyard's Elizabethan 'world picture'. Tillyard, it is now widely felt, assumed too readily that Elizabethan dramatists accepted the official view of authority, kingship, etc., as expressed in the *Homily Against Disobedience and Wilful Rebellion*. In many of the history plays, countered Wilbur Sanders, the orthodox attitude to kingship 'is continually being caught in compromising postures' (*The Dramatist and the Received Idea*, 1968, p. 75); in *Richard III*, for instance, Shakespeare shows 'the total inadequacy of blind obedience to whatever head happens to be under the crown . . . No simple rule of thumb can extricate us from the intense confusion about the nature of kingship which is generated'. As Leggatt explains, *Richard II* and *Perkin Warbeck* were particularly important in sharpening the audience's awareness of this confusion; and the dramatists, again, found their own solutions to technical problems, which were not always dictated by history or by the homilies.

Whether or not attitudes to the supernatural were equally adjustable remains open to dispute. Some commentators have plucked out the heart of this mystery with surprising confidence, ruling – in the case of *Hamlet* – that the Ghost comes from purgatory or from hell, is good or not good. After so much critical sparring with Hamlet's Ghost it is refreshing to turn to *Macbeth* and *Doctor Faustus*, with Kurt Tetzeli von Rosador, and to be asked to consider not so much the credentials of the supernatural as the tragic hero's imagination, his 'power to fantasise', the other side of the coin – and, arguably, the one that the dramatists knew more about.

Although Dieter Mehl is perhaps more specifically concerned than any other contributor with the 'influence' of one play upon another, this turns out to be the launching-pad for a far-ranging exploration of the 'ideas' and social attitudes in *Measure for Measure* and *The Revenger's Tragedy*, two of the most provocative plays of the period. Mehl's approach may be compared with Terence Eagleton's *Shakespeare and Society* (1967) or Michael Long's *The Unnatural Scene* (1976), or, in a more general way, with *Ideas in Drama* (ed. J. Gassner, 1964). More recent studies include Jonathan Dollimore's *Radical Tragedy* (1984), and *Political Shakespeare* (ed. J. Dollimore and A. Sinfield, 1985).

Two of the essays examine, from different angles, the narrative techniques employed in drama. In both Peele's *Old Wives Tale* and Shakespeare's *The Winter's Tale*, as Philip Edwards explains, 'segments of a very tall story are snatched from the inadequacies of narration and realised before us in action. Each dramatist tells us in his own way that this realisation does not one whit alter the improbability of the fiction.' Neville Davies, comparing *Pericles* and *The Travailes of the Three English Brothers*, also deals with the dramatists' 'preoccupation with the nature of stage illusion' and, in addition, writes illuminatingly about each play's symmetrical design. This last point follows up recent studies of numerology in poetry, notably Alastair Fowler's *Triumphal Forms* (1970). The reader will find it interesting to compare these two essays with Joan Rees's *Shakespeare and the Story* (1978).

The structure of Elizabethan plays did not escape scholarly attention in the age of structuralism. In the middle years of this century a number of books debated Shakespeare's 'five act structure', most of them (e.g. T. W. Baldwin's) firmly grounded in Renaissance practice and theory, and untouched by the whiff of modernism. The discussion then entered new territory, in Richard Levin's *The Multiple Plot in English Renaissance Drama* (1971), Ruth Nevo's *Tragic Form in Shakespeare* (1972), Mark Rose's *Shakespearean Design* (1972). Bernard Beckerman's work on 'scene patterns' grew out of the feeling that new methods of analysis were needed, and, of course, was influenced by his experience as a producer. A recent book with a similar approach is James E. Hirsh's *The Structure of Shakespearean Scenes* (1981), while an earlier one, Emrys Jones's *Scenic Form in Shakespeare* (1970), must be mentioned as an important stimulus for all that followed.

George Hunter's essay on 'bourgeois comedy', again, should be seen as a contribution to an on-going debate. The study of 'genre' owes much to Northrop Frye's *Anatomy of Criticism* (1957), and to other ambitiously 'synthesising' books (e.g. Rosalie L. Colie, *The Resources of Kind: Genre Theory in the Renaissance*, 1973; Alastair Fowler, *Kinds of Literature: An Introduction to the Theory of Genres and Modes*, 1982). Books devoted to a single genre are no less valuable, and have become increasingly popular; and Hunter's essay will no doubt be compared with Brian Gibbons's *Jacobean City Comedy* (1968) and Alexander Leggatt's *Citizen Comedy in the Age of Shakespeare* (1976).

Readers should note that Shakespeare is quoted throughout from *The Complete Works*, edited by Peter Alexander (1951). Other dramatists, where no source is indicated, are quoted from The Revels Plays.

E. A. J. Honigmann

GEORGE K. HUNTER

Bourgeois comedy:
Shakespeare and Dekker

⋅❧◦❧⋅

Kenneth Muir has remarked[1] that there is no such thing as Shakespearian Tragedy, only Shakespearian tragedies. The temptation to apply the same argument to Shakespearian comedy probably ought, however, to be resisted.[2] Clearly a number of the comedies belong together to a Shakespearian type, distinguishable from other authors'; most obviously, the so-called 'romances' form a single characteristic group, but with extensive parallels in the earlier grouping of Shakespeare's "romantic comedies". Yet other comedies seem to stand alone, as one-off experiments: *Love's Labour's Lost* is such a comedy; *The Merry Wives of Windsor* is another. One way of dealing with the fact that some plays are quite different from others is, of course, to devise histories of external circumstances which will explain the fact. The particular difference that separates *The Merry Wives of Windsor* from other Shakespearian comedies is sometimes thought to be succinctly expressible by the judgement that it departs from the norm only by being not up to it, that it is simply feeble or uninvolved Shakespeare. This feebleness is then often explained by the story (antique but not authoritative) that the play was written in a great hurry because the Queen – or, in another version, the Lord Chamberlain – needed it in a hurry. The story fits a judgement of the play conducted on the basis of a normative idea of "Shakespearian comedy"; but it hardly supplies a vocabulary for talking about it as it is, not as it might have been, for talking about what is present in this largely prose play dealing largely with contemporary life among the bourgeoisie. The usual vocabulary of imagery, themes, characterisation, mythic structure, seems to be inadequate to describe this case, and most of us would therefore welcome an alternative mode of address, if we could find a pertinent one.

In this impasse one reads with relief the following words from the Introduction to H. J. Oliver's New Arden edition:

> *The Merry Wives [of Windsor]* is not primarily satiric comedy, nor is it . . . either comedy of intrigue or romantic comedy as Shakespeare had . . . and was to develop it . . . *The Merry Wives* is in essence citizen comedy, of the kind also made famous by Dekker in *The Shoemaker's Holiday*, by Chapman, Jonson, and Marston in their fine collaborative work *Eastward Ho* (and by Webster and Dekker in the rival comedies *Westward Ho* and *Northward Ho*) and later by Middleton, and by Massinger in, for example, *The City Madam*.   (lxvi).

1

This offers a tempting way out of the impasse – *The Merry Wives* may be difficult to deal with inside the standard vocabulary of Shakespearian criticism, but it can be seen usefully in relation to the other members of its non-Shakespearian genre. It would certainly be comforting to one's sense of history to find that Shakespeare actually belonged to the aesthetic movements of his own time, for the theatrical conditions within which he worked would seem to have left him little option. A generic study of *The Merry Wives of Windsor* might thus hope to set up a slender footbridge between the conception of Shakespeare *then* (just another public play-wright) and the conception *now* (a unique seer and artist).

A beginning on the construction of such a footbridge reveals, however, some basic difficulties. Professor Oliver's presentation of the "genre" of citizen comedy is clearly enough not intended to raise the issue of the concept's definition; he takes over the word as it is generally employed and so he shows us the problems inherent in the standard usage. As he presents it, 'citizen comedy' is a kind of generic box inside whose standard dimensions one can file a large number of similar items. What his examples show, however, is that what he is describing here is a process rather than a repeating set of recurring characteristics. More particularly he shows that the invocation of a genre involves a process of exploiting the tensions and potentials that arise from our rudimentary expectation of recurrent features. The idea of genre thus liberates us into the discovery of appropriate differences rather than similarities.

The plays Oliver mentions are mostly concentrated in the few years between *The Shoemaker's Holiday* of 1599[3] and *Eastward Ho* of 1605, but the range of their variant features is clearly part of a larger drift of fashion or expectation that runs at least from Greene's *Friar Bacon and Friar Bungay* of 1589 to Massinger's *The City Madam* of 1632. Shakespeare's *The Merry Wives of Windsor* (usually dated 1600) occupies the niche inside this pro-gression that is appropriate for its date. This means that it is closer to *The Shoemaker's Holiday* in form and feeling than it is to the other plays mentioned, though some foreshadowing of later routines is also obvious. I shall therefore concentrate on *The Shoemaker's Holiday* as the companion-piece for Shakespeare's bourgeois comedy.

Both Dekker's play and Shakespeare's can be seen to be drawing on a stereotype whose presence may be defined most easily as a pattern of audience expectations, which is animated or suppressed as the very different stories these plays are telling move in or out of magnetising distance from it. The stereotype situation runs something like this: a nobleman is in love with/hopes to seduce a woman of lower social status whose protector (father/husband) opposes the relationship and seeks (*a*) to uncover, (*b*) to cut off the connection. The story will end satisfactorily if the lover is successful or if the would-be seducer is punished. The stereotype is obvious-ly capable of being exploited in various ways and the alternatives chosen will show up the playwright's purposes. For example, how is the author to handle the contradictory expectations imposed on the nobleman: that he should show himself ethically noble and marry the humble maiden or that he should show himself socially responsible and refuse to marry beneath him? And how is the protector to be judged: as a guardian of virtue or a tyrannical possessor?

Plays written on this theme before 1599 show different ways of dealing with the issues raised. Lyly's *Campaspe* of 1584 presents Alexander the Great enthralled by Campaspe, his chaste and humble captive. The play's strongly stratified social system leads (as it must) to Alexander's rejection of romantic entanglement as a lower-class weakness and his return to war, the proper passion for kings. The play's situation raises inevitably, however, the possibility of seduction: the situation of conqueror in love with captive requires us to see this as a probability, so that the refusal to take an obvious step can then be made to mark an extraordinary nobility. Lyly allows Alexander to combine ethical and social nobility: he does not ravish his captive, but neither does he stoop to the impropriety of marriage. Though suffering the pangs of love he none the less hands over the role of lover to the socially more suitable Apelles and contents himself with the part of the benevolent protector.

In Robert Greene's *Friar Bacon and Friar Bungay* (1589) the stereotype role of the aristocratic seducer is again doubled with that of the responsible prince – this time Edward, the Prince of Wales (later Edward I). The possibility of seduction is even nearer the surface here than in *Campaspe*, Edward being less oblique and self-controlled in expression than Alexander. The victory of the seducer over the noble gentleman seems to be an inevitability in this play and is only avoided by external pressure on the plot. Edward finally achieves Alexander's magnanimity by handing the girl over to his rival, Lacy, Earl of Lincoln; but he does so only after suffering the demeaning pangs of homicidal jealousy. The extent to which the social barriers of *Campaspe* have collapsed shows also in the ease with which the gamekeeper's daughter, the Fair Maid of Fressingfield, becomes the fair Countess of Lincoln.

That Dekker had Greene's play in mind when he wrote *The Shoemaker's Holiday* is made probable by the reappearance of Lacy of Lincoln as the romantic juvenile lead. And once again Lacy appears as the honourable aristocrat who has no aim beyond matrimony. But Dekker collapses the barriers of social rank even further than Greene. Greene's Lacy demeans himself only in his marriage. Dekker's Lacy is demeaned by the actions he takes to secure his marriage; he takes on himself the dishonouring status of a London tradesman (and a foreigner to boot). Still further, he seems willing to evade the activities that are most integral to the whole idea of aristocracy – leading troops in a patriotic war against the King's enemies. It may be supposed that it is this extraordinary rejection of the basic social hierarchy that makes it inevitable for Dekker to develop the stereotype in terms of class tensions rather than the ethical self-consciousness of the aristocratic hero. For the match of noble Lacy and citizeness Rose creates opposition in this play not simply in aristocratic minds – here represented by the elder Lacy, the Earl of Lincoln – but also in the mind of Rose's father, Sir Roger Oatley, the current Lord Mayor of London. Rose is no peasant beauty found in idyllic space, though Dekker secures some effect of this kind by placing her in her father's country house ('Old Ford'), where stags run through the garden, rather than in his town house in Cornhill. Sir Roger is a substantial figure in the realm of money and the bourgeois authority it can procure. As the representative of an unsubordinated social class his opposition to the Lacy match is as cogent as that of the Earl.

This is how the play begins: we see two kinds of class prejudice facing one another, temporarily combined but basically incompatible. Each thinks of the other as a 'subtle fox' (lines 38 and 71),[4] and each despises the motives of the other. The Earl sees citizen blood as inherently base; the Lord Mayor sees the nobility as culpably idle and spendthrift. One might guess that the class barriers are an important issue of discussion here (as not in previous plays) because they are no longer to be seen as simple facts of nature but as penetrable or exploitable on several fronts. The tension inherent in the interchange of merchant and gentleman – the issue that was to become central in the citizen comedies of the next decade – is thus placed in the forefront of our attention when we read or see *The Shoemaker's Holiday*. But Dekker's play shows no more interest than does *The Merry Wives of Windsor* in making economic conflict the centre of the action. The tension between Lacy and his potential father-in-law is not developed along the lines of class difference. On one side of the conflict we are shown a member of the nobility (Lacy), a city dignitary (Eyre) and a band of city workmen (the shoemakers); on the other side we have a member of the nobility (the Earl of Lincoln), a city dignitary (Oatley) and a merchant (Hammon); and over both sides, but not certainly committed to either, stands the King. The distinction between these two sides is thus not made primarily in terms of social classes; but is indicated rather as an issue of vitality, emotional spontaneity being set against hidebound legalism, hope for the future set against fixation on the past. On both sides we meet money and rank; what distinguishes them is the use to which these are put. Lacy may begin the play in the posture of an aristocratic seducer; but his openness and self-sacrifice soon disqualify him, and the role soon passes to Hammon, the rich merchant that Oatley approves of, whose attempt to buy Jane from the shoemakers attracts all the opprobrium and rejection that normally attaches to the aristocratic seducer.

The Merry Wives of Windsor treats the stereotype in an interestingly similar though eventually very different manner. Once again the nobleman/seducer role is doubled, Fenton being allowed to take over the 'noble' side while Falstaff retains the darker role. Falstaff begins with an assumption that his knighthood gives him an immense advantage over the bourgeoisie. But the play hardly endorses him; the only person to believe in this advantage is Falstaff, imprisoned as he is in self-imagination. Not even the jealous Ford imagines that class is an issue. The merchant class of Windsor – or rather its bourgeoisie, for the mercantile activity of the citizens is never mentioned – lives in undisturbed possession of the town. Indeed this group can hardly be called a 'class' since there is no other 'class' to set against it. The seducing knight is not opposed here by a 'protector' and does not even meet the resistance of a clearly defined economic group (like Dekker's shoemakers). Falstaff is frustrated instead by the free (and quite unideological) distaste of the wives themselves, backed eventually by the whole community in all its aspects (masters, servants, children) bonded together as townsfolk against the interloper.

The stereotype is thus played in both Dekker and Shakespeare against a 'reality' which allows its force but denies its sufficient truth. The fantasy that the stereotype describes the real world appears in both plays but animates only those who are found insufficient by the practicalities of the action. Those who are most central to the ethos of society – the wives, Simon Eyre – instead of accepting stereotypes, play with them, and become free of them by setting one against another, setting timid wives, for example, against bold adventuresses. In *The Shoemaker's Holiday* we see class hierarchy set against the egalitarian spirit of the London tradesmen, but without allowing that there is any real contradiction between them, especially in the case of the oxymoronically named 'gentle craftsmen', the shoemakers. The image of working-class life in Simon Eyre's shoemaking household or domestic factory is powerfully convincing, yet it is notably evasive about the economic basis of its truth. We are never told if Eyre's establishment makes substantial profits; no one talks about such matters, only about sleeping and eating and drinking and wenching, and about work as such another natural man's activity. Both in Dekker's play and in the Deloney tale which provided its source the economic ascent of Simon Eyre from shoemaker to Lord Mayor of London may be seen to be giving a fair enough representation of general economic truth, but the particularities appear as a species of accident or as the result of a providence which chooses to give wealth to those who can best use it to enjoy themselves.

The manic figure of the entrepreneur was to become another stereotype of those citizen plays that dealt with the conflict between spendthrift gentlemen on the way down and money merchants on the way up; but Eyre's energy differs from that of Middleton's Quomodo or Massinger's Sir Giles Overreach in the basic point that it is not overtly directed towards money-making or status-seeking. That Simon Eyre is a hard-driving employer is scarcely in question; but his commitment to hard work seems to express the quality of his native masculine aggressiveness rather than the profit motive: he is presented as unusually passive when it comes to the crucial issue of the huge profit to be made from a contraband shipload. Neither Deloney nor Dekker allows Eyre to take the lead in devising this economic coup: in Deloney it is Mrs Eyre who schemes to grasp the financial opportunity; in Dekker it is Lacy disguised as Hans who arranges everything and sets up the deal. Thus Eyre himself can remain a bully swaggerer and natural man and yet at the same time provide a model of the self-made millionaire, ending the play as a one-man Ford Foundation yet never losing touch with his old proletarian self.

The central theatrical point about Eyre is not, in fact, his commitment to the economic world he belongs to but rather the reality represented by his tone of voice, the strongly physical linguistic medium by which Dekker creates Eyre's presence and which allows him to dominate the ethos of the play:[5]

> Where be these boys, these girls, these drabs, these scoundrels? They wallow in the fat brewis of my bounty, and lick up the crumbs of my table, yet will not rise to see my walks cleansed. Come out, you powder-beef queans! What, Nan! What, Madge Mumblecrust! Come out, you fat midriff-swag-belly whores, and sweep me these kennels, that the noisome stench offend not the nose of my neighbours. What, Firk, I say! What, Hodge! Open my shop windows! (IV. 1–9)

What Dekker has created for Eyre is an entirely believable version of the comic-aggressive dialect that marks self-conscious male camaraderie in all ages.[6] It need not surprise us that the energy of the workshop language is directed most forcefully against the women in the household, especially against Margery, Eyre's wife. When she tries to assert some authority over the journeymen she is swept out in a flood of comic vituperation:

> Peace, you bombast-cotton-candle quean, away, Queen of Clubs, quarrel not with me and my men, with me and my fine Firk. I'll firk you if you do . . . Away, rubbish. Vanish, melt, melt like kitchen-stuff . . . Avaunt, kitchen-stuff; rip, you brown-bread Tannikin, out of my sight! Move me not. Have not I ta'en you from selling tripes in Eastcheap, and set you in my shop, and made you hail-fellow with Simon Eyre the shoemaker? And now do you deal thus with my journeymen? . . . Rip, you chitterling, avaunt! Boy, bid the tapster of the Boar's Head fill me a dozen cans of beer for my journeymen. (VII. 42–78)

The unfortunate Margery can only confirm her status as a standing target by her inability to handle this male dialect, by her constant misunderstandings and unintentional obscenities.

Eyre's loudmouthed assertion of masculine solidarity cannot be taken simply as an expression of truths elsewhere validated in economic and social terms. The language exists as a cause rather than an effect. In the passage quoted above Eyre calls for a 'dozen cans of beer for my journeymen'; but he immediately makes sure that no more than two cans will be delivered. The capitalist realities between employer and employees are absorbed but not concealed by the assertions of good fellowship and sexual solidarity. And yet, at the same time, the language does create its own level of reality. 'Prince am I none, yet am I princely born' is one of Eyre's favourite mottoes. In Deloney's *The Gentle Craft*, whence Dekker took the phrase, this begins at least as a literally true statement in the romantic stories told of Christian martyrdoms and princesses who marry shoemakers. In Dekker's play the motto cannot describe any such literal situation, for the making of money by sharp capitalist enterprise is the only way to change status in this realistic economic world. But the pride in craft that allows one to feel like a prince – this is allowed in the play as a genuine truth of an alternative non-economic kind, and is not to be dismissed as simply a piece of romantic self-deception. At the end of the action Eyre plays host to an anonymous King whose outlook seems to be modelled on the royal populism of Shakespeare's Hal and whose brief appearance establishes him as the patron of vitality rather than of rank. Of course Eyre would not be allowed into the royal presence if he were not Lord Mayor of London, and the King, before he meets him, has to be assured that

> In all his actions that concern his state
> He is as serious, provident, and wise,
> As full of gravity amongst the grave,
> As any Mayor hath been these many years.   (XIX. 6–9)

In the light of these remarks the play's praise of vitality might seem to be essentially shallow and the claim that vitalism is a solvent of class conflict to be mere rhetoric. But the King, as it turns out, is not only delighted by Eyre's 'wonted merriment' as a holiday jest but also endorses it as a proper outlook on life; and in the end he acts to re-establish the cross-class marriage of Lacy and Rose in defiance of the objections by their well-placed relatives. Lacy has already shown himself to be a 'good fellow' and boon companion with his workmates of the gentle craft (who are therefore gentlemen in this somewhat mystical sense). The marriage is approved not really as a class victory but more as a statement that the right kind of outlook makes class irrelevant.

In the scenes that lead up to the final royal endorsement of marriage and holiday we are obviously meant to approve as we see the shoemakers tricking and punishing those who oppose trade solidarity, male vitality and its consequence in female fidelity. But the confrontations here have no consequence as a class issue. The King as soldier has a vested interest in virility, and even in civil life is prepared to allow it expression as part of the holiday spirit. And so the play ends with the facts of the economic case set aside while 'all good fellows . . . of what degree soever' join together in a creative celebration marked not only by feasting and marriage and the promise of begetting (Eyre at sixty-five promises to beget 'two or three young Lord Mayors ere I die') but by the creation of a communal future for the London tradesmen of Elizabeth's reign – the Shrove Tuesday prentices' saturnalia in fulfilment of Eyre's youthful promise to his fellow prentices, and the erection of the Leadenhall as a covered market. And after the celebration these 'good fellows' will further express their renewed vigour by taking up again their war against France. The renewal of the war has been seen as an expression of the limit that attaches to holiday;[7] but it may be regarded instead as a further abrogation of the economic laws, when virility and a 'good heart' will, once again, count for more than money or social success.

I have noted above that the central expression of the anti-economic strain in *The Shoemaker's Holiday* is found in Eyre's joyful linguistic freedom. This dialect is central however not so much because it expresses Eyre's personality as because it is the shared language of the very group whose oxymoronic self-image (as 'gentle craftsmen') defies all expected social and linguistic separations.[8] Dekker uses this dialect, in short, to hold together the divergent pressures that appear in the play. When Shakespeare produces a highly idiosyncratic language of this kind (as for Armado, for Pistol, for Dogberry, or (closest of all) for the Host in *Merry Wives*) he seldom, if ever, places the dialect at the centre of the play. In such cases as I have mentioned, and in any others I can think of, the abnormal language is offered as a reflection of an abnormal angle of vision. Shakespeare's fictional worlds tend to be expressed by a balance of idiosyncratic styles so that when these are combined together they give us the sense of a range of social and linguistic possibilities that no one speaker can control. Elsewhere I have written about this in terms of the contrast between Shakespeare and Ben Jonson.[9] Jonson tends to give us his linguistic eccentricities arranged round a clearly defined normative style; Shakespeare, on the other hand, tends to leave the centre undefined or at least very unassertive.

Presumably the normative characters in *The Merry Wives of Windsor* are the two title characters, Mistress Ford and Mistress Page. If we ask ourselves how these ladies speak we run at once into the difficulties in Shakespeare's method I have been describing. Their talk is so normal (or normative) that we do not notice that they are using any style at all. Their prose is fluent and witty, of course, but seems to have no interest in drawing attention to itself; it seems to exist to achieve, with maximum efficiency, the easy exchange of facts and viewpoints on which community depends. This, I take it, is the central issue. *The Merry Wives of Windsor* shows a group of small town citizens whose community life depends for its survival on restraint, on a refusal to be tempted or even unduly excited by the chance to break out and proclaim individuality. We begin the play by hearing of one such breach of decorum. Falstaff, the courtly interloper, has offended Shallow, and now Shallow breaks out into frenzied (and comic) self-justification. But that is not how things are expected to proceed in Windsor. Though the cast of the play is almost entirely made up of touchy and self-important persons,[10] as a group they operate to anticipate and defuse quarrels. The scene ends with a meal, marking the resolution of this particular difficulty; the ruffled feathers have been smoothed down and social life can go forward, at least for a time, as it is supposed to. 'Citizen comedy', in these terms, is a comedy where the challenge to urbanity is met by deliberate acts of reconciliation and compromise, not, as in *The Shoemaker's Holiday*, by aggressive and infectious joyfulness; it presents an implicit statement that such challenges can only proceed from a mistaken sense of values. Hence there is no need for a reconciling king at the end of *The Merry Wives of Windsor*. In Windsor's world the healing of wounds is mainly achieved by self-medication.

The role of Falstaff in *The Merry Wives of Windsor* (and even in the *Henry IV* plays) might seem to contradict what I have said about the centrality of the social norms in the former play. Falstaff is commonly thought of as being, no less than Simon Eyre in *The Shoemaker's Holiday*, the dominating figure of the play; certainly his is the role that the star actor always wants to perform. But a comparison between Falstaff and Simon Eyre shows, I believe, that similar effects are made by the two men under totally different circumstances. Simon Eyre is a figure whose vitality manifests itself by its capacity to take over the lives of all those around him. Falstaff, on the other hand, flourishes by separation rather than absorption. He places himself characteristically at an oblique angle to the world he contemplates and challenges – and would eventually destroy, if he was given the chance. Both men create the impression of being larger than life, and in both cases our sense of their outsize vitality is conveyed principally by their power of speech, by their exuberant eloquence. To carry the description of similarity even to this point is to see, however, where it breaks down. It follows from Falstaff's oblique stance that his eloquence, in the *Henry IV* plays, and even more in *The Merry Wives of Windsor*, is an eloquence of comic self presentation. He is nearly always posing himself (and his companions) in brilliantly exaggerated colours that depend for their full comic force on our perception that they are designed as manipulations – of himself, his stage audience, and of us:

> my lord . . . do you think me a swallow, an arrow or a bullet? Have I, in my poor and old motion, the expedition of thought? I have speeded hither with the very extremest inch of possibility; I have found'red nine score and odd posts; and here, travel tainted as I am, have, in my pure and immaculate valour, taken Sir John Colville of the Dale, a most furious knight and valorous enemy. But what of that? He saw me, and yielded; that I may justly say with the hook-nos'd fellow of Rome – I came, saw, and overcame. (*2HIV*, IV.iii. 30–41)

> Well, on went he for a search, and away went I for foul clothes. But mark the sequel, Master Brook – I suffered the pangs of three several deaths: first, an intolerable fright to be detected with a jealous rotten bell-wether; next, to be compass'd like a good bilbo in the circumference of a peck, hilt to point, heel to head; and then, to be stopp'd in, like a strong distillation, with stinking clothes

9

that fretted in their own grease. Think of that – a man of my kidney. Think of that
– that am as subject to heat as butter; a man of continual dissolution and thaw. It
was a miracle to scape suffocation.   (*Merry Wives*, III.v. 94–104)

In his book on Ben Jonson's prose Jonas Barish quotes Harry Levin's
startlingly reductive characterisation of Simon Eyre as 'Shylock masquerading as Falstaff'.[11] The sharpness of the epigram almost succeeds in conceal-
ing its critical inadequacy. But then we remember that Falstaff spends even
more time masquerading as·'Falstaff'. Far more obviously than Simon
Eyre's, his rhetoric is self-consciously a manipulative game, and the world it
creates is designed to live parasitically on another, more practical and more
'authentic'. And this is the case whether the parasite's 'host' is the big
political world of the Lancastrian usurpation and the civil anarchy it
generates or the enclosed domestic world of Windsor's jealous husbands
and merry wives. If Simon Eyre's rhetoric is manipulative (and sometimes,
as I have indicated, it is so) there is much less self-consciousness involved in
the game he plays. The problem that arises in Eyre's case – the confusion
between a surface of unrestrictive good fellowship and a manipulative
intention behind it – is presented by Dekker as more than a picture of
appearance and reality, for both aspects are shown to be real. The contradiction is rather inherent in the nature of capitalism's joyful energy. The world
created by Eyre's eloquence is not parasitic on another more stable and more
serious world, but is itself the encompassing representation of the life the
whole play endorses, in which the workaday pleasure of making things and
making money and acquiring status at the same time provide a natural basis
for the free-wheeling holiday spirit. Falstaff is commonly regarded, and with
justice, as a notable festive or holiday figure; but he always brings with him
some awareness of the life outside his grasp, where it is not holiday, where
responsibility cancels fun and where self-advancement must be bought by
someone else's loss. Indeed we may suppose that the same is true of Eyre's
London; but Dekker does not mention it, and Eyre speaks as if he could
prevent it.

In both plays the principal challenge to comic harmony derives from class
distinction; and harmony is restored in both cases by the discovery that such
distinctions are unimportant. Falstaff arrives in Windsor convinced of the
stereotype that is to animate so many later citizen comedies – that bourgeois
wives will be set a-flutter by the advances of a belted knight (even when he is
an outsize-belted knight), and that their wealth will be entirely at his
disposal: 'I will be cheaters to them both, and they shall be exchequers to
me; they shall be my East and West Indies, and I will trade to them both'
(I.iii. 66–69). The stereotype of the courtly seducer is offered here, I need not
stress, only as a grotesque mis-match. The wives never think of their sweaty
suitor as other than a figure of fun. Here there is none of the thrill of real
danger that attaches to the wifely frolics in *Westward Ho* or *Northward Ho*.

Even the jealous passions of Master Ford are seen to be comic rather than dangerous. His violent threats are shown always in the communal context of the Windsor ethos; and by now we know enough about that town's ways to anticipate that he will be gradually nudged back into the old consensus, where his wife is already waiting for him. It is characteristic of the play that when Ford searches the house for Falstaff he brings the town worthies with him and makes them the judges whether or not he deserves to be a member of their society:

> If I suspect without cause, why then make sport at me, then let me be your jest; I
> deserve it. (III.iii. 132–4)

And the town is not slow to respond as requested. No one believes in Ford's eccentric claims, and when he fails to find the intruder Master Page makes a basic point about the worth of communal understanding: 'Fie, fie, Master Ford, are you not asham'd? What spirit, what devil suggests this imagination? I would not ha' your distemper in this kind for the wealth of Windsor Castle' (III.iii. 190–3).

There is, it will be noticed, something of a secular commination and exorcism here. Master Ford is possessed by a devil, and only the shared effort of the townsfolk can bring him back to normality. But the rebuke having been made pro forma, all the rest is healing and support. It is the business of these men to think well of one another, and their lives together offer continuous rituals of mutual encouragement: 'Well, I promis'd you a dinner. Come, come, walk in the Park, I pray you pardon me' (III.iii. 199–200). So far Ford; and Page is not far behind in seconding him: 'I do invite you tomorrow morning to my house to breakfast; after, we'll a-birding together; I have a fine hawk for the bush. Shall it be so?' (III.iii. 205–7).

Bourgeois life in Windsor proceeds by cajoling and joking and watching out for one another's pettinesses and aggressions, bearing with such excesses but pushing them all the time back towards the middle position. Even when Master Ford has come to his senses and acknowledges the truth, he has to be trimmed of a tendency to a new excess. He praises his wife:

> Pardon me, wife. Henceforth do what thou wilt;
> I rather will suspect the sun with cold
> Than thee with wantonness. (IV.iv. 6–8)

Master Page thinks that this is as unbalanced as the old jealousy: 'No more./Be not as extreme in submission as in offence' (IV.iv. 10–12). Too sweet is judged to be as unsocial as too sour; the town likes nothing so much as a temperate mixture.

The busybody efficiency of the community in holding individual self-assertion within acceptable limits depends for its theatrical effectiveness on our accepting that bourgeois calm cannot be relied on unless it is fought for. As I have pointed out already, the citizens are characterised by their prevailing tendency to indignant self-justification: the characters of Dr Caius and Parson Evans are largely derived from this 'humour'. On the other hand, it is true that the wives are never really threatened by Falstaff. But when Mrs Quickly is sent to confirm Falstaff's picture of the lie of the land she does so in brilliant colours that must be intended to draw on some degree of audience expectation:

> You have brought her into such a canaries as 'tis wonderful. The best courtier of them all, when the court lay at Windsor, could never have brought her to such a canary. Yet there has been knights, and lords, and gentlemen, with their coaches; I warrant you, coach after coach, letter after letter, gift after gift; smelling so sweetly, all musk, and so rushling, I warrant you, in silk and gold; and in such alligant terms; and in such wine and sugar of the best and the fairest, that would have won any woman's heart; and, I warrant you, they could never get an eye-wink of her. (II.ii. 54–64)

It is clear enough that Mrs Quickly is gilding the lily; there is no temptation to suppose that the events she describes actually took place. Yet the basic diagram of relations between courtiers and townswomen is surely plausible enough. Mistress Ford and Mistress Page may be immune to Falstaff; but it does not follow that all wives are immune to all knights. And that seductive picture of 'courtliness' that Mrs Quickly paints is given real substance in the play by the parallel wooing of Mrs Page's daughter Anne by Master Fenton. Fenton, we are told, 'kept company with the wild Prince and Poins' and is therefore a kind of duplicate Falstaff. But Fenton really possesses the courtly qualities that Mrs Quickly has described: 'he capers, he dances, he has eyes of youth, he writes verses, he speaks holiday, he smells April and May' (III.ii. 57–9). And in this case the qualities really are seductive. Even in his motives Fenton is set up to make us remember the stereotype of the fortune-hunting courtly seducer. As he ingenuously tells his beloved:

> I will confess thy father's wealth
> Was the first motive that I woo'd thee, Anne;
> Yet, wooing thee, I found thee of more value
> Than stamps in gold, or sums in sealed bags;
> And 'tis the very riches of thyself
> That now I aim at. (III.iv. 13–18)

Master Page has many of the same objections as we have already heard from Oatley in *The Shoemaker's Holiday*: Fenton is too great in state, is bound to be a spendthrift, and will despise Anne once he has got hold of her money. But for all the similarities, the wooing process here is pushed in quite a different direction from that found in *The Shoemaker's Holiday*. Rose and Lacy are not shown seeking parental compromise; their aim is to make it impossible for the old folk to intervene. It is characteristic of *The Merry Wives* on the other hand that the lovers should seek first of all to find ways of securing acceptance:

> Gentle Master Fenton,
> Yet seek my father's love; still seek it, sir.
> If opportunity and humblest suit
> Cannot attain it, why then – hark you hither . . .   (III.iv. 18–21)

Intrigue is to be indulged in only when compromise has failed. But the intrigue that Fenton and Anne Page undertake is not like that in *The Shoemaker's Holiday*, only resolved by permitting one social group to defeat another. The grouping of suitors around Anne Page is too complex to allow any such simple social split. And Master Page's opposition to the match is shown, like Master Ford's jealousy, not as a representative attitude but only as a piece of individual folly. It is, of course, a folly to which a closed community is particularly liable. But that does not lead Shakespeare to defend it. Renewal by exogamy is, after all, one of the standard methods by which such communities can achieve change without breakdown. Fenton and Anne (it is she who forms the plot) intrigue as members of the community and indeed simply join in revels and disguisings already under way.

The final episode of *The Merry Wives of Windsor*, like the final episode of *The Shoemaker's Holiday*, catches up the representative values of the community in large-scale festive action. It is characteristic of the plays that Dekker places his final action at a central point in the commercial topography of the City and seals the communal effectiveness of Simon Eyre's actions by showing us the establishment of long-lasting city customs. Shakespeare, on the other hand, moves his final event out of the town and into the forest, and seems to be relying less on the local values known to his London audience than on folk custom and mythology. For Shakespeare, as often in folk-tales and fairy-tales, the town seems to exist only as a clearing in the universal forest, where shadows and unexplained noises are the sanctions most easily invoked to enforce social propriety and cohesion. Even Windsor Castle, and so by extension the whole process of royal authority, seems to be less a stronghold of power to validate and govern and more a centre of the royal magic which ensures separation of the rank and indiscriminate from the carefully nurtured, so directing fertility away from the bestial and towards its socially approved manifestation in wedlock. It is presumably not inappropriate to the social self-consciousness of this comedy that Elizabeth as Fairy Queen should be invoked as the patron-saint of housemaids:

> Elves, list your names; silence, you airy toys.
> Cricket, to Windsor chimneys shalt thou leap;
> Where fires thou find'st unrak'd, and hearths unswept,
> There pinch the maids as blue as bilberry;
> Our radiant Queen hates sluts and sluttery.   (V.v. 40–4)

The bourgeois standards of neat housekeeping are easily associated with the mysterious magic of the Order of the Garter, the cleaning of the hearth with the purifying of the knights' stalls in the Garter Chapel. The magic of true knighthood redeems the humility (or impropriety) of the Garter emblem ("*Honi soit qui mal y pense*"); likewise, the 'fairies' in Windsor Forest are the real fairies of romance, ensuring that pure knights are reverenced while lustful knights (like Falstaff) are punished; but they are also the town schoolchildren having fun with the town victim.

The sense of a magic enclosed in the humdrum details of domestic life is achieved in this play only at the cost of setting up the ordinary as the permanent. The effort of Windsor is to avoid social change; and though Anne Page does marry outside the expected limits, her marriage is justified entirely inside the expected terms – religion, obedience, duty, compatibility. Her father is given the same sentiment of acceptance as is given to the king in Dekker's play: 'In love, the heavens themselves do guide the state'. But in Shakespeare the sentiment marks the end of the individual grievance; Fenton (like Falstaff) is accepted into the bourgeois circle and invited back to cosy laughter 'by a country fire'. The stability of the play has been extended to include some new members; but the new members gain admission by agreeing to the old values. In *The Shoemaker's Holiday*, on the other hand, the pressure of social change is everywhere evident; the king's hospitality to the new standards of behaviour, though it must be obeyed, is by no means universally approved of. Eyre's blustering contempt for social niceties, coupled to his deep patriotism and loyalty, makes his individual entre-preneurial success seem less offensive; but behind the individual career of Eyre it is not hard to see, at least in outline, the careers of Sir Giles Mompesson or Sir Giles Overreach; and we are free to suppose that the social process enacted is likely to be more pervasive than the benevolent energy attributed to one individual.

These plays of the opening years of the seventeenth century certainly raise the economic issues that are commonly supposed to have dominated the whole century. But it is their privilege as plays to raise them not as descriptions of the world-as-is but as possibilities only, as attitudes found among many others, and with no special leverage derived from the world outside the play. Indeed both comedies find it easy to reject class antagonism as the fuel of social advance. Hardly seeming to notice the contradiction, they absorb the energies of nascent capitalism into an older value-pattern of patriotism, marriage and parochial loyalty. These, they seem to say, are the permanences on which comic resolution can rest securely. From a present-day point of view *The Shoemaker's Holiday* might seem to have accepted the logic of a class struggle so far that it is only by rhetorical legerdemain that it can evade the consequences. Characteristically, Shakespeare stays on safer ground. In *The Merry Wives of Windsor* he raises the stereotype of aristocratic exploitation only as a misreading of reality. He assures his London audience that small town pieties can be expected, if handled with tolerance and liberality, to see us through the challenge offered by class consciousness. It can hardly surprise us that Shakespeare, as soon as he had made his pile, retired to another such small town – Stratford-on-Avon.

NOTES

1 Kenneth Muir, 'Shakespeare and the tragic pattern' (British Academy Shakespeare Lecture for 1958); reprinted in *The Singularity of Shakespeare* (Liverpool 1977), p. 2.

2 Not resisted, however, by Kenneth Muir. See *Shakespeare's Comic Sequence* (Liverpool 1979), p. 1.

3 The dates attached to plays are those specified in the Harbage/Schoenbaum *Annals of English Drama* (1964).

4 My references are all keyed to the Revels edition, edited by Smallwood and Wells (Manchester 1979).

5 Joel H. Kaplan has an excellent treatment of this topic in 'Virtue's holiday: Thomas Dekker and Simon Eyre', *Renaissance Drama* N.S. 2 (1969), 103–22.

6 The power of the stereotype even today is made clear by its employment in two highly successful television series – the British 'Till Death Do Us Part' and its American imitation, 'All in the Family'. The comic rhetoric of Alf Garnett (and of his suburbanised counterpart, Archie Bunker) shows the same self-consciously masculine bid for control of a domestic environment and its extended social context by loudmouthed verbal inventiveness.

7 See the Smallwood and Wells edition, p. 43.

8 See Kaplan, 'Virtue's Holiday': 'Eyre . . . stands at the centre of a charmed circle, exercising within its boundaries a magical power to animate or rejuvenate through language alone. The story of *The Shoemakers' Holiday* is the expansion of this circle and the enlargement of Simon's influence' (p. 108).

9 See G. K. Hunter, 'Poem and context in *Love's Labour's Lost*', in *Shakespeare's Styles: Essays in Honour of Kenneth Muir* (1980), pp. 25–38.

10 O. J. Campbell has argued that the cast list derives from the gallery of eccentricity found in the *commedia dell'arte*. See 'The Italianate background of *The Merrry Wives of Windsor*', in *Essays and Studies in English and Comparative Literature by Members of the University of Michigan*, 7 (1932).

11 See Jonas Barish, *Ben Jonson and the Language of Prose Comedy* (1960), p. 282.

R. A. FOAKES

The descent of Iago: satire, Ben Jonson, and Shakespeare's *Othello*

It is the habit of criticism to attend to the chronology of Shakespeare's plays in a general way, usually in terms of convenient groupings, such as the dark comedies, the central tragedies, the late plays, and so on. In this way we can conveniently preserve a sense of the rough placing of any play within the canon, and not worry too much about its specific dating, which in the case of most plays remains to some extent speculative. However, to the extent that we take the dating of the plays for granted, and think of them in conventional groupings, we are liable to ignore details that are both surprising and significant. The dating of *Othello* is a case in point. It is discussed usually in the context of Shakespeare's other tragedies, or, as by Reuben Brower in *Hero and Saint* (1971) or Richard Ide in *Possessed with Greatness* (1980), in the context of heroic tragedy.[1] Observing its position in the chronology of Shakespeare's plays suggests a quite different context. It is generally assumed that the sequence of plays after *Hamlet* is as follows:

Troilus and Cressida about 1602
All's Well that Ends Well about 1602–3
Othello 1602–4
Measure for Measure 1604

In other words, *Othello* belongs chronologically with the dark comedies. If at first sight this seems absurd, it is at least worth inquiring what significance this might have for an understanding of the play.

The plays of this period, beginning with *Hamlet*, have in general, as is well known, a strong connection with new departures in satire and satirical comedy. Shakespeare's own company staged Ben Jonson's *Every Man in his Humour* (1598), *Every Man out of his Humour* at the end of 1599, and *Sejanus* in 1603, a play in which Shakespeare himself took a leading part, according to the 1616 Folio. He also played in the revised *Every Man in his Humour*, performed at court on 2 February 1605, and perhaps staged earlier in 1604. Shakespeare knew Jonson's plays very well, and could hardly have escaped the impact of Marston too, whose *The Malcontent* was stolen, expanded and performed at the Globe before its publication in 1604. Although Shakespeare is not mentioned among the leading actors who played *Every Man out of his Humour*, this play is particularly interesting because it was the first of Jonson's works to be published, in 1600, and because it constituted a kind of manifesto for comical satire, including 'more than hath been publikely Spoken or Acted'.

The formal verse satires of Hall, Marston, Guilpin and others, published about 1598–9, characteristically invented a satirical spokesman, and various personae for him to attack as examples of vice or folly. In the boldest, most powerful and most sensational satires of this period, those grouped in Marston's *The Scourge of Villainy* (1598), some sketches are developed at considerable length, like that of the braggart soldier in Satire VII, 100–38, or the lover 'Publius' in Satire VIII, who is dramatised in passionate and lascivious adoration of the hairpin he has obtained from his mistress. What she used to allay the itch, he worships in his own extravagant words:

> Touch it not (by the Lord sir) tis divine,
> It once beheld her radiant eyes bright shine:
> Her haire imbrac'd it, ô thrice happie prick
> That there was thron'd, and in her hair didst sticke. (VIII. 104–7)

The dramatisation of a lover's absurd posturings anticipates the gentler and more humorous treatment of the romantic lover in Jonson's Puntarvolo. Shakespeare also made use of such sketches, as in his creation of the affected courtier Osric, who is exhibited, as it were, by Hamlet (and Shakespeare) the satirist to our mockery in V. ii.

In *Every Man out of his Humour* Jonson went much further both in theory and in practice. Marston's satires range across a spectrum from Juvenalian anger (Satire II) through cynic snarling (Satire VII) and malcontent spleen (Satire X) to laughter at the affectations of 'humours' (Satire XI). If there is no obvious overall design in Marston's *Scourge of Villainy*, he evidently tried out a variety of masks through which to satirise in different ways the follies and abuses dramatised in the numerous figures sketched within the satires. He also saw himself as a fool to write rhymes to be read by fools, and in Satire VII, he includes himself in condemnation of human degeneracy, showing the satirist to be himself vulnerable to attack, and tarred with the vices found in others. Jonson perhaps was stimulated by Marston's Satire XI, with its display of humours or affectations, to develop a theory of humours as anchored in the whole bent of the personality (*Every Man out of his Humour*, Induction 102–14), and so relate it to the greater depth necessary for developing a character through the five acts of a play. But Shakespeare had already shown, in his creation of figures like Nym, Bardolph, Silence and Shallow, that he did not need theories to teach him how to make characters.

Of much more interest is Jonson's concern with the role of the satirist in drama. His chorus of Cordatus and Mitis serves to explain the 'humours' of the play, to link them with classical antecedents, as in the reference to Plautus preceding III.ix, and to justify the claim that the absurdities of the characters are true to life, while at the same time arguing that they reflect on no one in particular. So in II.iii Cordatus claims it is 'very easily possible' that there should be such a 'humorist' as Puntarvolo, who makes advances to his wife 'in geometrical proportions', and at the end of II.vi, he counters the fears of Mitis by insisting that no 'noble or true spirit in court' will be upset at the display of Fastidious Brisk, any more than a 'grave, wise citizen' will see himself in Deliro. Jonson was evidently giving much thought to what he was about, in seeking to take care of the more obvious objections to satire, and he was also concerned with a profounder issue, which begins to emerge in the very design of his play. The induction presents to us Asper, the righteous man so indignant with the 'impious world' that he must, with a Juvenalian fervour (echoing too Marston's second satire in *The Scourge of Villainy*, which begins 'I cannot hold, I cannot I indure . . . my rage must freely runne'), 'strip the ragged follies of the time', expose vice, and be applauded, he thinks, by 'Good men and virtuous spirits' for doing so. Mitis raises an important question by asking, in effect, what gives Asper the right to take this stand:

> *Mitis*   I should like it much better, if he were less confident.
> *Cordatus* Why, do you suspect his merit?
> *Mitis*   No, but I fear this will procure him much envy.

For the purposes of the action of the play Asper is transformed into 'an actor and a humorist', becoming Macilente, who retains the function of satirical spokesman, as when he comments on the miserly Sordido, 'Is't possible that such a spacious villain/Should live, and not be plagued' (I.iii. 62–3), but whose judgement is undermined by his envy of others. Sordido he can hate and despise, as he can Carlo Buffone, who takes no moral position, 'bites at all, but eats on those that feed him' (I.ii. 203), and turns everything to jest. Carlo Buffone takes pleasure in misleading others, and describes himself in his advice to Sogliardo on his purchase of a coat of arms: 'Love no man. Trust no man. Speak ill of no man to his face: nor well of any man behind his back . . . Spread yourself upon his bosom publicly whose heart you would eat in private' (III.iv. 92–5). Jonson's own distaste emerges in Macilente's comments on him, and in Puntarvolo's linking of Carlo Buffone with Marston as the 'grand scourge; or second untruss of the time' (II.iii. 84–5), the 'black-mouthed cur' (I.ii. 202) whose voice Jonson apparently heard in the violent satire of *The Scourge of Villainy*. If Carlo Buffone deserves in the end to be punished, when Puntarvolo beats him and seals his beard with wax to prevent him from speaking in Act V, should Macilente escape untouched? His envy grows in the course of the play, from his understandable railing on fortune for making the foolish Deliro rich rather than himself, into a readiness to abuse others behind their backs, as Carlo Buffone prompts him to be spiteful about Fastidious Brisk in IV.iv; and finally, in V.i, it turns into mere malice in his poisoning of Puntarvolo's dog.

The treatment of Macilente at the end, when he acts as a supervisor in the discomfiture of Deliro and Fastidious Brisk, leaves him untouched, and able to become Asper again without even changing his appearance. This device enables Jonson to create an interesting and vulnerable character, and at the same time turn him into the upright judge Asper, 'eager and constant in reproof', who could hardly be developed without appearing conceited, self-important and didactic. The problem Jonson was trying to solve might be formulated thus: how is the satirical spokesman in a play to obtain leverage over the other characters? The writer of satires may give more offence by claiming, or appearing to suggest, that he is above the rest of humanity, than by glancing at particular people. Marston probably did so, even though he included himself among the sinners in Satire VII. An Asper stalking through the entire play would be intolerable and dull. So it was a good dramatic instinct which led Jonson to develop Macilente as the 'true picture of spite' (V.viii. 70), more malicious than Carlo Buffone, and distinguished from him by his self-awareness, his asides and soliloquies, which enable him to function to some extent as a moral commentator on the action, and give him a degree of superiority.

The unprincipled jester or railer like Carlo Buffone (a type Shakespeare developed into Thersites, Parolles and Lucio) may expose folly and vice in others, but remains contemptible himself. Even so, he draws our sympathy to the extent that he releases our frustrations by his exposure of others (as in Thersites' mocking of Ajax and Achilles, revealing their conceit and stupidity), or by being simply the thing he is, a scapegoat whose humiliation (as in the case of Carlo Buffone, Parolles and Lucio) soaks up blame for the offences of others, of Macilente in *Every Man out of his Humour*, of Bertram in *All's Well*, of society in *Measure for Measure*. Macilente is more complex, the malcontent scholar who feels his merits go unrecognised, and who knows he should, but cannot, control his 'blood and his affection', and is burnt up with envy. To the extent that we respond to his intellectual superiority (he has the best verse speeches in the play), and to the sense of self-laceration and defeat in one who might be better, our attitude towards him will be ambivalent. We have to balance his acts of petty malice (as when, after accepting a new suit from Deliro, and an introduction at court from Fastidious Brisk, he abuses Brisk as a 'poor fantastic' to Deliro and Fallace) against the justice of his perceptions, for instance, about the court itself:

> Here, in the court! Be a man ne'er so vile
> In wit, in judgement, manners, or what else;
> If he can purchase but a silken cover,
> He shall not only pass, but pass regarded . . .　　　　　(III.ix. 9–12)

It was Macilente's envy of fools wearing suits of satin (II.v) that led him to accept Deliro's gift: he would be as rich and splendidly dressed as the courtier, but cannot help then turning on those who have been kind to him; so Fallace comments, 'Here's an unthankful spiteful wretch! The good gentleman vouchsafed to make him his companion, because my husband put him in a few rags, and now see how the unrude rascal backbites him!' (IV.ii. 42–5). Carlo Buffone, who 'will sooner lose his soul than a jest' (Prologue), backbites for pleasure, Macilente backbites because he is torn between desire for the possessions of others and scorn of their stupidity or self-deception; and though their motives are different, the effect is similar, so that at this point these two kinds of satirist begin to merge.

The satirist's world is dominated by vice and folly, and the darker it becomes, the harder it is to maintain a comic tone. The genial solutions of a Justice Clement will not do, and Jonson's rescue of Macilente is contrived too palpably. In *The Malcontent*, Marston refined on this concept of the discontented railer who despises others as inferior, but envies them for possessing what he lacks, by creating Malevole/Altofronto. In this play Marston brings his Asper, so to speak, into the play as the good Duke Altofronto, but at the cost of making his *alter ego* Malevole innocuous. Malevole, it is true, strikes malcontent attitudes:

> Only the malcontent, that 'gainst his fate
> Repines and quarrels – alas, he's goodman tell-clock!
> His sallow jaw-bones sink with wasting moan;
> Whilst others' beds are down, his pillow's stone. (III.ii. 11–14)

In fact, he appears to be far from wasting with moan, and enjoys himself hugely in the action by intriguing and stage-managing the 'Cross-capers, tricks' (IV.iv. 13) by which fools and knaves are exposed or discomfited. The play turns into a comedy in which the wounding of Ferneze in II.iv is the only harsh moment (since the audience for a short time supposes he is dead), the nearest thing to Macilente's act of malice in poisoning Puntarvolo's dog.

The satirist (Macilente–Carlo Buffone) figure finds a more familiar and comfortable home in tragedy, most successfully in those Italianate plays where he joins or serves vicious princes like Lussurioso, Brachiano or Ferdinand; in considering the plays of Tourneur and Webster as tragedies of intrigue and revenge, it is easy to overlook the connections of Vindice, Flamineo and Bosola with earlier satirical comedy. It is ironic that the satirist figure of works like *The Scourge of Villainy* should, through his envy of others, his own contamination by the vices he attacks, in fact pass most readily into the service of the dramatist as the tool-villain of revenge tragedy. In a dramatic action in an evil world, the satirist, forced to take part in events and no longer merely a commentator, can join that world to serve it, however grudgingly, and he is thus given dramatic complexity through the conflict in himself as he condemns evil in others while participating in it himself; alternatively, he can stand aloof like Asper, in which case he is neutralised and unable to act at all. This is a difficulty in Jonson's finely wrought *Sejanus* (acted 1603, and another play in which Shakespeare took a part); in it Silius, Arruntius, Sabinus and Lepidus all function to greater or lesser degree as satiric commentators on the action, but can do nothing against Sejanus, Macro or Tiberius; they are reduced to following the counsel of Agrippina: 'stand upright, / And though you do not act, yet suffer nobly' (IV.i. 73–4). The strongest action possible, indeed the only one, is suicide, as staged in the presence of the Senate by Silius in III.i. In this world only Fortune, the goddess Sejanus prays to and denounces in V.iii, may one day bring a change, and the virtuous remain ineffectual.

The interest in the uses of satirical figures in drama at this time was shared by Shakespeare, as is evident in his dark comedies, and I would now like to consider what bearing this has on *Othello*, the tragedy that in time of composition most closely relates to *Troilus and Cressida* and *All's Well*. Here another factor has to be taken into account, namely Shakespeare's concern in this period with love, war and the heroic. This is implicit in *Hamlet*, in the hero's idealisation of his father as Mars or Hercules, his envy of Fortinbras, whose name embodies the heroic attribute of *fortezza*, and perhaps his rejection of Ophelia. It becomes explicit in *Troilus and Cressida*, which turns on the clash between love or lust and war, and in *All's Well*,[2] which shows Bertram as anxious to be off to the wars and dedicate himself to Mars, even as Helena abandons Diana for Venus (II.iii. 74–5) and chooses him for a husband. The play's action develops the tension between love and war, and allows neither to emerge unscathed. Perhaps Shakespeare had in mind the Renaissance vision of the hero as the godlike man, figured in Aeneas or Hector, and of love as an appopriate theme for an heroic poem, as proposed by Tasso, and exemplified in *The Faerie Queene*; perhaps too he conceived Othello, as Reuben Brower argues,[3] in relation to the conventional image of the tragic epic hero, but if so, he also had the experience of satire in mind, as an actor in *Every Man in his Humour*, *Sejanus* and perhaps other plays staged by his company. A familiar figure in the satires of the period is Marston's 'heroic' warrior, the 'dread Mavortian' of Satire VII, Tubrio, who swaggers with his experience of fighting in the low countries, but is wasted 'In sensuall lust and midnight bezeling' (VII.124). He reappears in Satire VIII as analogous to Hercules enslaved to Omphale, the warrior given over to the couch of Venus. Satire opened up new perspectives on the heroic by questioning the possibility of true nobility or moral authority and including all in the degenerate condition of man. Macilente envies the lover and the soldier, though one, Puntarvolo, is foolish, the other, Shift, a contemptible swaggerer. The most devastating critique of the heroic is perhaps Jonson's in *Sejanus*, in which no possibility of heroic action is left, merely stoic resignation in the face of corruption so pervasive and powerful that no individual can challenge it.

In its emphasis on love and war, *Othello* belongs thematically as well as chronologically with the early dark comedies. In them the image of the heroic warrior is challenged not only through the satirical commentary of Thersites and the empty flourishes of Parolles, but also in the presentation of Achilles as a 'dread Mavortian' corrupted by his lust for Polyxena and his 'masculine whore' Patroclus, and even of Hector as seduced by a desire for personal gain in pursuing to the death a Greek warrior solely for the sake of his rich armour. Here war itself is depicted less in terms of heroism and the 'chivalry' Hector speaks of, than as a matter of savage butchery and revenge. *Othello* at first sight offers a complete contrast in the figure of the noble, dignified Moor as he appears in Act I, stopping a brawl in the streets, or addressing the Senate in Venice; yet I think it has to be seen not as a kind of answer to *Troilus and Cressida*, an altogether different view, but rather as a play arising out of the same questioning that prompted both *Troilus and Cressida* and *All's Well that Ends Well*.

Othello's 'occupation' as a warrior has to be taken on trust, since he is not involved in any fight in the action of the play; what fighting there is involves Cassio, set on by Roderigo on the watch in Cyprus in II.3, and again attacked by Roderigo at Iago's behest in V.i. Othello's image as a warrior is created entirely in language, and the play has to do not with heroism, but again with the hero ensnared by love, and laid open to corruption. Implicitly, too, the critique of war itself is continued. Othello as warrior exists as a public figure: through much of the play he is seen with followers in the streets, at a meeting of the Senate, arriving with a crowd at Cyprus, or dealing with public business. By engineering the cashiering of Cassio, Iago is enabled to convert a business occasion into a personal conversation with Othello in III.iii, and so prompt his jealousy. Othello has no *private* scene alone with Desdemona until the murder in Act V, other than the scene in which he treats her as a whore in a brothel, converting this meeting in imagination into a less than private occasion, with Emilia transformed into a bawd listening at the door. The 'Pride, pomp and circumstance of glorious war' belong in the world of public affairs, and in so far as this is Othello's world, it leaves him without a private role.

Indeed, it might be claimed that Othello's habituation to 'glorious war' has incapacitated him for domesticity. Othello is not merely an alien black man of mysterious origin in the white world of Venice, and thus alone, but solitary too as a fighter who from his 'boyish days' (I.iii. 132) has known nothing but war and adventure in the perpetual motion of the professional soldier. He has no intimates,[4] until he is seduced into a kind of intimacy with Iago, as he has no small-talk, lacking 'those soft parts of conversation / That chamberers have' (III.iii. 268–9). His natural mode of utterance, as has often been noted, is magniloquent, a grand Othello music, 'spirit-stirring', like the drums of war, and splendid for calming a riot, ordering the watch and maintaining command. It also serves to tell the story of his life, which bowls over Desdemona, wooed not in a growing intimacy, but incidentally by a

narrative of adventures in war. Summoned to Cyprus immediately after
their marriage, and sailing in different ships, Othello and Desdemona are
reunited there in the one moment they have of sheer delight in their union:
here they embrace and kiss, the one occasion when the text requires them to
do so before the murder scene in Act V. Even their greeting in Cyprus,
however, is not a moment of simple intimacy. Othello may lose himself
momentarily in the absolute content of finding her safe on land after the
storm at sea (he uses the word 'content' three times in the space of a dozen or
so lines), but he seems to be aware, too, as an audience must be, that he is
speaking in public. His ship arrives after the others, and he makes his entry
late in II.i, when there are assembled on stage a group of Cypriots (Montano,
three Gentlemen and a Messenger), Cassio, Desdemona, Iago, Roderigo,
Emilia and attendants. Othello enters with more 'attendants' on to a
crowded stage, containing nine or ten actors with speaking parts, and an
unspecified number of extras. This scene of his reunion with Desdemona is
thus at the same time the biggest crowd scene, the largest public gathering, in
the play, after the scene of the Senate meeting in I.iii. Othello greets her

> O my fair warrior!
> Des.   My dear Othello!
> Oth.   It gives me wonder great as my content
> To see you here before me. O my soul's joy!
> If after every tempest come such calms,
> May the winds blow till they have waken'd death,
> And let the labouring bark climb hills of seas
> Olympus-high, and duck again as low
> As hell's from heaven. If it were now to die
> 'Twere now to be most happy; for I fear
> My soul hath her content so absolute
> That not another comfort like to this
> Succeeds in unknown fate.   (II.i. 180–91)

The last few lines, combining a sense of foreboding that their union cannot
last, with the hint of sexual consummation in 'to die', might be thought of as
privately addressed to Desdemona, but the whole speech is at the same time
a grand public declaration heard by all, as indeed the first part of the speech
could be addressed to the assembled company.

Othello is very much a public figure inhabiting the public arenas of war
and leadership. He is cut off from the play's private relationships, and the
scenes in which characters engage in small talk, convey a sense of being
relaxed, are those between Iago and Roderigo, the drinking scene (II.iii) in
Cyprus, the scenes between Cassio and Desdemona, Cassio and Bianca,
Desdemona and Emilia. Othello is marked off by his distance from these
others, by the extent to which he exists, is defined by, his role or 'occupation', his public standing as a great warrior. The play establishes a gap
between public and private worlds, between war and peace. Brabantio's

private anguish, his 'particular grief' (I.iii. 55), seems a small matter in relation to the threatened war with the Turks, but the arrival of Othello in Cyprus, where he greets Desdemona ironically as 'my fair warrior', coincides with the end of hostilities, as he announces 'our wars are done' (II.i. 200). Othello's 'occupation' is already gone, and Iago exploits his inability to adapt to peace, to domestic life, by filling his unoccupied mind with hideous suspicions.

Thus although it is important to start from the 'recognition of greatness' which Brower sees as essential in a reading of *Othello*, the 'heroic simplicity' of the 'noble moor',[5] the play is far from being an exposition of the noble perplexed by the diabolic. It seems to me rather that it stands in contrast to *Sejanus*: Jonson's play postulates a world almost wholly vicious, in which the few upright characters become innocuous Aspers, just satirical commentators reduced to impotence; *Othello* postulates a world almost wholly good, in which the one malicious character fulfils what is implicit in Macilente's 'true envy', which, followed out in its implications, leads not back to Asper as in *Every Man out of his Humour*, but on to Iago. In *Othello* the pursuit of Desdemona by Roderigo is made to seem absurd, as his folly is exploited by Iago, rather than wicked, and his ambitions would evaporate but for Iago's cunning exploitation. Also the peccadilloes of Cassio in getting drunk and later tangling with Bianca are not generally seen as blemishes on 'the daily beauty in his life' (V.i. 19) shown in his loyalty to Othello. In the world of the play, Roderigo and Cassio are not identified as corrupt, except in so far as Iago exploits their weaknesses.

In formal satires the poet or persona speaking takes on a role as presenter of characters displayed usually in savage caricature, such as Marston's Luxurio:

> looke who yon doth goe,
> The meager lecher, lewd *Luxurio*,
> Tis he that hath the sole monopolie
> By patent, of the suburb lecherie . . . (*The Scourge of Villainy*, Satire XI, 136ff.)

Macilente begins in similar vein in the early scenes in *Every Man out of his Humour*, as in his commentary on Carlo Buffone at the end of I.ii, or his railing, something in the fashion of Marston's cynic satirist in *The Scourge of Villainy*, Satire VII or Sordido:

> Is't possible that such a spacious villain
> Should live, and not be plagued? Or lies he hid
> Within the wrinkled bosom of the world,
> Where heaven cannot see him? . . .   (I.iii. 62ff.)

Here Sordido is on stage reading a 'paper' brought to him by a 'Hind', so that Macilente becomes a kind of presenter, and not merely a commentator (in I.ii he comments on Carlo Buffone directly to the audience when alone on the stage). As the play goes on, he inevitably becomes more involved, until in the final act Macilente functions as a kind of stage-manager within the action in putting characters out of their humours; he 'begins to be more sociable on a sudden', as Mitis points out at the end of Act IV, but only so as to 'unleash the torrent of his envy' in directly manipulating affairs. He thrives on the misery of others, 'O, how I do feed upon this now and fat myself! Here were a couple unexpectedly dishumoured: well, by this time, I hope, Sir Puntarvolo and his dog are both out of humour to travel . . .' (V.iii. 67–70); and in the final scene he gloatingly exposes and comments on the folly of Deliro, Fallace and Fastidious Brisk. The satirist as presenter of character-sketches and commentator on them naturally develops further dimensions in drama as a manipulator and intriguer exploiting the weaknesses of others in order to expose them for what they are.

Apart from his act of 'pure envy' in poisoning Puntarvolo's dog, this is where Macilente stops, and the resolution of the play is comic, allowing his conversion into Asper. In *Othello*, Iago may be seen as a Macilente developed into a tragic villain. A. C. Bradley thought of him as an artist, a figure into whom Shakespeare had put a good deal of himself, and Iago has sometimes been seen as expressing the malign as opposed to the benign artist (Prospero).[6] The connection with Macilente helps to show why this view is overpitched; Iago is not a creator, but a manipulator of what comes his way, an opportunist staging events he in the end cannot control, as they gather a momentum he does not foresee, when, for example, Othello demands that he kill Cassio (III.iii. 476–7), and when Roderigo and Iago together fail in the attempt. Like the satirist, Iago sees the worst in the other characters, and reveals their vices and follies; but he goes beyond the satirist in using this exposure to destroy others.

The play begins with the disturbance he stages in the streets of Venice, using Roderigo to work on the racial prejudice of Brabantio. Roderigo is the least plausible character in the play,[7] a 'silly gentleman' (I.iii. 307), doting so much on Desdemona that he does what Iago incites him to, however outrageous or dangerous, a prosaic fool who can nevertheless rise to the dignity of a powerful blank verse, as at I.i. 120ff., that seems out of keeping with his general nature. Roderigo serves, of course, as a necessary tool for Iago in bringing about the dismissal of Cassio from his office as lieutenant, and in the attempted murder of Cassio later; but we never hear the 'further reason' (IV.ii. 242) that might have persuaded Roderigo to such an implausible deed. Shakespeare is casual about this, and safely so, since our attention is so gripped by the main action involving Othello and Desdemona at this stage of the play that we do not stop to question why Roderigo turns murderer. The main function of Roderigo is not here, but in his role as interlocutor, setting off Iago's commentary, as a cynical and envious satirist, on the world. The long dialogues between the two, each dominated by Iago, at I.i. 1–80, I.iii. 301–79 and II.i. 211–79 establish Iago's perspective on everyone. Like Marston's cynic, all Iago sees is changed for the worse, as in his version of Othello's promotion of the 'counter-caster' Cassio, or is explicable in terms of appetite and sensuality; love becomes a 'sect or scion' of lust, and Desdemona's courtesy to Cassio in II.i is an 'index and obscure prologue to the history of lust and foul thoughts'.

The second and third of these prose exchanges end with the exit of Roderigo, while Iago remains on stage to deliver a verse soliloquy. In these two scenes, and also at II.iii. 325–51 and III.iii. 325–33, Iago, as it were, takes the audience into his confidence in speeches that are not, as Hamlet's soliloquies may be understood, largely expressions of an inner debate, overheard by an audience thinking of him as meditating on his own, but rather a means of subtly involving the audience in Iago's schemes and rationalisings. To describe them as direct self-explanation is not sufficient; through the first part of the play, Othello and Desdemona are seen only as public figures in crowd scenes, but we see Iago not merely in private talk with Roderigo, but with the audience too. His motives for 'practising' on Othello and Cassio may be unconvincing, but cannot be simply discounted as motive-hunting.[8] There is just enough plausibility in them to make them faintly disturbing; he has been passed over in promotion; Moors were assumed to be 'lusty', and the rumour that Othello had seduced Emilia might seem not incredible; Cassio is a 'proper man', and his courtesies to Desdemona and Emilia could easily be misinterpreted (indeed his kissing of Emilia and taking Desdemona 'by the palm', II.i. 166, parallel exactly the behaviour of Polixenes and Hermione which provokes such violent jealousy in Leontes). The point is that even if we reject Iago's particular imputations as unreliable or false, nevertheless, because of his privileged placing in the play's development, which allows him to confide in the audience directly, he involves us, draws us into a kind of complicity in his designs.[9]

His particular imputations may seem merely gross, but we have to assent in some measure to the general assumptions implicit in what he says, the assumptions of the envious satirist who sees folly and vice everywhere:

> And what's he then that says I play the villain?
> When this advice is free I give and honest,
> Probal to thinking, and indeed the course
> To win the Moor again? (II.iii. 325–8)

Iago's advice is indeed good, but it forces us to see Cassio and Othello in the satirist's perspective. Cassio's easy manner towards Desdemona and Emilia in II.i shows that he is 'handsome, young and hath all those requisites in him that folly and green minds look after' (II.i. 245–7); his loose behaviour with Bianca further warrants this perspective, suggesting how easily his constant suit to Desdemona to recover his office may be misconstrued, but in his self-concern Cassio is blind, and his contemptuous, self-satisfied dismissal of Bianca as a 'customer', a 'fitchew', in Othello's hearing, provides for him the final 'proof' of Desdemona's infidelity. Othello, of course, mistakenly supposes Cassio is speaking of his wife, but Cassio is to blame too, as Iago makes us see 'how he laugh'd at his vice' (IV.i. 167). Iago also exposes Othello, making us realise the gap in age, sympathy and manners between him and Desdemona (II.i. 218ff.), that incongruity which lends credence to the insinuation that the marriage cannot last, and is reinforced by general beliefs about the nature of moors, as lustful barbarians, 'changeable in their wills' (I.iii. 348). Iago generalises the prejudices that distort Brabantio's attitude to his daughter's marriage.

He also makes us see Desdemona in the context of general assumptions about women, jokingly brought out in the satirical verses with which he responds to Desdemona's invitation to praise her in II.i; his 'praise' of women is summed up in the lines

> There's none so foul, and foolish thereunto,
> But does foul pranks which fair and wise ones do. (II.i.141–2)

It is appropriate for the envious satirist to praise 'the worst best', as Desdemona says, to turn virtue itself into pitch, because he is 'nothing if not critical' (II.i. 119). Iago reiterates to Roderigo later in this scene, what he had argued in I.iii, that Desdemona is no different from other women, and as likely to do 'foul pranks' when she comes to her senses about the unnatural marriage she had made, and begins to 'heave the gorge' at it. If he misjudges Desdemona's virtue, he nevertheless forces us to be sharply aware of the incongruity in her marriage, the gap in colour, age, sympathy and temperament between her and her husband; he also makes us realise the potential fragility of a love that was excited by Othello 'bragging and telling her fantastical lies' (II.i. 221), an exaggeration too near the truth for comfort.

In these ways Iago's general satirical perspective in the first half of the play, his emphasis on the worst tendencies in human behaviour, shapes our view of the action. It is sometimes said that Iago poisons or infects Othello's mind, as evidenced by Othello's adoption of the animal imagery characteristic of Iago's perception of the beast in man; but Iago only draws out what is already there. He is at least partly right about Cassio, who laughs too easily about his 'vice', and about Othello, whose ability to transform in imagination Desdemona into a prostitute in V.ii confirms the possibility that the 'noble Moor' is at the same time an old black ram, whose world of experience includes a familiarity with the ways of brothels. The terrifying nature of the tragedy in this play is that it is brought about not by Iago, who can only trigger events, or take advantage of accidents, but by the potential for vice and folly that lies in everyone, and is held in check by a delicate balance that is easily disturbed. Iago knows this: 'If the balance of our lives had not one scale of reason to poise another of sensuality, the blood and baseness of our natures would conduct us to most preposterous conclusions' (I.iii. 329–34).

All he has to do is create a disturbance, and let the 'baseness of our natures' work.

If Desdemona escapes the general imputation of baseness, she is shown as headstrong and foolish, and again a partial truth emerges in Iago's perspective. The gap between her and Othello is also one of knowledge, and her innocence in part is mere ignorance, which leaves her amazed when he shows anger to her:

> My lord is not my lord; nor should I know him
> Were he in favour as in humour alter'd.   (III.iv. 125–6)

It is her failing that she does not 'know' him, and knows the world so little that she does not conceive how her advocacy of Cassio might be misinterpreted. So Iago's perception that 'her delicate tenderness will find itself abus'd' (II.i. 232) proves correct. Iago as the envious satirist serves as a presenter of the early stages of the action in *Othello*. He is the figure closest to the audience, who uses Roderigo as a foil in elaborating a general satirical vision of human beings as given to folly and vice, and makes us see Othello, Desdemona and Cassio in this context. In his soliloquies he talks us into a kind of complicity with him, to the extent that we are forced to allow his perceptiveness, to concede there may be some truth in what he says, and to enjoy his wit. As he 'knows' Othello, Desdemona and Cassio better than they know themselves, so we 'know' him better than we do the other characters, and because of this, his perspective provides a controlling view up to the third act. The key to the play is not the extent to which Othello is infected by Iago, but the extent to which we in the audience are seduced by him. For it is impossible to reject altogether the satirist's vision, even while we recognise and are horrified by the malice of a Macilente or Iago, since his truths come too near home. The power of Iago is rooted in the context of satirical poetry and drama which fed Shakespeare's imagination during the years that brought *Othello* to completion. A recognition of the connections between *Othello*, the dark comedies which belong chronologically with it, and the satire of the period, especially as represented in Jonson's *Every Man out of his Humour*, provides a context which helps us both to understand Shakespeare's method in constructing his play, and to explain why Iago is such a disturbing figure.[10]

NOTES

1 The main traditions in the criticism of the play are outlined by Robert Hapgood in the section on *Othello* in *Shakespeare: Select Bibliographical Guides*, ed. Stanley Wells (Oxford, 1973), pp. 159–70. If there has been a change in the years since then, it is best seen in a decline of interest in such questions as whether the Moor is noble or ignoble, and in a greater willingness to recognise what Hapgood called a 'full spectrum of interpretative possibilities' (p. 162), as marked, for instance, in the five different interpretations of Iago sketched in Stanley Hyman's *Iago* (1970). The most recent full-length study of the play, however, Janet

Adamson's *Othello as tragedy: some problems of judgment and feeling* (Cambridge, 1981), returns to old issues, dismissing Hyman's book (p. 65), and treating the characters as autonomous, 'real', and capable of being objectively analysed. She takes us back to the self-dramatising Othello of F. R. Leavis, and for her 'Iago's . . . is an essentially simple mind, for whom life is correspondingly simple' (p. 76). A subtler interpretation of Iago's 'secret motives' is offered in E. A. J. Honigmann's *Shakespeare: Seven Tragedies* (London, 1976), pp. 78–88. I have tried to show how varying, even contradictory interpretations of Othello and Iago are suggested by the text in 'Iago, Othello and the critics', printed in *De Shakespeare à T. S. Eliot: Mélanges offerts à Henri Fluchère* (Paris, 1976), pp. 61–72.

2 In *The Comic Matrix of Shakespeare's Tragedies* (Princeton, 1979), Susan Snyder relates *Othello* to Shakespeare's romantic comedies, and sees in the action up to the reunion of Othello and Desdemona in Cyprus 'a perfect comic structure in miniature' (p. 74). This seems a strained argument to me. Much more germane to the general issue here, though not concerned with *Othello* itself, is Lee Bliss's *The World's Perspective: John Webster and the Jacobean Drama* (New Brunswick, New Jersey, 1983), especially Chapter 1, 'The art of distance 1: Tragicomedy', pp. 13–53.

3 In R. A. Brower, *Hero and Saint*, (Oxford, 1971) p. 28ff.

4 It is true that Desdemona says Othello has known Cassio a long time (III.iii. 11), and speaks of him as many a time coming 'awooing' with Othello (III.iii. 71), but we are never *shown* this closeness between the two men, and what Desdemona says is contradicted by Cassio's complete ignorance about Othello's marriage in I.ii, and about the identity of his bride at I.ii. 52.

5 Brower, *Hero and Saint*, pp. 2, 28.

6 A. C. Bradley, *Shakespearean Tragedy* (London, 1904), pp. 225–32; see also Honigmann, *Shakespeare: Seven Tragedies*, pp. 78–82, and Hyman, *Iago*, pp. 61–100.

7 Roderigo is reminiscent of the comic butts satirised in plays like *Every Man out of his Humour* (see p. 18 above), but is presented without an assurance (as in the case of Jonson's Puntarvolo), that such extreme behaviour is 'very easily possible'. In his quirky, brilliant essay on *Othello*, published in *The Dyer's Hand* (London, 1963), and reprinted in *Shakespeare Othello: A Casebook*, edited John Wain (London, 1971), pp. 199–223, W. H. Auden remarked on the implausibility of Roderigo, and noted that 'when we first see Iago and Roderigo together, the situation is like that in a Ben Jonson comedy' (p. 204).

8 I am thinking, of course, of Coleridge's famous formulation, 'the motive-hunting of motiveless malignity' (*Coleridge's Shakespearean Criticism*, ed. T. M. Raysor, 2 vols., London, 1930, I. 49).

9 Moralistic critics tend to see Iago as a character designed 'precisely to arouse our intolerant loathing' (Adamson, *Othello as Tragedy*, p. 86); Nevill Coghill went so far as to claim that the function of Iago's soliloquies is to distance him from the audience and 'create hatred for him' (*Shakespeare's Professional Skills*, Cambridge, 1964, p. 147). Such approaches are insensitive to the way Shakespeare makes Iago fascinating through what Giorgio Melchiori calls 'The rhetoric of character construction in *Othello*', *Shakespeare Survey*, 34 (1981), 61–72. (He notes that Iago speaks 32.58 per cent of the words in the play, and Othello 24.09 per cent; however, Iago's proportion of the dialogue is even higher in Acts I and II, in which he has 43 per cent of the lines, about 606 out of 1398, and provides the dominant voice and perspective on the action.) See also Marvin

Rosenberg's study of the acting tradition relating to Iago, which led him to observe, in *The Masks of Othello* (Berkeley and Los Angeles, 1961), p. 183, that 'The drives we have learned to recognise as a badge of humanity are twisted and magnified in Iago, but we cannot disown them'.

10 *Every Man out of his Humour* is quoted from *The Complete Plays of Ben Jonson*, ed. G. A. Wilkes, Vol. I (Oxford, 1981).

BERNARD BECKERMAN

Scene patterns in
Doctor Faustus and *Richard III*

❧◦❧

The present essay is a further stage in my continuing examination of binary structures in drama. Elsewhere I have argued that the performance mode primarily though not exclusively employs unitary and binary organisation of agents.[1] Unitary arrangement prevails in celebratory presentations such as pageants which stress direct display. By contrast, binary arrangements underlie dramatic illusion which depends on dialectical interchange. Both types of presentations transcend the limitations of solo or duo performers by various patterns of redundancy, the unitary arrangement by replication of figures in a potentially infinite progression (crowds of identical marchers in a parade, for instance) and the binary arrangement by more subtle reiteration of secondary actors and actions. In the following essay, I compare Marlowe's and Shakespeare's use of binary structures in *Doctor Faustus* and *Richard III*.

One of the most graphic illustrations of alternate binary structures occurs in *Doctor Faustus* at the point when Lucifer appears to Faustus to warn him against calling on Christ.[2] He is accompanied by Belzebub. In the A-text (713–36) it is Lucifer and Lucifer alone who admonishes Faustus. In the B-text (654–76) the lines – they are virtually identical in the A- and B-texts – are divided between Lucifer and Belzebub. Neither text at this point is demonstrably more correct than the other. If the B-text suggests a more dynamic assault on Faustus by the companion princes of hell, the A-text by concentrating on Lucifer emphasises his primacy. The only other time Belzebub speaks (B 1904–5) is in the prelude to the final scene, a prelude that appears only in the B-text. The differences between the two texts cannot be attributed, as familiar argument would have it, to the assumption that the A-text represents a contracted version for provincial touring, since both texts require the same number of actors. Instead, the change is more likely to be dramaturgical, lending credence to the thesis that the appearance of Lucifer and Belzebub in Act II, scene ii of the B-text is an addition. But whatever the textual hypothesis, the alternate versions of Belzebub's role in the A- and B-texts exemplify two ways of maintaining a binary structure.

In these two versions we have what I term a complex duet, that is, a duet which includes more than two people on stage simultaneously, yet still functions as a simple dialectical exchange. But while both versions are complex duets, one is an arrangement using mutes while the other is an arrangement based on redundancy. In the A-text although Mephistophilis and Belzebub appear with Lucifer, they are silent throughout Lucifer's warning to Faustus. Following his chastisement of Faustus, Lucifer summons the Seven Deadly Sins to entertain the mortal (A 737 ff./B 677 ff.). He then becomes mute as Faustus queries each sin serially. This mode of concentrating action by confining dialogue to two figures while rendering others silent is a common one. It is a simple if obvious way of assuring dramatic focus.

A companion means for producing a complex duet is what I call redundancy. We find a cogent illustration of redundancy in the B-text, especially when we compare it to the A-text. In the A-text Lucifer's warning to Faustus comes forth as a single, continuous speech:

> we come to tell thee thou dost injure us,
> Thou talkst of Christ, contrary to thy promise
> Thou shouldst not thinke of God,
> thinke of the devil,/ And of his dame too.   (720–3)

In the B-text this same speech is divided as follows:

> *Belz.*   We are come to tell thee thou dost injure us.
> *Lucif.* Thou calst on Christ contrary to thy promise.
> *Belz.*   Thou should'st not thinke on God.
> *Lucif.* Thinke on the devill.
> *Belz.*   And his dam to.   (660–4)

As we see in the B-text, the lines allotted to Belzebub retain the same force and objective as they had when spoken by Lucifer alone. They merely take on an acceleration of energy as one voice reinforces another. This version demonstrates the principle of redundant action: the sharing of a dramatic line of action by two or more characters. Adroit manipulation of redundancy makes for subtle effects, as we will see. But in its fundamental structure, it allows a dramatist to multiply his stimuli without undermining theatrical cohesion.

Throughout *Doctor Faustus* Marlowe employs a crude form of redundancy, most obviously in those scenes with scholars. Initially, in the second scene of the play he introduces two scholars to question Wagner, later he utilises 'two or three'.[3] But whether two or three, the scholars function as joint agents, at one time querying Wagner about Faustus, at another admiring Helen of Troy. Their designation as Scholar 1 or Scholar 2, that is, as mere ciphers, only emphasises their redundancy. Yet even when redundant figures are given names such as Valdes and Cornelius, they continue to be reflections of each other.

The doubling or tripling of subordinate figures has purpose, of course. We need only imagine what the scene between Faustus and his friends Valdes and Cornelius would be like if only one of them were to appear. Valdes – if it were he – would have to carry the lines of both. By being alone, he would become a more significant person, and thus an alternate to Faustus. By introducing two friends, Marlowe dilutes their personalities, as Shakespeare did with Rosencrantz and Guildenstern later on, and thus avoids challenging or diffusing Faustus' centrality. In this way redundancy supplies dynamic variety as well as softening of focus.

On the other hand, mutes also perform vital functions in the unfolding of a play. They can dress a scene. They play the negative role of not drawing attention away from the focal action. In a more positive manner, they can also throw a scene into relief, as when Lucifer and his companion princes silently watch Faustus enjoy the show of sins. As in the matter of redundancy so in the matter of mutes, comparison of the A- and B-texts is illuminating.

Three times in scenes involving Lucifer there are differences between the A- and B-texts centring on mutes. One I have cited already, where we find a shift from the mute to the speaking Belzebub. Earlier Lucifer makes a mute entrance into the B-text (I.iii). Where the A-text has Faustus enter 'to conjure' (A 242), the B-text stage direction reads: 'Thunder. Enter Lucifer and 4 devils, Faustus to them / with this speech' (225–6). Supposedly in this version Lucifer mutely observes Faustus' conjuration and the raising of Mephistophilis. It is significant that the two texts for scene iii are virtually identical except for Lucifer's presence, and one might well argue that Lucifer's intrusion is a spectacular addition to the original scene. Aside from the textual questions, however, it is obvious that the introduction of Lucifer as a silent witness to Faustus' conjuration transforms the action, and makes what in the A-text is a daring but unpredictable attempt into a foredoomed and fatal act in the B-text.

A similar piece of business occurs in Act V, scene ii of the B-text (1894 ff.). Lucifer, Mephistophilis and Belzebub enter to the sound of thunder in order to see Faustus' end. After twenty lines announcing their arrival and relishing the coming fall of Faustus, they become mute observers of all the succeeding events. Which type of scene is dramatically more powerful, Faustus under the eyes of the devils or, as he is in the A-text, Faustus isolated on the large bare stage of the Elizabethan playhouse, is a matter of critical judgement. What does seem apparent, however, is that the introduction of Lucifer and the four devils in I.iii, the change of Belzebub from a mute to a redundant figure, and the final appearance of Lucifer, Mephistophilis and Belzebub were all efforts to expand the spectacular effects of the play. Unlike the procession-type sequences of devils with apparel (A 525/B 471) or of the Seven Deadly Sins (A 737/B 677), these spectacular additions were incomplete since they change the frame of the action, sometimes awkwardly, without touching the central action.

Although *Faustus* for the most part adheres to simple binary forms, it does include trios. Besides simple duets where Faustus and Mephistophilis are the only characters on stage and complex duets such as I have described, there are a number of scenes in which the presentation transcends binary form. The most obvious examples of triadic arrangement occur in the play-within-the-play sequences: Lucifer presenting the Seven Deadly Sins to Faustus, Faustus presenting Alexander and his paramour to the Emperor Charles V and later presenting Helen to the scholars. In all these scenes we have a show that is the centre of attention, a presenter, and an on-stage audience. Most dramatic in this type of triadic arrangement is the section in the A-text when the Old Man re-enters to hear Faustus eulogising Helen (A 1363).

Framed action of the play-within-the-play is a popular way to modify binary form. In the scenes just cited, Marlowe observes a simplicity by keeping the presenters relatively mute, allowing only slight action among the figures on stage. But if Marlowe does not exploit the trio of the play-within-the-play in the way Kyd did and Shakespeare was to do, he does employ it subtly in the psychomachean struggle of the Good and Bad Angels for Faustus' soul. In each of these brief segments the Angels exert contradictory pulls upon Faustus while Faustus, largely without signifying their presence, reacts to the inner thoughts they articulate. In one sense, this articulation of alternate thoughts can be considered a confrontation between two forces since the Angels represent opposite sides of Faustus' moral person. But since the pattern of action has the angels addressing Faustus rather than each other, Faustus acts as an inverted magistrate who passes judgement on himself. This trial scheme is traditionally triadic.

Throughout the play Marlowe repeats the same basic arrangement for the angels. Each alternately addresses Faustus while Faustus speaks to himself or, in the final encounter, to God. Only in the last appearance of the Angels, when first the Good and then the Evil Angel show Faustus what he has lost and won, is there variation from the repeated pattern. Yet if the earlier sequences are similar, they are not identical. Marlowe skillfully modulates the pattern of exchange to convey an interesting development.

In their first appearance the Good and Bad Angels each speak four lines in a formal exposition of their natures (A 101–09 / B 96–104).[4] In their second appearance, each speaks three lines, but this time divided irregularly with the Good Angel speaking one line first. Faustus answers. The Good Angel then speaks another line, only to be countered by two lines from the Bad Angel. Each then speaks a third line, the second of which by the Evil Angel is echoed by Faustus (A 452–61 / B 402–10). Here then Marlowe entwines the Angels and Faustus in a somewhat more intricate trio although the basic alignments remain the same.[5]

The Angels next appear in A scene vi, 640–6 / B II.ii. 581–7. Faustus's response grows while the Angels' lines serve as more pointed stimuli. As usual, the Good Angel speaks first, one line. The Evil Angel responds with a balanced phrase, so that the Good Angel's assurance 'God wil pitty thee' (A 641) is answered by the Evil Angel's cry, 'God cannot pity thee'. This time, however, it is Faustus who takes up the challenge.

> who buzzeth in mine eares I am a spirite?
> Be I a divel, yet God may pitty me,
> I God wil pitty me, if I repent. (A 643–5)

Since here it is Faustus who speaks what hitherto the Good Angel was wont to say, it is fitting that only the Evil Angel close the segment with 'I but Faustus never shal repent' (646). Significant here is the way the triadic arrangement shifts to a binary exchange where the Good Angel and Faustus grow in accord opposed to the Evil Angel.

Shortly thereafter the Angels return to a balanced exchange, but an exchange whose sequence is reversed (A 706–10 / B 647–51). In this fourth segment it is the Evil Spirit who speaks first, echoing Faustus' cry, 'Ist not too late?' 'Too late', retorts the Evil one while the Good Angel pleads, 'Never too late, if Faustus can repent' (B-text: 'will repent'). The Angels each speak another line; this time though the Good Angel is the last one to speak.

That sign of moral strength produces the most poignant appeal on Faustus' part. 'Ah Christ my Saviour / seeke to save distressed Faustus soule' (A 711–12 / B-text: 'Helpe to save' 652–3). This is the last we see of the Angels until their entrance in the penultimate scene. That entrance is preserved only in the B-text (1995–2034). Whether it is part of the original script or not remains open to debate. Yet given the almost absolute coincidence of the two texts for the first four appearances of the Angels, one has to wonder at the absence of any trace of them in the second half of the A-text unless the final scene, as preserved in the B-text, is a later addition. There are dramaturgic reasons for thinking so.

The last lines of the Angels in the A-text bring Faustus to the nearest point of repentance in the play. At that moment Lucifer arrives, overwhelming Faustus not only by threats but by displaying the deadly sins in all their essential viciousness to him. After this, Faustus loses the ability or will to repent. The Angels are needed no longer, for the die is cast, and as aspects of Faustus, struggle with each other no longer. By contrast, the Angels who enter in the fifth act are heavenly and diabolic in themselves, and serve to amplify the play's spectacle rather than crystallise its moral conflict.

Studying then all but the last sequence with the Angels, we can see how subtly Marlowe controlled the dynamics of the trio to reflect successive stages of Faustus' inner struggle. Indeed, the lines themselves are largely repetitive. It is the structure of delivery that carries the force and the message. From the formal statement of position in the first appearance to the irregular conflict of the second, the growing association of the Good Angel with Faustus in the third, and finally the assertion of the final line by the Good Angel in the fourth, we can follow the movement from a balanced trio to an implicit duet as Faustus shares the Good Angel's call for repentance. Nowhere else is there such eloquent testimony to Marlowe's dramaturgic craft.

Richard III is an apt play to set against *Doctor Faustus*. They both appeared in the early 1590s. They both centre on a superhuman figure who dedicates himself to diabolic power. Most pertinent to my purpose, however, is the way they illuminate contrasting approaches to scene structure.

It is too early in the study of Shakespeare's scenic structures to be categorical about his technique. The richness that we take for granted in his verse is matched by an equally rich variety in his scenic craftsmanship. So much remains to be understood, however, that we must regard any conclusions as tentative. Yet granting this necessary caution, I shall make some preliminary observations on how Shakespeare structures his scenes in *Richard III*.

An early play such as *Two Gentlemen of Verona* has a consistent binary pattern. Where Shakespeare introduces more complex arrangements, the trio in particular, he does so in a schematic manner, principally by using asides or observation scenes.[6] Later in his career, Shakespeare utilises complex duets and trios with far more subtlety, as evident in *As You Like It* and *Hamlet*.[7] By comparison, *Richard III* includes a mixed array of scene types that run the gamut from the morality-like soliloquy and common duet to group scenes of differing structures. Of the twenty-five scenes in the play, sixteen contain soliloquies or duets. Nine, on the other hand, show intriguing attempts to create more complex units.[8]

Among the sixteen scenes with solos and duets, few rely on the simple duet alone. Early in the play we find the well-known soliloquies of Richard. They fluctuate between direct address to the audience and self-address to the speaker though in either case they are sufficiently pointed to have a dialectical character. Simple duets appear distinctly as a series, most effectively and ironically in Act III, scene ii. In this scene Hastings, heedlessly defying warnings from Stanley, goes toward the conference on the coronation full of blind pride. First a messenger delivers Stanley's warning, and then Hastings, in a sequence of exchanges with Catesby, Stanley, a Pursuivant, a Priest, and lastly Buckingham, proceeds to his doom. Shakespeare uses a similar pattern of a duet series when Richard seeks someone to slay the Princes in the Tower (IV.ii).

But the most notable duets in the play are complex rather than simple although at first glance one is not likely to regard them as complex. They also happen to be the longest scenes in the play. Both are wooing scenes: the first the wooing of Anne (I.ii), the second the wooing of Princess Elizabeth through her proxy and mother Queen Elizabeth (IV. iv).

Structurally, these two scenes echo each other, though in reverse. Each wooing occurs before silent followers. In the first case, the mutes include Anne's guards as well as King Henry's corpse. Yet none of these help Anne to resist the blandishments of Richard. In the second case, the mutes are Richard's soldiers, and ironically, though their drums help Richard to silence his mother, they are no help to him in persuading the Queen. Artistically, of course, the two scenes are worlds apart. Whereas the first is one of the most daring and theatrical scenes in the play, if not in all of Shakespeare's works, the second is laboured and turgid. Yet it is no less daring than the first, perhaps more so, since Richard's attempt to deceive a mother whose children he killed is more outrageous than to seduce a wife whose husband he murdered. But the failure of the second wooing scene is evident in its insistent parallelism with the first. Instead of finding an organic means of portraying Richard's mad notion that his powers of deception are infinite, Shakespeare employs formal rhetoric that emphasises the duet itself rather than evokes the trio of king, mother and off-stage daughter.

The handling of these two scenes and the lack of other interesting duets suggests that in *Richard III* Shakespeare is trying to break the hold that binary form has on drama. His mixture of sharp, almost colloquial wit, flexible verse in the soliloquies, and rigid rhetoric in passages of lamentation argues for an inventive, even experimental attitude. One of his most artful variations of binary structure, for example, involves patterns of redundancy between Richard and Buckingham.

Richard and Buckingham reinforce each other wonderfully in the scene where they greet Prince Edward and then the young York (III.i). Without any overt sign of co-ordination, they work neatly in tandem. The scene opens with redundant greetings: 'Welcome, sweet prince', cries Buckingham to Edward. 'Welcome, dear cousin', echoes Richard, Duke of Gloucester (1–2). In reply to the Prince's dissatisfaction that his maternal uncles are absent, Richard seeks without success to convince Edward of his concerned protection. After the Lord Mayor and then Hastings appear, it is Buckingham who urges the Cardinal to violate sanctuary in order to bring York to his brother. Whether or not the actors playing Richard and Buckingham exchange glances or otherwise show that they act in collusion, the text in no way supplies clues indicating that the two men refer to each other and indeed the absence of overt signs that they are deliberately collaborating gives the action an uncanny terror.

While waiting for his brother, Prince Edward first asks Richard where he will reside until his coronation and then interrogates Buckingham about the history of the Tower. In turning from one man to the other Edward does not change his manner of address, thus suggesting their interchangeability. Moreover, as Edward and Buckingham converse, Richard overhears the boy's remarks and comments caustically on them: 'So wise so young, they say, do never live long' (79). Later, following a passage where York questions Richard, it is Buckingham who overhears the conversation and comments with a parallel aside: 'So cunning and so young is wonderful' (135). These interrogatory segments between young and old together with

37

the sneering comments emphasise the unity of Richard and Buckingham's action and thus create an indirect redundancy that permeates the entire scene. In form, the scene is flexible, even ambiguous, having the marks of both a duet and a trio.

Shakespeare plays with another kind of duality in the scene where Buckingham leads the Lord Mayor and Citizens to persuade Richard to accept the crown (III.vii). Instead of working in tandem this time, Richard and Buckingham now seem to be at odds. Richard is the reluctant bride, Buckingham the importunate bridegroom. The scene has all the features of a standard persuasion scene with the obvious difference that the game of persuasion is rigged. The structure of the game is ambiguous, however. On one hand, Buckingham leads the Lord Mayor, Catesby and the Citizens to plead with Richard. In that respect, we have a redundant structure. On the other hand, the Citizens are mute witnesses of this play-within-a-play. To the degree they serve as audience, to that extent we have a triadic arrangement. But whether the Citizens compose a hostile audience, as Buckingham's report of his meeting with them at Guildhall would suggest, or they play a positive part in Buckingham's game, remains unspecified in the text. Whichever choice a critic or producer makes determines the frame of the scene. What needs elucidation is the theatrical effectiveness of the choice. Is the scene stronger if the Citizens remain aloof? Or is it better if they reinforce Buckingham? Or perhaps, can their role change in the course of the scene?

Either in whole or in part, nine of the scenes, as I previously remarked, contain substantial groups of characters who have sufficiently contradictory objectives to inhibit neat binary structures. Among themselves, these nine scenes do not follow any single pattern but differ in arrangement one from another. The brief scene where Rivers, Grey and Vaughan are led to death (III.iii) has both binary and group features. Ratcliffe leads the prisoners to execution. His action frames the responses of the doomed men, responses that are presented in a highly formal manner. In order, Rivers, Grey and Vaughan berate those who have sentenced them to death. Ratcliffe briefly bids them on. Then Rivers, Grey and Rivers again curse the stones of Pomfret, recall Margaret's curse, and call upon God. Once again Ratcliffe urges them on. Rivers comments caustically, and they depart. The scene moves thus from redundant lament in the first three speeches, set off by Ratcliffe's single line, to the prisoners' growing hope that God will punish their enemies, and so seems to verge on binary usage without entirely following it.

One scene, however, if any, would seem to defy binary analysis. It is the third scene of the play, encompassing Richard, Queen Elizabeth and her kin, Hastings, Buckingham, Stanley and the vengeful Queen Margaret. Containing at least eight speaking parts,[9] the scene more than any other in the play has the largest number of active individuals on stage at one time. Each character has private interests that put him or her at odds with others present, thus contributing to a volatile ensemble. How Shakespeare manages to activate them all and yet retain dramaturgic coherence is what we shall see.

The scene has eight distinct segments. A prologue introduces Rivers and Grey attempting to reassure Queen Elizabeth about King Edward's health. The court begins to assemble. In response to Buckingham and Stanley's entrance, Elizabeth tries to convince them of her good will (17–40). The action intensifies as Richard enters, protesting to Hastings against his enemies; Elizabeth and Rivers take up the argument with him (62ff.). The arrangement becomes explicitly triadic in the fourth segment as Richard answers Rivers and Elizabeth while Queen Margaret comments aside on Richard's words (109ff.). For most of this fourth segment Richard castigates the silent Elizabeth and Rivers; Margaret is the only other speaker. The peers on stage mutely observe the argument, though not yet aware of Margaret. As this segment reaches its climax, Rivers and then Elizabeth answer Richard redundantly. Thus begins the fifth segment (156ff.).

In this fifth unit, dominated by Margaret's curses, seven people speak at one time or another. What is significant for us from a dramaturgic perspective is the way Shakespeare manages to order all these speeches.

This segment starts with Margaret attacking all those present. Richard is the only one to answer, and there is a short exchange between the two of them before Margaret again returns to the general attack.[10] Richard again answers her with Elizabeth, Hastings, Rivers, Dorset and Buckingham echoing him with one or, in the case of Hastings, two lines each. We here have a vivid example of redundancy as the characters all deplore Margaret's murder of Rutland:

> *Hastings*   O, 'twas the foulest deed to slay that babe,
>   And the most merciless that e'er was heard of!
> *Rivers*   Tyrants themselves wept when it was reported.
> *Dorset*   No man but prophesied revenge for it.
> *Buckingham*   Northumberland, then present, wept to see it.   (182–6)

This choral reply has the effect of unifying the peers into one group, all of whom join to meet Margaret's attack. At this point the diverse figures compose a binary arrangement.

Margaret renews her attack on the court, concentrating first at some length on Elizabeth, and then on Rivers, Dorset and Hastings as a group. She then, in reply to Richard, turns on him, venting her most heartfelt curses that rise to a shrill but unfinished peroration. As she falters at Richard's unforeseen interruption, Elizabeth exults, 'Thus have you breath'd your curse against yourself' (241), so beginning a second series as in turn Hastings, Rivers and Dorset abuse Margaret. Here too, Shakespeare uses a pattern of serial redundancy to provide direction for the action. Briefly follows an interpolative exchange in which Richard mocks Dorset. But soon Buckingham renews the previous line of action by bidding Margaret, 'Peace, peace, for shame, if not for charity' (274). Her appeal to him and his rejection of her brings this segment to a close. In this last sub-segment there is a genuine trio when Margaret warns Buckingham against Richard as Richard looks on. Otherwise, despite the number of speaking characters, the scene has a strong binary bias. By utilising a schematic pattern of redundancy and by arranging events into a series of duets, Shakespeare reinforces the dialectical interchange that is at the root of so much drama.

Before we finish with this scene, however, there remains one more factor to consider. When Stanley, the Earl of Derby enters with Buckingham in the second segment, Elizabeth and he have a short but pointed conversation about Derby's wife. After that, he is silent for the remaining action.[11] Usually, the reader forgets his presence and the director minimises or ignores it. Yet since Stanley is the one lord least deceived by Richard, his mute presence can provide a meaningful commentary, depending on where he is placed and how he reacts to the unfolding conflicts. Were there a way to accent his awareness of events, we would have a potentially powerful trio. The fact that Shakespeare makes no provision for him over so long a scene, on the other hand, indicates a problem of focus. Derby is just one too many a figure to consider, and so he is left dangling.

Our careful scrutiny of Act I, scene iii reveals several contradictory impulses. Shakespeare creates a fluid scene that has no natural organising principle (such as the ceremonial appearance before the King in Act II, scene i). He introduces several diverse issues between the Woodvilles and Stanley, Margaret and Elizabeth, Dorset and Richard. But as the action proceeds, the dramatist reduces the danger of diffusion by utilising obvious redundancy and more subtle serialising arrangements. At the core of the scene lies the conflict between Margaret and Richard and it is this conflict that Shakespeare so richly realises by having Richard battle not only directly but also indirectly through redundant surrogates.

Unlike *Doctor Faustus*, *Richard III* is dramaturgically adventuresome. In it Shakespeare employs a variety of techniques in order to elaborate planes of action. While Marlowe is content to perfect an older, more settled binary form, as in his dramatisation of the Angels, Shakespeare seems to contest the limits of that form repeatedly. *Richard III* is a storehouse of such efforts. He gives a virtuoso demonstration of how to write a duet in the Anne and Richard scene. He also explores how to create choral effects in the lamentations of the Queens (IV.iv) or the meeting of Clarence's children, the Duchess, Queen Elizabeth and Dorset (IV.i). In the scene between Margaret and the court, moreover, we have a vivid model of the tension between extending the limits of action and concentrating the lines of conflict. Preliminary study of other Shakespearean plays suggests that this tension pervades his work and that he continually strives to transcend performance limitations.

In the process he transforms the binary foundation of drama into a peculiarly resonant instrument.

NOTES

1 See 'Shakespeare's industrious scenes', *Shakespeare Quarterly*, 30 (1979), 138–50; 'Theatrical Perception', *Theatre Research International*, n.s. 4 (May 1979), 157–71; and especially, 'Shakespeare's dramaturgy and binary form', *Theatre Journal*, 33 (March 1981), 5–17.

2 Scene vi, lines 713–736 / Act II, scene ii, lines 654–76. All citations to *Doctor Faustus* refer to either the A-text or the B-text as printed by W. W. Greg in his edition, *'Doctor Faustus': 1604–1616; Parallel Texts* (Oxford, 1950).

3 Both the A-text (1275) and the B-text (1785) stage directions specify 'two or three Schollers' although both texts show three speaking scholars.

4 Except for minor variations in spelling, punctuation and capitalisation, the speeches in both texts are identical.

5 The B-text differs from the A-text by prefacing the segment with a line spoken by the Evil Angel (B 403). This line is a repetition of the first line spoken by him in his first entrance: 'Go forward Faustus in that famous Art' (A 106 / B101), and cannot be regarded as an integral part of the second appearance.

6 'Shakespeare's dramaturgy and binary form'.

7 Barbara Barran in her doctoral dissertation, 'Scene Structure in Shakespeare's and Jonson's Comedies' (Columbia University, 1984) demonstrates the intricate handling of binary form in *As You Like It*; also see my 'Shakespeare's dramaturgy', pp. 12–13.

8 Scenes utilising solos, simple duets and complex duets: I, i, ii, iv; II. iii; III, ii, v–vii; IV, ii, iii, v; V, i–v (16); other scenes: I, iii; II, i, ii, iv; III, i, iii, iv; IV, i, iv (9).

9 Whether the scene contains eight or nine characters depends on how one treats Lord Grey and Dorset. The stage direction at the opening of the scene as well as speech-prefixes up to Richard's entrance include Grey but make no mention of Dorset. In the dialogue following Richard's entrance, Dorset speaks and is spoken to. He has no entrance, however. Meanwhile, Grey disappears. If we assume both are on stage, then Dorset is mute during the first half of the scene and Grey during the second half.

10 Three lines from the Folio copy of *Richard III* do not appear in the Quarto copy of this segment (166–8). The effect of the cut is to make Margaret's challenge to the entire group more forceful and direct.

11 Since there is no exit marked for Stanley and Richard includes him in the list of people he is deceiving (330), we can presume he remains on stage throughout the scene.

K. TETZELI VON ROSADOR

'Supernatural soliciting': temptation and imagination in *Doctor Faustus* and *Macbeth*

⟡⟡⟡

Temptation has played a crucial role in Christian history and cosmology. Yielding to its first, archetypal instance, man exchanged the glorious, yet static totality of Paradise for time's ravages and history's irresistible movement, for mortality and the necessity of (moral) choice, for drama. The mystery of iniquity presented itself to him. He had to come to terms with the existence and justification of evil in a God-created universe. And ever since he has, like Milton's devils or the critics of *Doctor Faustus* and *Macbeth*,

> reasoned high
> Of providence, foreknowledge, will and fate,
> Fixed fate, free will, foreknowledge absolute,
> And found no end in wandering mazes lost. (*Paradise Lost*, II, 558–61)

If drama, by its very form and aesthetic quality, cannot solve such questions, it can certainly stage the dynamics and experience of temptation, the conflict between tempter and tempted, and what it feels like either to tempt or to be tempted. If it cannot decide in so many words whether it is the tempter or the tempted who sins most, it can embody in action the human cost of temptation and the subtle interdependence of tempter and tempted; it can picture forth the results of temptation, both the promised end and the image of horror.

All drama based upon or related to Christian cosmology has therefore frequently, if not invariably, made good dramatic use of temptation. In Lucifer, who fell self-tempted, self-depraved, in Adam and Eve, the victims of satanic suggestion, and in Job, the human pawn of a wager between God and Satan, the Bible offers three models of temptation, differing in motive, technique and result, for further use, be it for nice theological distinction and interpretation or be it for literary imitation and variation. Of these models sixteenth-century English drama in its progress from moral allegory to a richly varied poetic symbolism has insistently availed itself for its presentation of the mystery of iniquity.[1] Satan himself enters the stage as Lucyfer in *Wisdom* or Titivillus in *Mankind* and tempts the *humanum genus* figures of the moralities, to be succeeded by the Vice, embodiment of a smaller moral or social evil, in the more concrete and more restricted world of the interludes. Among the figures inhabiting the socially and psychologically still more concrete world of late Elizabethan drama and fathered by the Vice are the magician and the witch.[2] They are almost ideal subjects of a drama firmly dedicated to holding the mirror up to nature and equally firmly determined not to relinquish its macrocosmic inclusiveness, a drama in which the stage-world is still capable of meaning the world-stage. By their profession the magician and the witch reach up to heaven and down to hell; they are the agents or may become the objects of cosmic conflict. At the same time, they are creatures of everyday reality, to be met with, like Cornelius Agrippa, at the courts of princes or, like Mother Sawyer and her ilk, in dirty village hovels.[3] Being figures of the perennial moral and cosmic drama and of everyday reality the magician and the witch are highly popular on the Elizabethan and Jacobean stage: their appearance in more than fifty plays between 1530 and 1640 bears ample witness to this popularity.[4]

This dual nature of magicians and witches corresponds, with regard to temptation on and off the stage, to a dual function. As descendants of the Vice, they are instruments of the devil, tempters; as real and fallible human beings, their souls are the battleground of good and evil, they are tempted. This double function of theirs as the devil's instruments or as his victims is frequently dealt with in the extensive literature of demonology.[5] Still, in order to describe the process and experience of diabolical or magical temptation, there is no need to enter into all the subtleties of demonological theory and controversy. The basic and widely accepted tenets of the literature of demonology and faculty psychology provide a frame of reference sufficient for an understanding of the process of temptation in contemporary Elizabethan terms. This reliance on an 'understood background'[6] does not reduce either *Doctor Faustus* or *Macbeth* or any other work of art presenting magical phenomena to a narrow and historically limited demonological or psychological meaning, does not by itself 'explain' them in orthodox terms.[7] On the contrary, the mechanism of temptation so understood operates as a foil against which Marlowe's and Shakespeare's handling of it can be seen and evaluated in its particularity and complexity.

Who tempts whom in *Doctor Faustus* and *Macbeth*? How does temptation operate in both these plays? These seemingly easy questions have been a matter of some critical debate. For A. C. Bradley, speaking about *Macbeth*, 'we are admitting . . . too much when we use the word 'temptation' in reference to the first prophecies of the Witches'.[8] For him, and recent critics have tended to agree,[9] the witches simply make an announcement about the future. Is then Macbeth his own Iago? Similar objections have been raised about the function of Mephostophilis in Marlowe's *Doctor Faustus*. According to Harry Levin, Mephostophilis 'proffers no tempting speeches and dangles no enticements; Faustus tempts himself'.[10] In *Doctor Faustus*, the matter is further complicated by the differing accounts the A and B versions give of Mephostophilis's machinations.[11] Are Faustus and Macbeth, as is Lucifer, self-tempted, self-depraved? Pointing to Faustus's and Macbeth's own experience and words – to Faustus who discourses with the devil about temptation (B 429) and who finally in the hour of death is told how he has been deceived (B 1986–92), to Macbeth who feels supernaturally solicited (I.iii. 130) – provides no easy solution to the problem: subjective, deceptive feeling might easily have replaced objective reality; an explanation like Mephostophilis's coming so very late in the play is of little persuasive force, if contradicted or not borne out by what the spectator has witnessed.

If placed within a context of general Elizabethan ideas about perception and diabolical or magical interference, the mechanism of Faustus's and Macbeth's temptation can be illuminated. Both processes can then be seen as basically identical, the devil and the witch proceeding by the same means.[12] (The difference resides in the treatment and the consequences to be discussed later on.) If Mephostophilis and the witches are to tempt Faustus and Macbeth they must somehow creep into their minds and souls to work mischief there, they must distort their victim's perceptions. A glance at Elizabethan ideas about the process of perception will help to understand how this can be done. A sufficiently general outline of this process has been provided by Theodore Spencer:

> Through the working of the animal spirits, the outward senses perceive an object, an impression of it is conveyed to the imagination, the imagination refers this impression to the affections as pleasing or displeasing, reason debates the matter and presents its verdict to the will, the Queen of the soul, who finally dictates back to the sensitive appetite (the function which desires), telling it to act or to refrain from action, according as the object is seen as good or evil.[13]

Of course, nomenclature may vary from author to author, and Spenser may base his allegory of Archimago's magical temptation in *The Faerie Queene* on a slightly updated version of the medieval ventricle theory of perception. Nevertheless, for our purposes the summary is comprehensive and uncontroversial enough. Moreover, it hints at the crucial importance of the imagination or fantasy for the process of perception, a function well described in more detail by Pierre Charron:

> The fantasticke or imaginatiue facultie, hauing recollected, and withdrawne the kindes and images apprehended by the senses, retaineth and reserueth them; in such sort that the obiects being absent and far distant, yea a man sleeping, and his senses being bound and shut vp, it presenteth them to the spirit and thought, *Phantasmata idola, seu imagines dicuntur*, and doth almost worke that within in the vnderstanding, which the obiect doth without in the sense.[14]

No doubt, the right functioning of the imagination is of the highest importance. It is, in a quite modern sense an image-receiving, an image-combining, and an image-making capacity. Its creative power, which makes the true nature of things appear, is consequently praised by George Puttenham:

> Euen so is the phantasticall part of man (if it be not disordered) a representer of the best, most comely and bewtifull images or apparances of thinges to the soule and according to their very truth. . . . of this sorte of phantasie are all good Poets, notable Captaines stratagematique, all cunning artificers and enginers, all Legislators Polititiens & Counsellours of estate, in whose exercises the inuentiue part is most employed and is to the sound & true iudgement of man most needful.[15]

This is an overtly optimistic view, fully expressive of Renaissance aspiration, although it is not of Renaissance origin.[16] It relies on the possibility of rational order and human perfection and stresses the importance of imaginative creation not only for the individual but also for the body politic. The poet, the warrior, the politician and the engineer are all in equal need of it. But in a fallen world such perfection is unattainable. Thus Puritan and Calvinist thought with its profound distrust of man and the senses can see nothing but the dangers inherent in the workings of the imagination and declares it, in the words of William Perkins, the influential Cambridge divine, as partaking fully of man's postlapsarian corruption: 'The imagination and conceite of euery man is naturally euill'.[17] Of course, this Calvinist distrust attests *e contrario* to the power the imagination is believed to possess. For Puttenham it is a power which makes for order and creation, for Perkins one which, unreformed and unrestrained, makes for distortion, corruption and damnation.

It is because of this dual potential that the imagination or fantasy is invariably considered to be the proper and main point of attack or gateway for the temptations of either devil or witch. This is a matter frequently discussed in demonological treatises and elsewhere. For Thomas Wright, author of a well-known psychological study, 'the Diuell immediately by his suggestions allureth vs to sinne, he being a spirite, by secrete meanes can enter into the former parte of our braine, and there chop and chaunge our imaginations'. The problem, to give only one other example, is similarly phrased by Walter Raleigh: '. . . by the same way that God passeth out, the Deuill entreth in, beginning with the fantasie, by which he doth more easily betray the other faculties of the soule: for the fantasie is most apt to bee abused by vaine apprehensions'.[18] With the corruption of the fantasy, temptation has almost done its work. A fantasy thus corrupted loses its firm hold on reality and thrives on appearances. It receives, combines and produces images without testing and evaluating them; it breeds, in Puttenham's words, 'Chimeres & monsters'.[19] From a mind so diseased, the corruption of the whole being inevitably ensues. There is not the slightest doubt, however, that, as Job's example teaches and demonologians unanimously and repeatedly confirm, such temptation will succeed only if something in the tempted answers it.[20] A fantasy on which something illusory, something which is not, some vague ambitious dream, has fastened is most liable to succumb to temptation. Else, to quote Chapman's unambiguous statement from *The Tragedy of Charles Duke of Byron*, 'Witchcraft can never taint an honest mind' (V.ii. 174).

The concrete method of devilish or magical temptation can now without difficulty be deduced. It must be the aim of the tempter to present as real to the fantasy of his victim something which is not and, like Comus, thus to 'cheat the eye with blear illusion'. All images of illusory character, dreams, apparitions, prophecies and suchlike, may be used by the tempter for his purposes. If appearance is taken for reality by the tempted, moral judgment inevitably loses its foothold. And this is indeed how temptation generally proceeds and is presented in Elizabethan and Jacobean literature, as a glance at the detailed and extensive treatment in Spenser's *Faerie Queene* may demonstrate.[21] There Archimago sends an 'ydle dreame' to the Red Crosse Knight and bids it 'with false shewes abuse his fantasy' (I.i. 46). After some resistance Spenser's Everyknight is corrupted and, in his 'falsed fancy', takes Duessa 'to be the fairest wight, that liued yit' (I.ii. 30). He is no longer able to distinguish appearance from reality; a total reversal of values takes place. An imagination corrupted by illusion, the dominance of appearance, the reversal of values – these are the symptoms and results of supernatural solicitation. And from an observation of the symptoms conclusions about the character of the disease may be drawn.

In the case of *Macbeth*, however, there is no need for such an indirect procedure. It is the protagonist himself who explains, in highly concentrated form, the psychological process underlying temptation:

> This supernatural *soliciting*
> Cannot be ill; cannot be good. If ill,
> Why hath it given me earnest of success,
> Commencing in a truth? I am Thane of Cawdor.
> If good, why do I yield to that *suggestion*
> Whose horrid *image* doth unfix my hair
> And make my seated heart knock at my ribs
> Against the use of nature? Present fears
> Are less than horrible *imaginings*.
> My *thought*, whose murder yet is but *fantastical*,
> Shakes so my single state of man
> That *function* is smother'd in surmise,
> And nothing is but what is not.   (I.iii. 130–42; my italics)

This much-discussed passage contains an abstract of the entire process of perception and devilish temptation. Correct technical terms of psychology and theology are used to express personal experience with stirring immediacy. For Macbeth, it is a moment at once of terrible clarity, of perfect insight, and of equivocation and temporising, a moment in which decision is wilfully suspended. He realises that he is yielding to suggestion – and suggestion is the traditional theological term for the first stage of temptation, delight and consent being the other two:

> Sin, as write the Schoole Doctors, hathe three procurators or tempters, Suggestion, Delight, and Consent.
>
> Suggestion, draweth vs with the vaine thoughtes and desires of the gaine of this life, and worldly pleasures inwarde or outward, enticing the fraile fleshe to sinne.[22]

That suggestion can enter Macbeth, that he is, as it were, temptable, has been indirectly and subtly impressed upon the spectator from the very first scene onwards. He is sought out by the Weird Sisters. His first words echo, as is well known, the blurring, the reversing of values, that fair is foul and foul is fair. He is identified with their paradoxical perspective, the simultaneity of loss and gain: 'What he hath lost, noble Macbeth hath won' (I.ii. 68). And, what is more, in his extensive aside the rhythm, the music, of the Weird Sisters' verses can be heard again in what L. C. Knights has called 'the sickening see-saw rhythm' of 'Cannot be ill; cannot be good'[23] which is sounded again in 'nothing is but what is not'. A prior affinity of Macbeth's mind, of his imagination, to the world and thought of the Weird Sisters is thus established. This is what, retrospectively, the aside implies. At the same time, it dramatises the process of the progressive corruption of Macbeth's imagination and thus of his whole being.

The vehicle for this corruption, for the tempting of Macbeth, is the prophecy, a verbal image. This is no mere announcement. Macbeth, in classifying it euphemistically as 'soliciting' and correctly as 'suggestion', is undoubtedly right – and this not only subjectively, because he experiences it as such. What the Weird Sisters confront Macbeth with is something illusory, something which is not, simply because it is not yet. The degree of Macbeth's affinity to the Witches' world and thought can be deduced from the fact that he never doubts the truth, the reality, of the prophecy. Unlike Banquo, the possibility of deception, of being purposely deceived, never occurs to him. Instead, he confounds the future in the instant and takes something which is not (yet) for fact. All he meditates on is ways and means. The illusory verbal image sets the imagination furiously to work. Due to its combinatory and creative power the fantasy conjures up horrible imaginings, other illusory or delusive images, images of murder. Thought, understanding, is subordinated to the fantastical image, the murder which is not yet; and function, act, is stalled by the unreality of the mind-obsessing image. Illusion or appearance begins to occupy Macbeth's mind. He is no longer capable of distinguishing it clearly from reality: 'And nothing is but what is not'. Like the Red Crosse Knight's, his imagination is corrupted, reason is dominated by imagination, which is itself subservient to appearances.

What distinguishes Macbeth from Spenser's Knight is the terrible lucidity with which he is able to describe his state of mind, although he is unable to stop the destructive and deluding workings of his imagination. This is not a relatively simple case of an Ovidian 'video meliora proboque, deteriora sequor',[24] because it is not one of a known *summum bonum* which is deserted for a lesser good.[25] Macbeth's case is of a much richer complexity. The ability to picture forth, to describe lucidly and concretely, his own state of mind is a quality of his imagination just as is the compulsion to produce illusory images.[26] What is poet-like in Macbeth, the ability to see imaginatively into the truth of things, is at war with what is hallucinatory and produces horrid images. Imagination, in both its creative and its deluding, destructive quality, is thus the battleground on which Macbeth's fate is decided. Although temptation has made a breach, Macbeth has not totally succumbed to it as yet; he awakens from his 'rapture' into a state of indecision. Thus evil must attack again and it does so by repeating the process. It is Lady Macbeth who now takes over the Weird Sisters' functions, for which she has prepared herself by invoking evil ('Come, you spirits . . .') and by becoming virtually possessed. Her vehicle of temptation is identical with the Weird Sisters', whom she paraphrases: 'Great Glamis! Worthy Cawdor! / Greater than both, by the all-hail hereafter!' (I.v. 51–2).

The effect of this temptation on Macbeth is revealed in his two soliloquies. Macbeth's ability to picture forth, to create images, is not a whit weakened. The images his fantasy produces now, however, are almost surrealist in character, transcending, like the 'naked new-born babe / Striding the blast' or 'heaven's cherubin hors'd / Upon the sightless couriers of the air', in their cosmic expansiveness reason's limits – they are images of a hallucinated great apocalypse. His attempts at moral reasoning ('He's here in double trust . . .') are swamped by this compulsory production of images, images which like the dagger possess or rather usurp the status of reality. Reason has abdicated its proper functions, Macbeth is of imagination all compact. Yet self-division has gone even further: the truly creative power of imagination, that part which according to Puttenham is necessary for the poet and the politician, is starved and atrophies. That part reigns which pervertedly apes the poet's ability and breeds chimeras and monsters. Consequently, Macbeth, having surfeited repeatedly on temptations' illusory images, fantasises an imaginary, yet experientially real world of evil where witchcraft celebrates pale Hecate's offerings and withered murder moves like a ghost.[27]

With the killing of Duncan this world of nightmarish hallucination closes in on Macbeth and becomes all-encompassing. The scene of his return from the murder is indeed, as E. A. J. Honigmann has observed, his sleep-walking scene.[28] It shows a Macbeth terribly troubled by thick-coming fancies which his imagination produces unrestrainedly. Practical necessities, the objective world, his dearest partner of greatness, have no hold on him. Communication is broken. Macbeth lives in a world self-contained, 'of sorriest fancies (his) companions making' (III.ii. 9). His imagination, assuming the dramatist's office, recreates the scene of murder replete with action and dialogue, aping poetic creation, it rattles off periphrases of sleep, time-honoured literary clichés, such as have been used in the apostrophes to care-charmer sleep by a host of poets, Virgil, Statius, Desportes, Sidney, Daniel, Griffin, Drummond among them:

> – the innocent sleep,
> Sleep that knits up the ravell'd sleave of care,
> The death of each day's life, sore labour's bath,
> Balm of hurt minds, great nature's second course,
> Chief nourisher in life's feast;   (II.ii. 36–40)[29]

This automatic production of images is a horrible parody of the true creative function of the imagination. It progresses without control and direction and has to be stopped by a sorely puzzled Lady Macbeth: 'What do you mean?' (II.ii. 40). It demonstrates both the licence and the barrenness of an imagination which has completely lost touch with reality and moral reasoning and feeds on itself.

At the same time the spectator is ironically made aware that Macbeth's fantasising anticipates his future fate. The voice he hears echoes what has tempted him, namely, the prophetic verbal image based on his names and titles, and, in addition, transforms it with devastating effect:

> 'Glamis hath murder'd sleep; and therefore Cawdor
> Shall sleep no more – Macbeth shall sleep no more.'   (II.ii. 42–3)

The climactic arrangement of the Weird Sisters' and Lady Macbeth's tempting speeches is broken at the exact moment the prophecy is nearly fulfilled and the sweet fruition of the golden round seems within easy reach. The murderer can envision himself as nothing but Macbeth and a man, a man, moreover, haunted by sleeplessness, a man self-divided, in whom perception and act, eyes and hand, are violently at odds. Temptation has done its worst.

In *Doctor Faustus*, it is the A text which, quite early in the play, points to the crucial importance of the imagination for the process of temptation. Faustus, having summoned the German magicians Valdes and Cornelius, acquaints them with his decision:

> Know that your words haue woon me at the last,
> To practise Magicke and concealed arts:
> Yet not your words onely, but mine owne fantasie,
> That will receiue no obiect for my head,
> But ruminates on Negromantique skill . . .   (A 134–8)

49

As the Red Crosse Knight, as Macbeth, so is Faustus under the sway of his fantasy, a fantasy cut off from objective reality.[30] This function of the fantasy is similarly emphasised in the *Damnable Life*, the English translation of the *Historia von D. Iohann Fausten*, where, in the first chapter, it is said of Faustus that he 'fell into such fantasies and deep cogitations, that he was marked of many'. This is in perfect accordance with the general Elizabethan ideas about diabolical and magical temptation. The fate of Faustus thus conceived will necessarily present a study in the workings and effects of the imagination.

These verses (A 136–8), however, are missing in the B version. Is imagination of lesser importance there? In any case, how is Faustus's imagination influenced and corrupted? By the words of Valdes and Cornelius which have won Faustus 'at the last'? Can, as is regularly assumed in Marlowe criticism, Faustus's first soliloquy then be taken to present a personal decision, the result of self-temptation? Is an opposition between internal and external influence implied in Faustus's statement 'Yet not your words onely, but mine owne fantasie'? And if so, what part do the books of magic play in tempting Faustus? After all, Faustus is urged by the Good Angel to 'lay that damned booke aside, / And gaze not on it least it tempt thy soule' (B 97–8). And how does Mephostophilis's retrospective account of the temptation, his gloating triumph that it was he who 'turn'd the leaues / And led thine eye' (B 1991–2), agree with all this? Must we reluctantly come to the conclusion variously advanced that the play, if greatly planned, is much less well executed and offers contradictory explanations of Faustus's temptation and responsibility?[31]

A look at the introductory Chorus and its effect on the play's structure can help us to understand the causal sequence and the implied chronology of Faustus's temptation. The Chorus's rapid survey of the hero's curriculum vitae is not restricted to providing preliminary information about character, time and place. Faustus, as portrayed by the Chorus, has already been tempted and is far advanced on his way to corruption. A complete reversal of values has apparently taken place:[32]

> For falling to a diuellish exercise,
> And glutted now with learnings golden gifts,
> He surfets vpon cursed Necromancie:
> Nothing so sweet as Magicke is to him;
> Which he preferres before his chiefest blisse . . .   (B 23–7)

The Faustus who is now discovered has already found his chiefest bliss in the pursuit of magic. Does this make the first soliloquy redundant? Obviously not, as the fascination of critics and theatre audiences alike proves. What the Chorus does is to place the soliloquy both morally and chronologically. The norm against which Faustus's fortunes, good or bad, are to be measured is firmly established by him. Moreover, the Chorus acts as a presenter. His deictic gesture – 'And this the man that in his study sits' – explains the exemplary nature of the play to follow. (And acting as an epilogue the Chorus will point the moral of this *exemplum*.) As an *exemplum* of the fate of too forward wits, Faustus's course is thus morally prejudged and framed by a prim and proper perspective.

Against the Chorus's evaluation, the first soliloquy sets Faustus's own view and thinking. The process which the Chorus had abstracted in moral terms is recapitulated as living experience. A dual perspective is thus dramatised.[33] Attention is directed away from the foregone conclusion of such a recapitulation and towards the argumentation. And the argumentation certainly needs attending to, for it is astonishing indeed: a Doctor of Divinity, who made the schools ring with *sic probo*, misquotes basic texts, attributes a Ramistic idea to Aristotle, and formulates and meditates a syllogism unworthy of a freshman. Does that prove that Faustus possesses only patchy learning and a superficial mind, that he is nothing but a dilettante, a fool, a numskull, an ass, as recent critics have assumed? Certainly such scholarly misdemeanours as misquotations, wrong attributions of texts, and facile syllogisms are signs of a mind gone wrong. Yet to ascribe these academic failures to professional incapacity is to reduce Faustus to an academic nonentity. Such a reduction, surely, would totally destroy the possibility of feeling any serious interest in his life and fate, let alone the possibility of tragedy. If the Chorus is taken seriously, however, and not only as the pious mumbling of orthodoxy, Faustus's soliloquy merely recapitulates what has already happened. The Chorus's "Nothing so sweet as magic is to him" corresponds to Faustus's "These Metaphisicks of Magitians, / And Negromantick bookes are heauenly" (B 76–7). In other words: Faustus is never shown in a state of relative innocence. The soliloquy does not so much epitomise Faustus's academic career, leading step by step to a reversal of values, but is from the first misquotation to the final decision a symptom of intellectual and moral blindness resulting from, and partaking of, temptation.

Mephostophilis's taunt at the end of the play that it was he who manipulated Faustus's scholarly *sortes Virgilianae* is therefore no new explanation. It puts in so many words what the spectator has witnessed in action. A Mephostophilis, however, turning the leaves *in persona* would be a ludicrous or rather anachronistic sight, very much in the manner of a Titivillus who hangs a net in front of Mankind "to blench hys syght" and buries a board to make him lose his labour. Yet Marlowe does not leave everything to be inferred. That Faustus, like Macbeth, has entered the realm of evil he makes excitingly visible with Faustus's next entry: Lucifer himself presides invisibly over the conjuration scene, a striking scenic emblem of hell's power encroaching on the protagonist. And this power has been tempting Faustus not only through Mephostophilis's machinations. Faustus's greeting of Valdes and Cornelius proves, as does the Chorus, that temptation has preceded the action of the play:

> Know that your words haue woon me *at the last*.
> To practise Magicke and concealed Arts.   (B 128–9; my italics).

Thus temptation has been at work before the play's opening, its effect on a scholarly mind is demonstrated in the first scene, and it is an ongoing process throughout the play. For although both Faustus and Macbeth succumb to temptation, enter the realm of evil, and create hell on earth with the one's *"Consummatum est"* (B 462) and the other's more indirect version "I have done the deed" (II. ii. 14), only Marlowe's play thematises a theological issue, the possibility of salvation.[34] It is most clearly presented in the two externalisations embodying Faustus's *psychomachia*, the Good and the Evil Angel. The frequency of their appearance in the first part of the play (B 96, 402, 581, 647) testifies by itself that Faustus's fate is not predetermined. The ever-present possibility of repentance and salvation means that temptation's heaviest artillery must be employed throughout the play to lead Faustus further into evil. The three traditional enemies of man, the devil (Mephostophilis), the world (the tour of the universe and through the princes' courts), and the flesh (Helen of Troy), are moved against him.[35] He is tempted to be "on earth as *Ioue* is in the skye" (B 103), that is to presume, and he is tempted to despair and to commit suicide when Mephostophilis "giues him a dagger" (B 1831).[36] And he is tempted with the scholar's basic tools, with the "words" of Valdes and Cornelius which have won him "at the last", and with books – the books Mephostophilis manipulates and the "heauenly" books of magic (B 77) which he is sporadically given by Mephostophilis (B 548, 736). Quite appropriately Faustus's final scene, his full realisation of how he has fallen, opens with "O would I had neuer seene *Wittenberg*, neuer read book" (B 1942) and finishes with the desperate cry "I'le burne my bookes" (B 2092).[37]

The faculty which in *Doctor Faustus* as in *Macbeth* has to bear the brunt of the devil's attack is, quite expectedly, the fantasy or imagination. The A text expressly points to it as corrupted, while B explains the method of temptation as the traditional misleading of the senses. In accordance with the literature of demonology and in analogy to *Macbeth*, the symptoms of Faustus's corrupted imagination and darkened reason are an inability to distinguish between appearance and reality, a reversal of values, a breeding of chimerical visions. But these are general and conventional terms, which, when applied indiscriminately to Red Crosse, to Macbeth, and to Faustus, as well they might be, tend towards the small common denominator and towards reduction. What seems of more importance: Marlowe, like Shakespeare, dramatises the dual nature of the imagination as both a potentially creative and delusive faculty. In *Doctor Faustus*, however, creation is generated by delusion. It temporarily attracts to it wondering and uneasy admiration, while carrying at the same time within itself the seeds of ultimate destruction. Neither a romanticising praise of Faustus's aspiring mind nor the harsh dismissal of the deceived and foolish trickster, ignorant of the absolute vacuousness of his achievements, seems therefore justified. A more complex appreciation and reaction is called for.[38]

In Faustus the deluded fantasy becomes an image-making and image-combining faculty of compulsive intensity. The tedium and weariness surfacing again and again during his error-ridden tour of the academic disciplines quite vanish:

> O what a world of profite and delight,
> Of power, of honour, and omnipotence,
> Is promised to the Studious Artizan?
> All things that moue between the quiet Poles
> Shall be at my command: Emperors and Kings,
> Are but obey'd in their seuerall Prouinces:
> But his dominion that exceeds in this
> Stretcheth as farre as doth the mind of man:
> A sound Magitian is a Demi-god,
> Here tire my braines to get a Deity.   (B 80–9)

Even without the A version's Medea-inspired claim – "Nor can they raise the winde, or rend the cloudes" (A 89) – or with B's general toning down ("mighty god" to "Demi-god"), this is a world-encompassing aspiration. Faustus fantasises a new creation, a new world, to be dominated and inhabited and used by him. Inhibitions and restrictions are left behind. A feeling of liberation seems to accompany Faustus's verbal flights: the world of power and omnipotence is also meant to be a world of freedom. In its thrust and range this fantasising is stunning indeed, resuscitating in the spectator long-forgotten or repressed infantile visions of omnipotence.

Yet this is certainly no true creation; it only apes the method and achievement of either poet or god. It is the result of temptation, the product of a deluded imagination, unhampered by, in modern terminology, the reality principle. Each temptation scene is almost invariably followed by such a speech of mock-creation. And as *Doctor Faustus* consists of a string of temptations by the devil, the world and the flesh, vision is followed by vision: the tempting by means of "that damned book" evokes in Faustus the dream of knowledge, riches, and power ("How am I glutted with conceipt of this?" B 105). Mephostophilis's promises make him visualise the possibility of being "great Emperour of the world" (B 329); the Evil Angel triumphing once again makes him hanker after riches ("Why the Signory of *Embden* shall be mine" B 411); and the verses which the appearance of that devilish succuba, Helen of Troy, provokes are too well-known to need quotation. No doubt, these soaring speeches carry the spectator along, make him experience a feeling of elation inasmuch as this uninhibited fantasising expresses and touches needs normally and shamefacedly hidden.

Yet to be nothing but attracted were to disregard the criticism and ironical undercutting which Marlowe has carefully inserted into these speeches. Not only does their structural position explain them to be the direct results of temptation and delusion, they also flaunt an egoism of monstrous dimension. "I'le haue . . . I'le haue . . . I'le haue . . . I'le haue . . . I'le leauy . . . I'le make" (B 109–24) – both the prominently anaphoric position and the frequency of the personal pronoun emphasise the absolute self-centredness of Faustus's aspiration. The lines on Helen's beauty, certainly poetically the most alluring, also partake of this crude egoism:

> I will be *Paris*, and for loue of thee,
> In stead of *Troy* shall *Wittenberg* be sack't,
> And I will combat with weake *Menelaus*,
> And weare thy colours on my plumed crest.
> Yea, I will wound *Achilles* in the heele,
> And then returne to *Hellen* for a kisse. (B 1881–6)

"I will . . . I will . . . I will": Marlowe uses again the device he had employed in Faustus's first vision of power and omnipotence. The parallel has a levelling effect. What Helen evokes are nothing but the dreams and rhapsodies of a deluded imagination. Moreover, Helen's beauty is, as has frequently been noticed, destructive in itself and the cause of destruction in others. She creates havoc similar to the "flaming Iupiter" and, as Faustus's love-token, Wittenberg is to be sacked, Menelaus fought, and Achilles wounded. All of Faustus's grandiose speeches deploy such images of destruction. The poetic visions of a new creation, a new earth, are not only baseless fabrics but also contain in themselves the seeds of destruction – their own, that of Faustus, and that of others.[39]

It is within such a context that the attraction of the problem of supernatural solicitation for the two greatest poet-dramatists of the Elizabethan age must be seen. Not only is the whole universe – heaven, earth and hell, God, man and the devil – spectacularly brought before the gaping crowd, but diabolical or magical temptation externalises, provides a fascinating objective correlative for, a central aspect of the dramatist's art. It is the fantasy or imagination as the image-receiving, image-filtering organ which is first and foremost attacked and abused by the devil's temptation; and it is the fantasy or imagination as the image-making and image-combining faculty on which all creative art depends. Thus all works dealing with supernatural temptation become necessarily in some way or other works dealing with the power, the shortcomings, the abuse of imagination in both its creative and delusive potency. (That the dual nature of such fantasising is a very modern concept should need no special emphasis in a post-Freudian age with its free association techniques and its conflicts between the pleasure and the reality principle.)

Of all the many Elizabethan and Jacobean plays on magic, *Doctor Faustus* and *Macbeth* present this dual nature of the imagination most fully.

Having been tempted, both Faustus and Macbeth become of imagination all compact. In this, and it needs no Theseus to tell us that, they resemble the lunatic and the poet or rather the lunatic poet. They envision and create alternative worlds and confound the future in the instant. This, it seems to me, lies at the root of those numerous critical statements stressing the poet-like and imaginative nature and ability of Faustus and Macbeth. No doubt, the tempted and deluded imagination creates for itself an unreal and artificial universe, resembling and mocking the poet's images of truth. The spectator's ambivalent reaction towards Faustus and Macbeth, the simultaneity of attraction and repulsion, the admiration for the wide sweep and evocative richness of the world imagined, and the realisation that these visions are only chimerical and hallucinatory, spring from here.[40]

This is what both protagonists have in common. The worlds they fantasise, however, and the results of their fantasising differ radically. Macbeth, confronted with evil presences, can discern and set no limits to the world of evil. Apocalyptic images, visions of foul murder and Night's black agents inhabiting the earth, crowd upon him and obsess him. What is obsessively fantasised, he then sets out to realise. Action supplants imagination. No more visions and poetic flights for him – Macbeth acts to kill imagination:

> From this moment
> The very firstlings of my heart shall be
> The firstlings of my hand. (IV. i. 146–8)

Such a Macbeth, an automaton of murderous action, is quite properly relegated to the background of the play's action during a whole act. When he reappears next, he can only ask prematurely for his armour, for something bloody to be done. He has now forgotten the taste of fears. With the creative aspect of the imagination deadened, life shrinks to a tale told by an idiot, signifying nothing.

In contrast, Faustus's power to fantasise never fails until his final hour. His imagination, being deluded again and again by the seduction of the devil, the world and the flesh, produces vision after vision of power, of pleasure, of omnipotence. While Macbeth's moral reason works with frightening clarity until the deed is done, Faustus's is clouded from the beginning. As rational and moral restraint first weakens and then is lost, a liberating effect seems to derive from the worlds Faustus imagines, from the upward lift of the imagery and speech-forms employed. Faustus's programme:

> My foure and twenty yeares of liberty
> I'le spend in pleasure and in daliance (B 862–3)

contains the attempt to live what has been so exhilaratingly imagined. And it contains an ironical shrinking of the scope of the original aspiration. This shrinking, the discrepancy between the limitless fantasy and the banal reality, determines, as is well known, the structure of the rest of the play. What never shrinks is Faustus's fantasising capacity:

> Stand still you euer mouing Spheares of heauen,
> That time may cease, and midnight neuer come.
> Faire natures eye, rise, rise againe and make
> Perpetuall day: (B 2039–42)

> And see a threatning Arme, an angry Brow. (B 2053)

> You Starres that raign'd at my natiuity,
> Whose influence hath allotted death and hell;
> Now draw vp *Faustus* like a foggy mist,
> Into the entrals of yon labouring cloud,
> That when you vomite forth into the aire,
> My limbes may issue from your smoky mouthes,
> But let my soule mount, and ascend to heauen. (B 2058–64)

In Faustus's last hour, cataclysmic images of horror take the place of those earlier grandiose ones of power and aspiration. Their essence, however, is little changed. Faustus's thought still moves in cosmic dimensions, although the perspective has been totally reversed: a negative fantasy is the result, as inhuman in its despairing desire to be annihilated as was the earlier one in its presumption of godlike dominance and unrestrained indulgence. Such compulsive fantasising only death, the one ineluctable reality, can put a stop to.

Few tragedies present the human cost of temptation and error in such uncompromising and pitiful terms as *Doctor Faustus* and *Macbeth*. This is achieved by first displaying fully the creative potential of the protagonists, the god- or poet-like power of their imaginations. In *Macbeth*, the barren futility of a life without imagination and thus without the possibility of alternatives is then starkly contrasted to this early image of the protagonist's potentiality; in *Doctor Faustus*, the dangers of an imagination without moral or rational restraint are acted out. Imaginative atrophy and imaginative licence: surely these are the anxieties most profoundly haunting all artists.

NOTES

1 For a useful survey of various kinds of temptations, tempters and temptation scenes see Dieter Mehl, "Versucher und Versuchte im Drama Shakespeares und einiger Zeitgenossen", *Shakespeare Jahrbuch West* (1966), 146–72.

2 The best account of this literary development is still Bernard Spivack's *Shakespeare and the Allegory of Evil* (New York, 1958), although Spivack does not discuss magicians.

3 Cf. the rich material in R. H. West, *The Invisible World: A Study of Pneumatology in Elizabethan Drama* (Athens, Ga., 1939), which should be augmented by the folkloristic perspective of K. M. Briggs, *Pale Hecate's Team*.

An Examination of the Beliefs on Witchcraft and Magic among Shakespeare's Contemporaries and His Immediate Successors (London, 1962), and the historical one of Keith Thomas, *Religion and the Decline of Magic* (London, 1971).

4 See the full list of plays in my *Magie im elisabethanischen Drama* (Braunschweig, 1970), pp. 9–11. The following interpretation of *Doctor Faustus* and *Macbeth* uses, in a much revised and extended form, some material drawn from Chapter III.

5 The magician as the devil's victim figures prominently in those contemporary real life accounts from Peter Stubbe (1590) to John Lamb (1628) in which the magician is in the end deserted by the devil, left to the mercies of the secular arm or else horribly killed. The instrumental function of magicians is an oft-repeated commonplace of demonological lore; cf., among many others, Henry Holland, *A Treatise against Witchcraft* (Cambridge, 1590), p. 40.

6 This is West's term (p. 93) and procedure.

7 This is an objection frequently and, by and large, rightly raised against such works as W. C. Curry's *Shakespeare's Philosophical Patterns* (Baton Rouge, La., 1937); cf. for example, the criticism of Wilbur Sanders, *The Dramatist and the Received Idea. Studies in the Plays of Marlowe & Shakespeare* (Cambridge, 1968), pp. 277f.

8 *Shakespearean Tragedy* (London, 1905), p. 344.

9 Cf. the views of R. A. Foakes and Robin Grove in the recent volume of essays, *Focus on Macbeth*, ed. J. R. Brown (London, 1982), pp. 11, 116.

10 *The Overreacher. A Study of Christopher Marlowe* (Cambridge, Mass., 1952), p. 116; cf. also Philip Brockbank, *Marlowe: Dr. Faustus* (London, 1962), p. 37.

11 As has become increasingly clear no interpretation ought to be based on a conflated text, both the A and the B text representing autonomous concepts of the hero and of the form of his fortunes good or bad. Cf. my "*Doctor Faustus*: 1604 und 1616", *Anglia*, 90 (1972), 470–93, and the more thorough discussion of Michael J. Warren, "*Doctor Faustus*: the old man and the text", *ELR*, 11 (1981), 111–47. I shall use the B text as the one which dramatises more fully the process of temptation, to which an analysis of A 136–8, lines not found in B, is added. All quotations are taken from W. W. Greg's great parallel edition of the texts (Oxford, 1950).

12 Thus there is no need here to discuss once again the nature of the Weird Sisters: their function as tempters does not differ, whether they are assumed to be demons or witches (and surely they possess some characteristic features of both); cf. R. H. West's sensible discussion in *Shakespeare and the Outer Mystery* (Lexington, 1968), Chap. 5.

13 *Shakespeare and the Nature of Man* (New York, repr. 1961), p. 24. Cf. also the important and detailed studies of R. L. Anderson, *Elizabethan Psychology and Shakespeare's Plays* (Iowa, 1927), and Hardin Craig, *The Enchanted Glass. The Elizabethan Mind in Literature* (Oxford, 1952).

14 *Of Wisdome Three Bookes* (London, 1612), pp. 45f.

15 *The Arte of English Poesie*, ed. G. D. Willcock and A. Walker (Cambridge, 1936), pp. 19f.

16 Cf. M. W. Bundy's extensive history, *The Theory of Imagination in Classical and Mediaeval Thought* (Urbana, 1927).

17 *A Treatise of Mans Imaginations. Shewing His naturall euill thoughts: His want of good thoughts: The way to reforme them* (Cambridge, 1607), pp. 21f. As a basic maxim the sentence is printed in italics.

18 *The Passions of the Minde* (London, 1601), p. 294; *The History of the World* (London, 1614) p. 210. An earlier formulation of this commonplace may be found in the late fifteenth-century *Malleus Maleficarum* by the two inquisitors H. Institor and J. Sprenger, frequently reprinted during the sixteenth century. They claim that "sicut Daemon potest interiorem Fantasiam immutare, sic etiam Intellectum obtenebrare. Et hoc quidem non erit immediate agere in animam, sed mediantibus fantasmatibus" (Frankfurt, 1580), p. 108.

19 Puttenham, p. 19.

20 Cf. the full statement in Alexander Potts, *A Treatise of Witchcraft* (London, 1616), p. 24: "So then to conclude, in euery Magicall action, there must be a concurrence of these three. First, the permitting will of God. Secondly, the suggestion of the Diuell, and his power cooperating. Thirdly, the desire and consent of the Sorcerer."

21 Cf. for a competent analysis Kerby Neill, "The degradation of the Red Cross Knight", in *That Soueraine Light. Essays in Honor of Edmund Spenser 1552–1952*, ed. W. R. Mueller and D. C. Allen (Baltimore, 1952), pp. 93–110.

22 John Jones, *The Arte and Science of preseruing Bodie and Soule* (London, 1579), p. 65. Hunter's hint, recorded in the Furness Variorum, has been strangely neglected. In *Wisdom*, Lucyfer summarises the whole process:

> To þe Mynde of þe Soule I xall mak suggestyun,
> Ande brynge hys Wndyrstondynge to dylectacyon,
> So þat hys Wyll make confyrmacyon. (365–7)

It may be of interest to add that, in Shakespeare, *suggest* and *suggestion* are fairly regularly associated with devilish or supernatural interference; cf. *Richard II*, III.iv. 75 f., *Othello*, II.iii. 340f., Sonnet 144.

23 *Some Shakespearean Themes* (London, 1959), p. 121. A fine analysis of the Witches' verse-rhythm is Robin Grove's " 'Multiplying villainies of nature' ", in *Focus on Macbeth*, pp. 113 ff.

24 This, "the absolutely shocking contradiction that man could be and think and feel the way Macbeth is and thinks and feels – and still do what Macbeth does", has been suggestively argued by Richard Waswo, "Damnation, Protestant style: Macbeth, Faustus, and Christian tragedy", *JMRS*, 4 (1974), p. 67.

25 This traditional view of evil and Macbeth's ambition has been vehemently attacked by Sanders, Chap. 14.

26 The crucial importance of the imagination for an adequate understanding of *Macbeth* has, ever since Bradley pointed to it as Macbeth's best faculty, frequently been recognised. What, to the best of my knowledge, has not been adequately treated is the relation of magical temptation to an imagination seen as both creative and destructive.

27 It does not follow from this that the vision of the dagger is nothing but the product of a heat-oppressed brain. Like the objective status of the Weird Sisters, that of the dagger cannot be definitely decided. The dagger belongs to that world of evil, Macbeth's hell-in-life, where nothing is but what is not. The most recent extensive study of the question is Ninian Mellamphy, "Macbeth's visionary dagger: hallucination or revelation", *ESC*, 4 (1978), 379–92.

28 *Shakespeare: Seven Tragedies. The dramatist's manipulation of response* (London, 1976), p. 128.

29 The Folio's full stop after *feast* is best replaced by some lesser mark of punctuation, such as a comma or semicolon; Kenneth Muir's editorial decision in the (New) Arden *Macbeth* is adopted here.

30 The passage has been similarly glossed by F. S. Boas in his edition of the play (London, 1932): "My imagination that will not be impressed by solid realities, because my thoughts are running only on the practice of necromancy".

31 Cf. among others Greg (ed.), pp. 102 f., and Constance Brown Kuriyama, "Dr. Greg and *Doctor Faustus*: the supposed originality of the 1616 text", *ELR*, 5 (1975), p. 177.

32 This reversal of values is here and throughout the play expressed through the use of Christian and theological terminology to describe and evaluate magical practice; cf. the fine analyses of Douglas Cole, *Suffering and Evil in the Plays of Christopher Marlowe* (Princeton, 1962), Chap. 5, and C. L. Barber, " "The form of Faustus' fortunes good or bad" ", *TDR*, 8, 4 (1964), pp. 98 ff.

33 That this is a central Marlovian characteristic and "involves a genuine ambivalence (not an ambiguity) of feeling" in all the plays has been proposed by J. R. Mulryne and Stephen Fender, "Marlowe and the 'comic distance' ", in *Christopher Marlowe*, ed. Brian Morris (London, 1968), pp. 49–64.

34 This has been frequently and controversially discussed; cf. especially the classic statements of W. W. Greg, "The damnation of Faustus", *MLR*, 41 (1946), 97–107, and L. B. Campbell, "Doctor Faustus: a case of conscience", *PMLA*, 67 (1952), 219–39.

35 As pointed out by Michael Hattaway, "The theology of Marlowe's *Doctor Faustus*", *Ren D.*, N.S. 3 (1970), p. 69.

36 That this is to be seen as temptation the corresponding scene in Robert Greene's *A Looking-Glasse for London and England* (2236ff.) makes perfectly clear. There a usurer, having echoed and quoted Faustus's last soliloquy, is thus given knife and halter: "The Euill Angel tempteth him, offering the knife and rope" (2261).

37 This makes the nature and power of language and the use of books and book-learning live issues in Marlowe's play, as criticism realises ever more clearly. For a speculative, but stimulating essay see A. B. Giamatti, "Marlowe: the arts of illusion", *YR*, 61 (1971/2), pp. 532 ff.

38 Such a more complex appreciation seems increasingly to gain critical support; cf. the thought-provoking essays assembled in *Two Renaissance Mythmakers: Christopher Marlowe and Ben Jonson*, ed. A. Kernan (Baltimore and London, 1977).

39 It should be noted that Faustus's way through the world is strewn with the victims of his magical practices, of whom some are jocularly, others more seriously harmed: the metamorphoses of Robin and Dick, the beating of the Pope and the Cardinals, the transformation and wounding of Benvolio and his crew, the torturing of the Old Man are the most important instances of this. It should also be noted that, quite in accordance with current Elizabethan opinion, the tempted Faustus becomes Faustus the tempter. This is certainly but briefly and implicitly dramatised in Marlowe's play. The Emperor, however, who mistakes the shadows of Alexander and his paramour for substances and whose "thoughts are so rauished / With sight of this" (B 1305–6), echoes Faustus's being ravished by magic (B 132). And the two scholars who count Helen a "blessed sight" (B 1809) are witnesses to the reversal of values which follows upon magical temptation, just as the tempted Faustus had felt "blest" by the sage conference of two infamous magicians (B 126).

40 This ambivalence has been analysed from various points of view: the most recent attempts are Johannes H. Birringer's *Marlowe's "Dr. Faustus" and "Tamburlaine"* (Frankfurt, Berne, New York, 1984) and John Bayley's *Shakespeare and Tragedy* (London, 1981), pp. 184–200.

EDWARD PECHTER

Julius Caesar and *Sejanus:*
Roman politics, inner selves
and the powers of the Theatre

For *Julius Caesar* and *Sejanus*, all critical roads must start from Rome. Both plays take the Roman setting seriously as an historical ground. Jonson's fidelity to his sources, scrupulously recorded in his own notes, is well known, but Shakespeare too stays close to the historical material he found in Plutarch, closer in fact than to the comparable material he drew upon for the English history plays. Dryden and Pope were impressed with the sense Shakespeare gives of genuine Romanness,[1] and today it is a commonplace to see the Roman plays as endeavouring to respect the style and values of the ancient world. But to say both playwrights were interested in historical accuracy, in getting Rome right, immediately raises some vexing questions. Getting it right implies an easy objectivity, as if the past ('it') were an object external to ourselves, who as interpreting subjects simply see it for what it is. But as recent theorists of history insist, the past does not exist except in our reconstructions of it.[2] To judge from the English histories Shakespeare himself must have understood this very well, and Jonson too, since he wrote it into the action of *Sejanus* in the figure of Cremutius Cordus.

Cordus enters the play, seventy-three lines into the action, just as Silius speaks of the pervasive spy network in Tiberius's Rome: 'our wordes, / How innocent soeuer, are made crimes; / We shall not shortly dare to tell our dreames, / Or thinke, but 'twill be treason.'[3] As if to prove Silius right, Natta and the other spies observe the Germanicans across stage (as Caesar and Antony observed Cassius and Brutus, themselves being observed), and then '*They whisper* . . . Who's that salutes your cousin? . . . one, that has writ / Annal's of late . . . How stands h'affected to the present state? . . . Haue you or seene, or heard part of his worke? . . . Not I, he meanes they shall be publike shortly' (74–84). By the time Cordus is accused in Act III, his annals have been published, but the point is that they are already public documents by the beginning of the play. As Silius says, everything in Rome is paraded out to view in the public arena. Cordus makes a great speech defending his Annals from the taint of topical relevance:

> But, in my worke,
> What could be aim'd more free, or farder of

From the times scandale, then to write of those,
Whom death from grace, or hatred had exempted? (445–8)

But the authorities think otherwise. For them, history, like everything else, can be understood only within the perspective of contemporary political concerns. And if they think this way of history, then history perforce becomes in effect what they think. (Jonson must have been irritated when the Council called him in to account for *Sejanus*, but not, I suppose, altogether surprised.)

We have come a long way apparently from the Roman setting; in fact we have never left it. For whatever else it may have meant to Shakespeare and Jonson, 'the matter of Rome' meant the public world, civic duty, acting in history, political power in action. There can be political plays not set in Rome, but no Roman play that is not a political play, at least not by Shakespeare or Jonson. *Antony and Cleopatra* is arguably an exception, but part of that play takes place in a world elsewhere. There is no such place for Coriolanus. Pindarus, the bondsman who gains his freedom by killing Cassius, his master, imagines such a place:

So, I am free; yet would not so have been,
Durst I have done my will. O Cassius!
Far from this country Pindarus shall run,
Where never Roman shall take note of him.   (V. iii. 47–50)

But where can he go? Rome *is* the world.

In this world of Rome, the characters in *Caesar* and *Sejanus* reveal and discover themselves in terms of politics, the needs that impel to public action. Yet both plays are concerned also with an alternative to Rome, existing not outside the geographical limits of the empire, but inside the self, in a space of consciousness that remains private and somehow detached from the demands and pressures of political action. The plays move us to the felt need to believe in such a refuge, though they also make us sceptical whether this autonomous inner self is a reality, or at least whether there is any access to it by theatrical means. I want to argue that the admixture of such belief and scepticism, the crossing of these contrary needs within a self-conscious sense of the power and limits of the theatrical medium, are at the heart of the dramatic energies in *Caesar* and *Sejanus*.

It is privacy that Brutus seeks at the beginning of *Julius Caesar*. 'I'll leave you', he tells Cassius in his first speech, and in his next he refers insistently to 'conceptions only proper to myself'. Cassius, though, won't allow Brutus his privacy:

Cas.   Tell me, good Brutus, can you see your face?
Bru.   No, Cassius; for the eye sees not itself
       But by reflection, by some other things.

61

> *Cas.* 'Tis just;
> And it is very much lamented, Brutus,
> That you have no such mirrors as will turn
> Your hidden worthiness into your eye,
> That you might see your shadow . . .
> *Bru.* Into what dangers would you lead me, Cassius,
> That you would have me seek into myself
> For that which is not in me?
> *Cas.* Therefore, good Brutus, be prepar'd to hear;
> And since you know you cannot see yourself
> So well as by reflection, I, your glass,
> Will modestly discover to yourself
> That of yourself which you yet know not of.   (I.ii. 51–70)

Self-knowledge, Brutus grants, is mediated: you can know yourself only as others represent you. Brutus nonetheless clings to a self, a 'me' in 'that which is not in me', but Cassius smoothly and slyly contradicts him. The danger is there, but 'you yet know not of' it. Cassius gets the last word here, and this leaves us with a disturbing question. If you do not know what's inside except as others tell you, in what sense do you have a self, a stable and independent core of being properly your own?

This exchange effectively originates the conspiracy, and it serves moreover to define the limits of the self in the play. The self in *Julius Caesar* is volatile; hence the shifts of belief throughout the play. Caesar 'is superstitious grown of late', and Calphurnia, though she 'never stood on ceremonies', yet 'now they fright' her. (II. i. 195, II ii. 13–14). At the end, Cassius cannot sustain his Epicureanism ('Now I change my mind / And partly credit things that do presage'), and Brutus wavers ('I know not how') between Stoic disapproval of suicide and disdain for the prospect of being led in triumph through the streets of Rome. As belief tends to disintegrate under the force of circumstance, so it is subject to manipulation. The mob, when we meet them in the first scene, have already transferred allegiance from Pompey to Caesar, and in the Forum they will shift twice again, from Caesar to Brutus to Antony. The mob, of course, is mindless, but high-mindedness, as in Brutus's case, is no protection: as the mob's 'basest mettle' is moved by the Tribunes at the beginning, so Cassius sees Brutus's 'honourable mettle may be wrought / From that it is dispos'd'. As Cassius 'would work' Brutus, so Decius would Caesar: 'Let me work, / For I can give his humour the true bent'. And Brutus is not merely the passive victim of manipulation. He 'fashions' the argument in his soliloquy, and as he is led into danger by Cassius, so he 'fashions' Caius Ligarius 'To do I know not what; but it sufficeth / That Brutus leads me on'.

If the self is so malleable in *Julius Caesar*, then the question of identity cannot be referred for an answer to any presumed inner core of being, but must rather be directed into the public world. Character is not to be defined psychologically but politically or historically. A man is what he does. The idea is introduced at the very beginning, in Flavius's words to the mob: 'you ought not walk / Upon a labouring day without the sign / Of your profession. Speak, what trade art thou?' The words point to something beyond the nasty class consciousness of Shakespeare's Rome, namely to the subsuming of all human identity into the actions of the body: you are your work. 'Speak hands for me', says Casca, and he becomes the deed's creature. Caesar's name, Cassius tells Brutus, is an empty abstraction; what's real about him is his falling sickness, his lack of stamina in the Tiber and so on. Or: what's in Cinna's name?

This reduction of meaning to action is what Brutus strives mightily against. He would transform the murder into a purgative sacrifice, not a butchery of the body, and metamorphose the dead man's blood on his sword and arms into a sacramental symbol of 'peace, freedom, and liberty'. He begs Antony to look through the body of the deed into the generating spirit of intention:

> Though now we must appear bloody and cruel,
> As by our hands and this our present act
> You see we do; yet see you but our hands,
> And this the bleeding business they have done.
> Our hearts you see not; they are pitiful;
> And pity to the general wrong of Rome —
> As fire drives out fire, so pity pity —
> Hath done this deed on Caesar. (III. i. 166–73)

Antony will have none of this. He shakes their bloody hands, one by one, but alone, he makes it clear that the blood is blood, and that if Caesar's spirit survives it has no abstract meaning — peace or tyranny or whatever — but remains the body's blood, begetting more blood, ranging for pitiless revenge against 'these butchers'.

At the centre of the play is a contrast between Antony, an extrovert who lives in the body, and Brutus, an introvert who lives in the mind. Obviously Antony succeeds and Brutus fails, but we would expect such a political animal to triumph in his own sphere. The larger question is whether we are expected to judge the terms of his triumph, to be aware of the limits of the sphere (no one, for instance, would want to call *Hamlet* the success story of Fortinbras). This larger question becomes especially important during the fifth Act. Brutus's last words are about his heart's joy in the loyalty of his friends, in contrast to Octavius and Antony's 'vile conquest'; and the last words about him in the play are Antony's, distinguishing Brutus's intentions from the other conspirators'. Both passages point towards qualities of being — honour, gentleness — that seem really to belong to Brutus's name and heart. But for all the power of this closural rhetoric, it is not clear that this image of Brutus can survive the corrosive ironies of the very words that create it. Whatever Antony says, Brutus's main action was a brutal not a gentle one, and the elements were not so much mixed in him as mixed up, 'an insurrection' in his 'state of man'. Brutus's own remarks about the loyalty of friends are even more problematic. To distinguish friendship from vile conquest assumes a realm of personal relations free from politics and self-serving, but like everything else in the play, friendship is bound up with political interests and vulnerable to the instability of political fashions. Cassius's manipulation of Brutus originates in an appeal to friendship:

> Brutus, I do observe you now of late;
> I have not from your eyes that gentleness
> And show of love as I was wont to have. (I.ii. 32–4)

and the 'quarrel-scene' in Act IV, with a neat symmetry, originates with Brutus's second-hand observations of Cassius: 'Thou hast describ'd / A hot friend cooling'. Caesar invites the conspirators to share wine before going with them 'like friends' to the Senate. Brutus's heart 'earns to think upon' the irony of this, but after the assassination he says without apparent irony that 'we [are] Caesar's friends, that have abridg'd / His time of fearing death'.

Above all, it is Antony who will not allow us to see the bond of friendship outside of a political context. 'Therefore I took your hands. . . . Friends am I with you all, and love you all.' This gesture of Antony's repeats the meaning of the play's central action; as bodies embrace on the sword, so flesh meets flesh through blood. These same gestures are enacted repeatedly in the last Act. Brutus himself appeals to Volumnius to kill him 'Even for that our love of old'. Volumnius refuses (though Strato agrees, provided Brutus will 'give me your hand first'), and the terms of his refusal are interesting: 'That's not an office for a friend, my lord'. But clearly it is, in Rome, where all human energy and relationship seem to be defined in terms of political action, and in which all political action takes the form of the same bloody deed. 'Slaying is the word' as Brutus says to Clitus. 'It is a deed in fashion.'

In making the existence of a private inner self highly problematic, *Julius Caesar* is not unique. In *Henry V*, written a few months earlier, and in *Hamlet*, which is imminent, Shakespeare makes us wonder whether there is or can be an interior self apart from represented public actions. The problem isn't even particularly Shakespearean; it is common to drama. 'Character gives us qualities, but it is in our actions – what we do – that we are happy or the reverse. In a play accordingly they do not act in order to portray the Characters; they include the Characters for the sake of the action' (*Poetics*, 1450ᵃ). Whether Cassius moves Brutus to find something not in himself, or whether it is there without Brutus's knowledge, how can this *it*, this *something* – these 'qualities' – be represented on stage, except in action? In the theatre, to borrow the Duke's words in *Measure for Measure*, 'if our virtues / Did not go forth of us, 'twere all alike / As if we had them not' (I.i. 34–6).

The problem is at the heart of *Sejanus*. Like Shakespeare's, Jonson's Rome is a totally politicised world, but beyond Shakespeare's the politics of Jonson's Rome are wholly and irredeemably corrupt. In the play's opening words, Silius's 'rarely met in court' becomes Sabinus's 'therefore, well met', and Silius agrees, 'Indeed, this place is not our sphære'. Right from the beginning, the official values of the play are unambiguously clear: disengagement from political intrigue, and withdrawal into the stability of the virtuous self. The authority of these values is nowhere more striking than in Lepidus's answer to Arruntius in the fourth Act, what arts preserve him against the omnipresent threat of absolute and arbitrary power:

> Arts, ARRVNTIVS?
> None, but the plaine, and passiue fortitude,
> To suffer, and be silent; neuer stretch
> These armes, against the torrent; liue at home,
> With my owne thoughts, and innocence about me,
> Not tempting the wolues iawes: these are my artes. (293–8)

But how can Jonson convincingly dramatise disdain for the court when the disdainers are voluntarily present? If the court is not their sphere, why are they there? why isn't Lepidus 'at home' where he belongs?

The simple answer is that Jonson needs the Germanicans, not for the action, to which they contribute nothing, but for their point of view upon the action. A more interesting kind of answer emerges if we interpret the Germanicans' speech metaphorically. The 'home' Lepidus refers to is not then a place, a Sabine farm, say, but a space of consciousness, once again the freedom of an individual's mind, the 'centred self' so richly embodied in Jonson's poetry.[4] But this answer raises more questions about Jonson's dramatic skill or success. As the imitation of speech, lyric can dramatise the qualities of consciousness, and Jonson's lyrics do so brilliantly. But the means to such dramatisation in lyric – wit, the play of allusion, tonal modulation – are not in themselves sufficiently effective in the theatrical drama, the imitation of action. Just how do you put 'living at home' on stage? Or consider the versions of this same ideal that precede Lepidus's speech in the fourth Act. The first is Agrippina, learning that Sejanus is now apparently absolute in his 'power, to turne those ruines all on vs', the second Sabinus, in response to Latiaris's exhortation that 'it must be actiue valour must redeeme / Our losse, or none':

> then stand vpright;
> And though you doe not act, yet suffer nobly:
> Be worthy of my wombe, and take strong cheare;
> What we doe know will come, we should not feare. (73–6)

> 'Twere better stay,
> In lasting darkenesse, and despaire of day.
> No ill should force the subiect vndertake

> Against the soueraigne, more then hell should make
> The gods doe wrong. A good man should, and must
> Sit rather downe with losse, then rise vniust. (161–6)

These speeches not only describe the same ideal as Lepidus's, but in sequence, and they all occur within 225 lines, from standing firm against adversity, to sitting down with loss, to suffering in silence, they systematically strip that ideal of any actively heroic dramatic presence. How can standing upright be presented as a theatrical action? In *Paradise Lost*, though we see the heroic angels falling, the epic voice can assure us that they 'stand faithful'; plays, though, have no epic voice. Harder still, how can Jonson represent sitting down with loss? In Thomas Lodge's *The Wounds of Civil War*, arguably the first real Roman play on the English Renaissance stage, Marius rejects the 'stales of fortune . . . / That still mislead the thoughts of simple men', and a few lines later the stage direction tells us that '*He lies down*'.[5] Or consider Chapman, most critics' candidate as Jonson's collaborator in the original version of *Sejanus*. Bussy in his first speech says that 'Fortune, not Reason, rules the state of things', and his way of disengaging himself from such an alien sphere is the same as Marius': '*He lies down*'.[6] Both rise, of course; the plays couldn't go on if they didn't. But their re-emergence into the action also places terrible strains upon those of us who wish to find consistency and coherence in the characters. With Lepidus, the problem is the other way round. Coherence and consistency he has in plenty, but no dramatic presence. For all his moral authority, he remains – suffering in silence, never stretching his arms against the torrent, living at home – effectively just not there.

One conclusion to draw from this is that Stoics are unsuitable for the centre of a play, as the later Chapman tends to demonstrate. Maybe Jonson knew this and turned it to his advantage, but this surmise brings us to more complicated hypotheses. Perhaps the inner self, private and free, is an impossibility not just for theatrical representation, but an impossibility *tout court*, an illusion. This is the claim of a number of recent theorists, oriented towards social history, who argue powerfully from the position that we exist not in heroic contrast to the culture we inhabit, but as its artifacts, constructed by its conventions.[7] In this view our presumably free thoughts are imprisoned in the language, not to say body, we inherit, everywhere marked by the traces of history. 'History', Fredric Jameson tells us, is 'the experience of Necessity, [it] is what hurts, it is what refuses desire and sets inexorable limits to the individual as well as collective praxis . . . we may be sure that its alienating necessities will not forget us, however much we might prefer to ignore them.'[8] Or to put this in terms of *Julius Caesar* and *Sejanus*: Brutus and the Germanicans try to ignore politics, but politics won't forget about them.

Such an approach sorts well with the still prevalent distaste for 'character criticism', and with the critical shift away from Brutus in favour of the representatives of power, Caesar and Antony. *Sejanus* too may seem enriched and illuminated: seeing the Germanicans as the victims of their own illusions suggests that Jonson, far from sacrificing dramatic effectiveness to a high-minded Stoic morality, was in good, and typically satiric control of his materials. Still, the power of this hard-nosed approach to represent the plays is also a power to misrepresent them, as witness Jonathan Goldberg, one of the most interesting of the new political critics, from whose brilliant recent book I have been shamelessly looting in the preceding pages:

> In *Sejanus* and *Julius Caesar* the tragic experience lies in the failure of the hero to become Caesar . . . The heroes insofar as they are attractive (and Brutus is, of course) are so precisely because they fail to become what they aspire to be (and Brutus, only at the very end, with the ghost, even sees what it was he wanted when he allowed Cassius's words to find out his spirit).[9]

'With the ghost', we are told, Brutus sees his own lust for power. How can Goldberg be so sure? Whatever Brutus sees, in any event, the perception does not occur 'at the very end' of the play – not, as Goldberg puts it elsewhere, 'finally' or 'at last'.[10] Though the critic's interpretation ends at this point, the play gives us and Brutus another whole Act of experience, including Brutus's sense of heart's gladness in the loyalty of his friends, and Antony's insistence on the gentleness which distinguished Brutus from all the other conspirators, who *were* motivated by the desire for power. Whatever the reasons not to take these words as the whole truth, it cannot be pretended that they and the whole fifth Act are simply not there. The new political criticism tends to be generated from a self-conferred position of privilege which almost inevitably tends to limit sympathy. Here the only reference to Brutus's attractiveness comes in a bored parenthesis, and its kind limited to that accorded to a misled child, who comes only gradually, 'finally', to know what the critic knew all along – that everything is politics, that *il n'y a rien hors la politique*.

Such detachment systematically pushes tragedy towards satire, and thus works better for a play like *Sejanus*, but even *Sejanus* is oddly represented by the statement that 'the tragic experience lies in the failure of the hero to become Caesar'. Sejanus is not at the centre of this play. He might have been another Richard III, or a Tamburlaine, but he totally lacks Richard's wit and charm, and he is much too small to support the weight of Tamburlaine's rhetoric which, when it descends upon him near the end, leaves us with nothing so much as '*scenicall* strutting, and furious vociferation' (*Jonson*, VIII. 587). In fact, Goldberg makes a better case for Tiberius as the play's centre. Tiberius has some great moments in the play, especially as he comes gradually to reveal his authority. His 'H'mh?' (III, 515) when Sejanus asks to marry into the royal family ought to be terrific. But Jonson puts definite limits on Tiberius's interest for us. The brilliance by which he maintains power is no doubt meant to astound the Romans on stage, but hardly ever the spectators. Jonson scrupulously flattens the angularities he found in Tacitus's Tiberius, and removes him from the action during the last two Acts. We well understand that he is ruling *in absentia*, but this abstraction does not alter the impression of his absence, and in drama the impression is the fact, as Maurice Morgann once remarked. What Sejanus and Tiberius lack as single figures, moreover, they lack equally in their relationship. Herford and Simpson are right to see Sejanus–Tiberius as the enactment of a favourite Jonsonian idea – the biter bit, the master of his master (*Jonson*, III, 17–18). But the enactment here is thin and diluted compared to Mosca–Volpone or Face–Subtle. Whether Jonson wasn't ready yet for the magnificent villainies of his subsequent masterpieces, or whether he deliberately diminished the power of these materials to engage our interest, the effect is the same. Sejanus and Tiberius even together cannot carry this play. The insight that allows us to remove the Germanicans from the centre of the dramatic experience can put nothing in their place, and the play must still look radically flawed.

Sejanus is something less than a fully realised masterpiece, but the play I see is a lot better than this one. It is also a more old-fashioned play, whose ethical function is, in Jonas Barish's words, to 'teach us to steel ourselves against disaster, and so defeat it'.[11] In this view we realise that in Tiberius's Rome all is indeed politics, but this is a fact from which we recoil in horror, not triumphantly patronising the Germanicans for their naive illusions about the autonomy of the Stoic self, but admiring them for the nobility of their desire to imagine and inhabit a space of consciousness free from the anxiety of power relations. It is also a relatively traditional *Julius Caesar* that I see before me. Brutus may have a *libido dominandi*, but as Honigmann says, 'the gentleness of Brutus survives as a general impression'.[12] The tragedy then, the pity of it, is not that Brutus fails to realise or to recognise his political ambitions, but that the total politicisation of experience in Rome blocks access to any area of self free from these ambitions, or allows no possibility for the expression of such a self apart from the murder of Caesar.

But this claim, that what Brutus and the Germanicans are matters more than what they do, returns to the same problem: how can such 'qualities of character' be presented in the drama? For Shakespeare, there is a rich critical tradition of answers to this question, available once more (however modified) now that Bradley-damning has ceased to be obligatory. With Jonson, though, the problem is more acute, and no help comes from the critical tradition to solve it. 'Whereas in Shakespeare the effect is due to the way in which the characters *act upon* one another, in Jonson it is given by the way the characters *fit in* with each other.' This is Eliot,[13] who effectively established the modern interest in Jonson, but in terms that pretty clearly yield character to Shakespeare without contest. And rightly so: Jonson smoothed out not just Tiberius, but all the figures in *Sejanus*; they are black or white, tragical humours as it were, for whose elemental simplicity change is out of the question. Yet if Jonson's characters lack the depth to change, his spectators do not, or at least might not, and this is what I want to consider now – what happens to us, the shifts in our relation to the action, the growth in our consciousness of that relation and its meaning. (This suggests an answer in passing to the question that kept coming up earlier, what is at the centre of the dramatic experience in *Sejanus: we are*.)

At the beginning, the Germanicans' speech is studded with echoes of *Julius Caesar*. Silius refers to a lost freedom: 'We since became the slaues to one mans lusts; / And now to many' (63–4); and he sounds like Cassius ('When went there by an age . . . / But it was fam'd with more than with one man?'). Arruntius carries on from Silius: speaking of 'god-like CATO' who 'had power, / As not to liue his [Caesar's] slaue, to dye his master' (91–2), Arruntius too sounds like Cassius ('Cassius from bondage will deliver Cassius'). He speaks of Brutus who 'did strike / So braue a blow into the monsters heart / That sought vnkindly to captiue his countrie' (95–6), and then sounds like Brutus, indeed virtually quotes him, though in the dramatic fiction it is Cordus's Annals he is quoting: '*Braue* CASSIVS *was the last of all that race*' (104; 'The last of all the Romans, fare thee well!'). Such echoes, and there are many more as the first Act continues, lead me, as they have led others, to think that Jonson was very conscious of *Julius Caesar* when he wrote *Sejanus*, and expected at least part of his audience to share the consciousness.[14] But the point need not be pushed. Whether we know *Caesar* or not, we know enough about plays to imagine that we are witnessing the origins of a conspiracy. How long before the violent language ('brests . . . rip'd vp to light', 'cut / Mens throates with whisprings' [24–5, 30–1]) erupts into action?

With Arruntius, the most verbally aggressive of the Germanicans, it very nearly does. 'I'ld hurle his panting braine about the ayre', he says about Sejanus, and actually moves across stage towards Sejanus's toadies, 'Death! I dare tell him so; and all his spies: / You, sir . . .' but Sabinus gets him to 'forbeare' (255–60). This little action, or frustration of action, is performed twice more in the Act (425–34, 505–6). With the departure of the court, Arruntius is still raging, and now for the fourth time restrained. 'Checke your passion', says Silius, but his addition, 'Lord DRVSVS tarries' (548) is the pivot by which we move from passion checked to passion expressed. Drusus picks up Arruntius's rage towards Sejanus in four staccato speeches, each punctuated by Arruntius's encouragement. At this point Sejanus re-enters, Drusus blocks him and strikes him: 'Take that'. Drusus is given nine provocative and exultant lines during which Sejanus stands transfixed, 'at gaze', presumably too callow to respond. 'A noble prince!' says Arruntius, then all four of the Germanicans shout "A CASTOR" four times in unison and exit triumphantly from the stage.

It is the grand climactic action we have been promised by the affective structure of the whole first Act, grander for its being so long in coming, grandest of all in what it promises for the future. Having seen so brave a blow struck upon the monster that sought unkindly to captive his country, how long now before we can share in striking a blow into the monster's heart? A long time indeed, maybe never; so we find out in what follows. Sejanus is alone on stage, and his three couplets end the Act. Whether callow or not, he had been calculating in his silence, bearing his wrong with patience, covering his wrath. Drusus's blow in no way weakens Sejanus's position, and has indeed no repercussions for Drusus himself. Sejanus was already committed to eliminating Drusus anyway, so the murder to come is simply 'styled . . . new', turned from 'my practice late' to 'my fell iustice'. Drusus's blow accomplishes exactly nothing.

The anti-climactic effect is unusual, and even more remarkable for its recurrence in the middle of the play. At the end of Act II, Jonson carefully sets up the indictment of Silius. In the beginning of Act III, the Senate convenes, Silius enters, is charged, and the scene is set: 'SILIVS accus'd? sure he will answere nobly' (34). But then, unexpectedly, Tiberius enters with a long speech conferring the sons of the murdered Drusus upon the care of the Senate. 'By IOVE', says Arruntius, 'I am not OEDIPVS inough / To vnderstand this SPHYNX' (64–5). Neither are we, but if Tiberius's purposes are clouded in mystery, so are Jonson's. Why cut across the impetus of the action with this apparent irrelevancy? After Tiberius's speech, the Senate waxes rhapsodic about Tiberius, who interrupts them – that is, interrupts the interruption he has caused – and puts the play back on track: 'We will not hold / Your patience, *Fathers*, with long answere . . . / Proceed to your affaires' (149–53). Finally, after 118 lines, which is long enough to be patient, Silius gets his chance to answer nobly. And so he does, in powerful speech and powerful, if self-directed, action: 'Looke vpon SILIVS, and so learne to die' (339). But as the climactic power of Silius's suicide is weakened by Jonson's prior interruption, so now Jonson refuses to let us dwell upon it. 'Be famous euer for thy great example', says Arruntius (343), but we are made almost immediately to forget him. First Tiberius takes a step to regain the initiative: he intended to pardon Silius, so he says. At this point there is a squabble about what to do with the estate. Heroic climaxes are decisive events, but here the unheroic life of legality and death duties goes on.

And on, as Cordus is now arraigned. Cordus's speech is by no means without interest. He claims his Annals are irrelevant to 'the times scandale', but the phrase itself, which is not in Tacitus, says that the times *are* a scandal. Cordus gets it both ways, but in terms of the overall rhythm of the action, the very interest of his speech is problematic, for his foxy rhetoric tends further to displace Silius's leonine gesture from our thoughts. What is more, or rather less, even its own diminished climax is not allowed to stand. Cordus 'puts 'hem to their whisper' (463), thus departing from the action as he had entered it; but he leaves a prisoner, and his books will be burnt. In Tacitus he 'walked out of the senate, and starved himself to death',[15] but we have no dramatic basis to know this. Near the end of the play Cordus's death is listed by Sejanus among his accomplishments (V. 247), but this is too late to be of much interest, and here and now his fate is left undecided, indecisive, unclimactic.

Where are we then at the end of this third-Act sequence? The answer comes immediately with the clearing of the stage and Tiberius alone with Sejanus. 'This businesse hath succeeded well, SEIANVS' (488), he blandly says, and we must recognise that the apparent climax of the Senate scene accomplishes what Drusus's blow did in the first Act: nothing. In both cases, moreover, anti-climax looks like a deliberately contrived effect. Jonson takes events from the background or narrative periphery of his sources, enacts them prominently on centre stage, then leaches from them all significance. Why? Why twice build up our expectations only to disappoint them?

An answer is available in the form of a hypothesis about Jonson's attitude towards his audience. For the spectators of the popular theatre, Jonson's contempt is well-known.[16] So is his pride in *Sejanus*. Whether or not it is *Sejanus* to which Jonson is referring at the end of *Poetaster* – something 'That must, and shall be sung, high, and aloofe, / Safe from the wolues black iaw, and the dull asses hoofe' (*Jonson*, IV. 324) – this is clearly *his* play, the one he wanted to write. Yet *Sejanus* is not altogether the product of an intransigent aloofness. In their editions, Barish and Herford and Simpson point out that *Sejanus* furnishes many instances in which Jonson mediated classical ideals of decorum to suit popular theatrical taste, Drusus's blow and Silius's suicide on stage among them. Yet I wonder if Jonson would thank us for such apologies, as if he reluctantly debased his material somewhat, simply to please us. Jonson was not a great compromiser, and *Sejanus* remains one of his least compromised achievements. To be sure, he must respect – that is, pay attention to – what Aristotle calls 'the defects of our hearers'.[17] In 'these Iig-giuen times' (*Jonson*, V. 431), without gambols or thrasonical struttings, his audience will sleep, or indeed hoot him off stage. So he gives us some big actions, even some blood and gore. This is not much compared to *Julius Caesar*, which is itself a relatively cool play for Shakespeare. Even this, moreover, is not so much to please us, for as I have argued these climactic moments turn into profoundly frustrating anti-climaxes, as to move us (and this, at last, is the hypothesis I wish to make) beyond the base desires we bring into the playhouse towards satisfactions of a nobler kind.

The last Acts suggest what these are. After the Senate scene, we get Tiberius's 'h'mh'. From now on it is clear that the effective struggle in the play is not between good and evil, but between the evils of Sejanus and Tiberius. This is a struggle from which we are detached, and the removal of

Tiberius can only increase the detachment. We hear of the episode at Spelunca, and Jonson does not give us any privileged information whether Sejanus's rescue restored him to Tiberius's favour. We are as ignorant as the on-stage characters, but if we share their ignorance, do we share their interest as well? Spelunca is juxtaposed with Agrippina's standing upright, Sabinus's sitting down with loss, Lepidus's living at home; in this context, how much does Spelunca matter? If we have attained to something like Lepidus's disengagement, Jonson rewards us in the final Act with the pleasures of satire. We get Sejanus's high terms, but they are too silly to astound us, especially juxtaposed with his fawning upon his followers when it looks as if he might need them. On the other side we get the silliness of Regulus and Macro.[18] And of course we get the immensely funny grand finale, with cartoon Senators like Sanquinius 'with his slow belly, and his dropsie' (455), and Haterius, whose 'gout keepes him most miserably constant' (623) when the other toadies scramble away from Sejanus's side.

We watch all this, I think, with amused detachment. Arruntius has an exultant moment at the fall of Latiaris ('O, the spie! / The reuerend spie is caught' [650–1]), but Arruntius's authority has by this point been supplanted by that of Lepidus, who knows better and cares less. Nor can we be expected to join those cartoon Senators now calling for blows on the monster that sought unkindly to captive his country. Sejanus's death is politically meaningless, his dismemberment the expression of mob violence. Arruntius predicts Macro will be worse, and we can be sure he's right whether or not we know our Tacitus. Fear, though, is not relevant here, and as Arruntius says in the play's penultimate speech, 'he that lends you pitty, is not wise' (897). The moral, then, true wisdom, is the traditional Stoic ideal, living at home:

> Make playn thyn hert that it be not knotted
> With hope or dred, and se thy will be bare
> Ffrom all affectes whome vice hath ever spotted;
> Thy self content with that is the assigned,
> And vse it well that is to the allotted.
> Then seke no more owte of thy self to fynde
> The thing that thou haist sought so long before,
> For thou shalt fele it sitting in thy mynde.[19]

Such wisdom may not be accessible to the representations of the stage, but if Jonson's stage representation works on us as I have suggested, then we will leave the theatre feeling it sitting in our mind.

What sits in our mind at the end of *Julius Caesar*? Shakespeare's designs upon us are more ambivalent and complex than Jonson's, and hypotheses about them must be even more tentative. I think that Brutus's honour and gentleness are a major part of the final effect, but not merely because of the impressions we get of a character external to ourselves. If a belief in such qualities of Brutus sustains itself against irony, it is because of what the play does to us as well as what it shows us. I shall limit myself to the play's action upon us during the climax in the middle, building on Kenneth Burke's witty and endlessly suggestive essay, 'Antony in behalf of the play'.[20] Burke's premise is that the play brings us first of all to participate in Brutus's enterprise, however reluctantly, with whatever doubts: 'the conspirators would not so much as touch him until you also had been brought into the band' (332). Then, as Antony transforms the mob from conspirators to Caesarians, so the play bends our allegiance, from Brutus to Antony himself. With this reversal our doubts about the conspiracy, subordinate at first, become available for exploitation, and Antony now guides us through the play's second half.

Burke's *Caesar*, then, moves its spectators through a simple but powerful arc of experience, first engaging us, then turning us against our own engagement. Not the least advantage of Burke's essay is allowing us to recognise in *Caesar* a characteristically Shakespearean design (think of *Richard III* and *Richard II*, even *Lear* in part). But *Caesar* remains an odd sort of play with eccentric movements of its own. It gives us not just one but a succession of three distinct climactic actions in the middle – assassination, oration, and finally the murder of Cinna the poet. It seems fair to suggest that Antony's oration is pivotal, both for the on-stage and the off-stage mob, but what are we to make of Cinna's murder? In this scene, we witness a group surround and kill an isolated individual. The stage action must remind us of the assassination, and the echoes in the language reinforce the sense of connection: as Brutus would stand up against Caesar's spirit without dismembering Caesar, so *1. Pleb.* would 'pluck but his name out of his heart' and then turn Cinna going. Presumably we are, at both the assassination and here, at once killer and killed, but do the proportions change, and does the meaning of the action change?

For one version of the scene's meaning, we can look at John Ripley's description of Byam Shaw's 1957 production:

> as Antony cried, 'Here was a Caesar! when comes such another?' ... a star appeared, a reminder of vanished constancy in the midst of cataclysm. Suddenly Cinna entered, and the mob surged back, bearing lighted torches. When they left, the mutilated body of the poet hung, like some bloodstained rag, over the pulpit. And in the blue-black heavens the star shone on, a dispassionate witness to bloodlust and anarchy as the curtain fell.[21]

Here the lighting and backdrop carefully shape the meaning of Cinna's murder into an extension of Caesar's assassination: the murderers of Caesar have brought chaos, including this chaos. Shakespeare's theatre, however, did not have the manipulative resources of the modern stage, and without them it is difficult to see how Cinna's murder can be hung on the conspirators. Most productions suggest that Cinna's blood is on Antony's hands, not

Brutus's, and though modern versions from the left as it were, as with Welles's brown shirts, can be equally manipulative in their pre-packaged meaning, the textual sequence seems to support this interpretation: Antony stirs up the mob, the mob kills Cinna, and as they drag him off the stage on one side, Antony enters on the other with 'these many, then, shall die; their names are prick'd'.

This in fact is how Burke understands the scene, but he nonetheless takes it as confirming the reversal of our feelings from Brutus to Antony. In order to allow us to participate in the mob's action, or at least not be wholly repelled by it, Burke asserts that we 'somehow know that the poetic Cinna will suffer no fundamental harm. He will merely be slain-unslain, like a clown hit by cannon balls' (343). There is some element of truth in this: 'all facts and personages of great importance in world history occur . . . twice . . . the first time as tragedy, the second as farce'.[22] But the authority of stage history suggests that the scene is more of a horrific black comedy than a circus, a lynching at the end of which Cinna is definitively dead (sometimes, indeed, dismembered). A quasi-comic nobody he may be, but nobody can come close to Everyman, and to whatever extent we had become the mob created by the action of Antony's words, we cease to be members of that body when Cinna falls.

I am arguing that the succession of three climactic moments here serves not just to reverse the flow of our feeling, but to reverse it twice, from Brutus to Antony and back again. Antony, then, doesn't have the second half of the play, but merely a moment at its beginning. It is a powerful moment, constituted of everything Brutus is or has not: pathetic rather than ethical rhetoric, feeling rather than noble abstractions, tears of compassion for the bleeding body rather than a pitiless pity for the general wrong of Rome. Antony lives in the flesh, and he loves plays. His 'passion . . . is catching', but such instinctive warmth, unsullied by cold ideals, itself chokes pity with custom of fell deeds. Just after Cinna falls, we see Antony casually trading Lepidus a nephew for a brother, then coolly determining how to change Caesar's will. Dorsch points us backwards to 'a contrast with Brutus's refusal to take the precaution of killing Antony himself',[23] and we might look ahead to another version of the same contrast, Brutus's fastidiousness about monetary bribes in the 'quarrel-scene'. Such contrasts seem to me to radiate affectively from the contrasting sides of the climactic succession in Act III: the murder of Caesar by Brutus, the murder of Cinna by Antony. The unambiguously repellent mob violence of the latter does not retroactively remove the horror of the former. Brutus's desire to transform his murderous action into a purgative ritual remains wrong-headed and radically flawed. But having been moved by the play back and forth so swiftly between the aggressor's and the victim's role can not only make us experience contradictions, but can make us conscious of the experience. In such a consciousness, which opens into genuine differences of intention hidden under similar actions, pity and gentleness of heart, though unseen, can seem to be real enough, as real as the guilty blood visible upon the hands.

The first recorded comparison of Shakespeare and Jonson's Roman plays is in Leonard Digges' commemorative poem about Shakespeare, published in the Folio of 1640:

> So have I seene, when Cesar would appeare,
> And on the Stage at halfe-sword parley were,
> *Brutus* and *Cassius*: oh how the Audience,
> Were ravish'd, with what wonder they went thence,
> When some new day they would not brooke a line,
> Of tedious (though well laboured) *Catilines*;
> *Sejanus* too was irkesome, they priz'de more
> Honest *Iago*, or the jealous Moore.[24]

We know Digges was right; *Caesar* was a great success in its own time, *Sejanus* a failure. Moreover, theatrical history has sustained this initial reaction; *Caesar* is still and has virtually always been popular, *Sejanus* always and still ignored. We are likely to confer special authority on Digges' remarks, in part because they are a contemporary witness, and even more because their emphasis upon ravishing audiences corresponds nicely with our own interest in Shakespeare's theatrical power. This, of course, is the flow with which I have been going in the preceding pages, but I want here at the end to issue a few sceptical caveats, if not actually to block these currents, at least to turn them awry.

In the first place, we cannot properly understand Digges unless we understand his context. The immediate context for Digges is Jonson's 1623 memorial poem, which he echoes (or conceivably which echoes him). The larger context, I suggest, includes a wide range of seventeenth-century texts, mentioning sometimes one or the other of Shakespeare and Jonson, sometimes both, sometimes neither, but in this last case concerned with literary qualities or figures that can be associated with either Shakespeare or Jonson: ease and labour, genius and craft, sublimity and decorum, wit and judgement, Homer and Virgil, *inventio* and *dispositio*, nature and art, emotional and intellectual appeal, theatrical and literary power.[25] Part of our problem in trying to understand this context is that we come to it backwards, through a figure like Hazlitt, by whose time it has become a set of rhetorical gestures from which the original significance has been displaced by the desire to use Shakespeare's virtues to demonstrate Jonson's defects.[26] We do better to understand this context in terms of its origins in the rhetorical critics of antiquity, especially Horace: the living monument outlasting brass or marble, familiar from Shakespeare's own Sonnets, which we find in both Jonson's and Digges's commemorative verses and in Milton's 'On Shakespeare', goes back to the Odes, II. 20 and III. 30.

This classical tradition of critical judgment is aimed not at valuing one kind of quality or writer at the expense of the other, but rather at finding a balanced response to a variety of different and potentially conflicting values. If we try to put Digges into this context, he is still saying the same thing, that Shakespeare excelled Jonson in his power to move audiences in the theatre, but not meaning the same thing, for his statement now acknowledges that there are advocates of literary-cum-intellectual power as superior to theatrical power. Digges is disagreeing with such advocates, but without the implied acknowledgement that they exist, and exist to be taken seriously, his statement would be tautological or empty – like telling a Montrealer that winter is cold.

Are we capable of such an acknowledgement ourselves? Only with difficulty, I suppose. In these days especially of the theatrical Shakespeare, we admire his professionalism, and his apparent indifference, except in financial terms, to the publication of any of his plays; and on the other side we find misguided Jonson's loathing of the stage, and his aspiration not just to readers but to extraordinary ones. But as Barish has demonstrated, the anti-theatrical prejudice has been around far too long not to be taken seriously, even respected. There is a case to be made, and Jonson, who worked both within the terms of the prejudice and the conditions of the theatre, makes it in a way whose brilliance and thoughtfulness should not be patronised.

The fact that *Julius Caesar* has almost always been a theatrical success and *Sejanus* almost always a failure is rather a point of departure than a place to end. Whatever their similarities, the two plays are in some ways like chalk and cheese. There are different values in them, different ideas and themes: one propounds Stoicism, the other judges it; one makes us seek to find ourselves in public action, the other in a withdrawal from it. Yet as this last suggests, they differ particularly in their willingness to work within the constraints of the theatrical medium. *Caesar* succeeds after all in large part because it gives us a powerful emotional involvement in the dramatic action; *Sejanus* doesn't because it doesn't. Yet theatrical effectiveness is not a transcendental signified; it does not encompass the whole field of value. We are poorer if we cannot admire the austerity and intelligence of *Sejanus*, a play which does not subdue Jonson to what he works in like the dyer's hand.

Putting it that way should remind us that Shakespeare himself acknowledged the limits of the theatre. And of course his plays can respond to the requirements placed upon them to cohere intellectually and even morally, as well as to be potent in the theatre (Shakespeare is not Fletcher). But Jonson also was not without the other kind of virtue. It can be claimed that *Sejanus* fails because it tries to do something profoundly anti-theatrical, but it knows what it is doing, and it makes careful use of the very theatrical appetites it would transform into something arguably nobler than themselves. I can imagine theatrical circumstances in which it might succeed, and it is depressing to think that I shall almost certainly never get the chance to find out whether these imaginings are right.

NOTES

1 See T. J. B. Spencer, 'Shakespeare and the Elizabethan Romans', *Shakespeare Survey*, 10 (1957), pp. 27–38.
2 See J. H. Hexter, *Doing History* (Bloomington, Indiana, 1971); Nancy S. Struever, *The Language of History in the Renaissance: Rhetoric and Historical Consciousness in Florentine Humanism* (Princeton, 1970); and Hayden White, *Metahistory: The Historical Imagination in Nineteenth-century Europe* (Baltimore, 1973).
3 *Ben Jonson*, ed. C. H. Herford and Percy and Evelyn Simpson (11 vols. Oxford, 1925–52), IV, p. 357. All references to Jonson's works will be to this edition, interpolated henceforth parenthetically in the text, Act and line numbers for *Sejanus*, volume and page numbers for other works.
4 See Thomas M. Greene, 'Ben Jonson and the centered self', *SEL*, 10 (1970), pp. 325–48. See also Richard S. Peterson, *Imitation and Praise in the Poems of Ben Jonson* (New Haven, Conn., 1982).
5 Ed. Joseph W. Houppert (London, 1970), III.ii. 22–3, 58.
6 Ed. N. S. Brooke (1964; rpt. Manchester, 1979), I.i. 33.
7 Foucault's works are seminal here. See also Stephen J. Greenblatt, *Renaissance Self-Fashioning from More to Shakespeare* (Chicago, 1980), and as editor, *The Forms of Power and The Power of Forms in the Renaissance* (Norman, Okl., 1982); Fredric Jameson, *The Political Unconscious: Narrative as a Socially Symbolic Act* (Ithaca, N.Y., 1981); Frank Lentricchia, *After the New Criticism* (Chicago, 1980); and Edward W. Said, *The World, the Text, and the Critic* (Cambridge, Mass., 1983).
8 Jameson, *The Political Unconscious*, p. 102.
9 *James I and the Politics of Literature: Jonson, Shakespeare, Donne, and Their Contemporaries* (Baltimore, 1983), pp. 185–6.
10 'So, *finally*, Brutus sees "that which is not in me" . . . the spirit of Caesar mighty yet. *At last*, Brutus sees the very form of power before him' (176, my emphases).
11 'Introduction' to his edition of the play (New Haven, Conn., 1965), p. 15.
12 E. A. J. Honigmann, *Shakespeare: Seven Tragedies: The Dramatist's Manipulation of Response* (London, 1976), p. 41.
13 *The Sacred Wood* (1920; rpt. London, 1964), pp. 112–3.
14 See Herford and Simpson, II. 9; John Dover Wilson, 'Ben Jonson and *Julius Caesar*', *Shakespeare Survey*, 2 (1949), pp. 36–43; and Robert Ornstein, *The Moral Vision of Jacobean Tragedy* (Madison, Wisconsin, 1960), p. 90.
15 *The Annals of Imperial Rome*, translated with an introduction by Michael Grant (1977; rpt. Harmondsworth, 1981), p. 175.
16 See Barish, 'Jonson and the loathèd stage', in *The Anti-theatrical Prejudice* (Berkeley, California, 1981), pp. 132–54. See also Peter Carlson, 'Judging spectators,' *ELH*, 44 (1977), pp. 443–57.
17 *Rhetoric*, 1404[a]. The passage is worth looking at in full: 'the whole business of rhetoric being concerned with appearances, we must pay attention to the subject of delivery, unworthy though it is, because we cannot do without it. The right thing in speaking really is that we should be satisfied not to annoy our hearers, without trying to delight them: we ought in fairness to fight our case with no help beyond the bare facts: nothing, therefore, should matter except the proof of those

facts. Still, as has been already said, other things affect the result considerably, owing to the defects of our hearers.'

18 Barish comments on V.117–70: 'it is hard to discover much point to Regulus's comings and goings in this scene, or to Macro's sarcasms on them. They would seem to be a rare instance of Jonson's hamming his material so as to make it more palatable for the stage' (201). For a different interpretation, however, see Anthony Miller, 'The Roman state in *Julius Caesar* and *Sejanus*', in *Jonson and Shakespeare*, ed. Ian Donaldson (London, 1983), pp. 179–201, 193.

19 *Collected Poems of Sir Thomas Wyatt*, ed. Kenneth Muir (Cambridge, Mass., 1950), p. 190.

20 *The Philosophy of Literary Form* (Berkeley, California, 1973), pp. 329–43.

21 *'Julius Caesar' on Stage in England and America, 1599–1973* (Cambridge, 1980), p. 257.

22 Karl Marx, *The Eighteenth Brumaire of Louis Bonaparte* (New York, 1963), p. 15.

23 *Julius Caesar*, ed. T. S. Dorsch (1955; rpt. London, 1966), p. 91.

24 We actually have two poems by Digges, one of which was published in the 1623 Folio. It seems likely that both were ready for 1623, but cut for reasons suggested by E. A. J. Honigmann, *Shakespeare's Impact on His Contemporaries* (London, 1982), pp. 38–40. Both poems are printed in E. K. Chambers, *William Shakespeare: A Study of Facts and Problems* (2 vols.; Oxford, 1930), II. 231–4, from which my quotation is taken.

25 The best known of these seventeenth-century texts are *Timber*, Milton's 'On Shakespeare' and 'L'Allegro', and Dryden's essays *passim*, but especially the comparison of Shakespeare and Jonson in *An Essay of Dramatic Poesy* in *Essays of John Dryden*, ed. W. P. Ker (1900; rpt. 2 vols.; New York, 1961), I.82–3.

26 See the editor's 'Preface', in Ian Donaldson's *Jonson and Shakespeare*, pp. viii–x.

PHILIP EDWARDS

'Seeing is believing': action and narration in *The Old Wives Tale* and *The Winter's Tale*

Whether or not Shakespeare had Peele's *Old Wives Tale* in mind when he was writing *The Winter's Tale*, the resemblances are striking.[1] Peele's play (of uncertain date, published in 1595) twice mentions 'winter's tale' in its induction:

> a merry winter's tale would drive away the time trimly.　(85–6)

> I am content to drive away the time with an old wives winter's tale.　(98–9)[2]

Here we see the affinity of the offhand titles of the two plays; they both imply an idle and foolish tale to which you couldn't give credence. Shakespeare, of course, has an extra level of meaning in his title; and when Mamilius, chief victim in the *wintry* tale, gives the play its ambiguous name, the passage seems to hark back to the first of Peele's phrases just quoted.

Hermione	'Pray you sit by us,
	And tell's a tale.
Mamilius	Merry, or sad, shall't be?
Hermione	As merry as you will.
Mamilius	A sad tale's best for winter . . .　(II.i. 22–5)

In starting to tell his tale, Mamilius only gets as far as 'There was a man . . . dwelt by a churchyard' when Leontes, the real-life man of winter, storms in. Is this interruption an allusion to the most famous element in Peele's play, the electrifying appearance of Madge's characters as she begins to tell her tale?

Other resemblances between the plays include the prominence of references to the passage of the seasons, the appearance of a figure representing Time in the middle of the play, and the theme of resurrection. Much more important than these, however, is the resemblance which gives rise to this essay: the sudden shifts of focus in presenting what is proclaimed to be a very unlikely story, and especially the movement between narration and performance.

We should look first, however, at an important feature of *The Winter's*

Tale which came directly from Peele, though not from *The Old Wives Tale*. This link makes it more likely that the resemblances already noted are not fortuitous. The feature in question is the handing out of appropriate flowers by Perdita, costumed as Flora.[3] In *The Arraignment of Paris*, the goddess Flora is literally preparing the ground for the entry of Pallas, Juno and Venus:

> The primrose and the purple hyacinth,
> The dainty violet and the wholesome mint,
> The double daisy and the cowslip, queen
> Of summer flowers, do overpeer the green. (I.iii. 23–6)

Like Perdita, by sheer force of language, 'the queen of flowers prepares a second spring' (I.iii. 32). Flora then describes the flowers which she has prepared for the individual goddesses; for example, for Juno 'yellow oxlips bright as burnished gold'; for Pallas 'flowers of hue and colours red' including 'Julie-flowers'; for Venus 'sweet violets in blue, / With other flowers infixed for change of hue'. There is a curious additional premonition of *The Winter's Tale* when in admiring these gifts Venus says:

> Hadst thou a lover, Flora, credit me,
> I think thou wouldst bedeck him gallantly. (I.iv. 50–1)

It is hard at this point not to think of Perdita making a garland for Florizel 'to strew him o'er and o'er'. Florizel is, like Paris, the hero of Peele's play, a prince in the guise of a shepherd.

It is common for Peele to use framing techniques in his plays to suggest different layers and levels in the fiction. The most sophisticated example is in *The Arraignment of Paris*. The play starts with a grim prologue by Ate, who explains that the play we are about to witness is the first stage of the destined destruction of Troy. The 'fatal fruit', the golden apple which is to begin it all, is in her hand. This beautiful play therefore has both its own nature and a much changed nature when viewed as part of a whole cycle of events. The light which bathes it is the strange light of a sunlit landscape seen against the intense black of an approaching storm. But by a sleight of hand, Peele makes the storm disappear from our minds. Paris is arraigned before the gods for awarding the golden fruit to Venus, and Diana is given the task of resolving the quarrel. Diana moves to the centre of the hall and gives the apple to Queen Elizabeth in person. By making her thus step out of the fiction into the life of the audience, Peele changes the status of his play from an induction to the collapse of Troy to an induction to the self-created destiny of the second Troy. The fiction of the play is given threefold definition: as itself, as modified by the prologue, as modified by the conclusion.

In both *The Battle of Alcazar* and *David and Bethsabe*, Peele uses a presenter to comment on and explain the action, and to fill in bits of the story. From *David and Bethsabe*, for example:

Urias in the forefront of the wars
Is murdered by the hateful heathen's sword,
And David joys his too dear Bethsabe.
Suppose this past, and that the child is born,
Whose death the prophet solemnly doth mourn.   (570–4)

The presenter in *Alcazar* uses dumbshows, mostly allegorical, to underline the moral significance of the action. The use made of the presenters in these two plays looks forward to the use of Gower, the presenter of *Pericles Prince of Tyre*, and by this route establishes another important link between Peele and *The Winter's Tale*.[4] By means of Gower, Shakespeare ostentatiously places *Pericles* as a medieval romance, a very old tale which gives perennial delight. Gower moves his play forward by varying means of presentation: narration, dumbshow, and performance. In the Chorus to Act III, for example, he introduces a dumbshow in which it is revealed that the distressed knight is a prince, who is then summoned home with his bride to Tyre. Gower then tells of their perilous sea-journey, and concludes:

And what ensues in this fell storm
Shall for itself itself perform.
I nill relate, action may
Conveniently the rest convey.

('Action' means, as usual, 'acting'.) Narrative is an integral part of the play; it is offered as an alternative to performance, which is to vivify the most important parts of the story. *The Winter's Tale* handles its alternation of narration and performance very differently, but the arrow which points from Peele's presenters to Gower points directly forward to *The Winter's Tale*.

To return to Peele, everyone agrees that the technique of the frame which Peele uses in *The Old Wives Tale* is unique. Three young men are lost at night in a wood, and they are given shelter in a cottage. The old woman begins to tell them a tale to pass the time, and the characters in her tale suddenly materialise on stage and act the story out. It is an imaginative opening for a very subtle work. In general, critics have made heavy weather of trying to describe its strange blend of artlessness and sophistication, though some recent studies have considerably deepened our understanding of how the play works.[5]

Part of the difficulty in getting to grips with the play comes from a misunderstanding of the frame. The three who are lost in the wood are called Frolic, Antic and Fantastic, and for some reason editors and critics have always called them 'pages'. They are evidently young men, and they refer to 'our young master'. But when Clunch their rescuer answers their question, 'tell us what thou art', with a firm 'I am Clunch the smith. What are you?', they are pointedly evasive (37–40). It is repeatedly said that they are lost in the wood, and their words, as Susan Viguers says, 'conjure despair and figurative death'.[6] ('No hope to live till tomorrow'; 'never in all my life was I so dead slain' (4, 6–7).) Fantastic wonders that Frolic should be surprised at their situation 'seeing Cupid hath led our young master to the fair lady, and she is the only saint that he hath sworn to serve' (11–13). Surely these three are figurative characters, as much shadows as the eerie beings who materialise in the main action – indeed, more shadowy, since those characters have real names: even the ghost is called Jack. The only characters in the play who have proper substance are Clunch and Madge. There is great force in Clunch's solid words: 'What am I? Why, I am Clunch the smith. What are you? What make you in my territories at this time of the night?' For his visitors have strayed out of allegory into realism. They are personifications of qualities which the 'young master' has discarded now he is dedicated to serving his lady and which are withering away, deprived of their life-support. They are the qualities that Mercutio was sorry to lose in Romeo, the high spirits of unattached young men out to enjoy themselves: 'Cupid . . . hath cozened us all' (44). It is not anything so gross as food they want to revive them, and they rather rudely refuse Madge's 'piece of cheese and a pudding'. It is 'chat' they want, and a song, and 'a merry winter's tale'. The tale they are provided with shows an extraordinary medley of characters seeking and finding love, then returning home. When it is over, Madge offers her guests the cheese once more, for breakfast. And we assume they are reconciled to their master's inevitable enlistment in the ranks of love and will take ordinary food and accommodate themselves to his new life.

A second important point about the play which is not always understood is that the tale is not Madge's. As (again) Susan Viguers recognises, 'her tale has a reality not wholly dependent on her . . . The tale moves by its own energy'.[7] Everyone notices that Madge makes a mistake in saying that the harvesters at their first entry 'will sing a song of mowing' when their song is in fact about *sowing* (258–64). This is a bad mistake! For the two entries of the harvesters are fundamental to the structure and meaning of the play. Their first entry is spring:

> All ye that lovely lovers be,
> Pray you for me.
> Lo, here we come a-sowing, a-sowing,
> And sow sweet fruits of love.
> In your sweet hearts well may it prove. (260–4)

Their second entry is autumn; they enter '*with women in their hands*':

> Lo, here we come a-reaping, a-reaping,
> To reap our harvest fruit;
> And thus we pass the year so long,
> And never be we mute. (561–4)

Madge, who knows about the harvesters, hasn't comprehended the significance of the order of the entries. This haziness is reflected in the opening of her narrative – all that she is allowed to tell.

> Once upon a time there was a king – or a lord – or a duke – that had a fair daughter . . .
>
> O Lord, I quite forgot! There was a conjurer . . .
>
> O, I forget! She (he, I would say) turned a proper young man to a bear in the night . . .   (113–14, 122, 128–9)

Given this incompetence, it is little wonder that the characters come alive to take over from her and put the record straight, telling the story as it really was. At the end of the play, it is discovered that Madge is fast asleep (956), though as she awakes she has no difficulty in continuing with her hazy explanations. Finally, Fantastic asks (with a note of irony in his voice?): 'Then you have made an end of your tale, gammer?' and she replies: 'Yes, faith. When this was done, I took a piece of bread and cheese, and came my way. . . .' The phrase 'when this was done' is extraordinary. What she has haltingly tried to relate was something that actually happened, which she observed; and when it was done she took a piece of bread and cheese and came her way. As she hesitates in re-telling it to her audience, the indignant story re-enacts itself – as does the story of the terrible bridal night in Yeats's play, *Purgatory*. This of course is our retrospective view, with the hindsight of Madge's closing words. As in *The Arraignment of Paris*, the bracket which closes the play is not one of a pair with the bracket which opens it.

'Why, this goes round without a fiddling stick', marvels Frolic as the characters act out their story. But what is it that the characters are so anxious to demonstrate the truth of? It is still only an old wives' tale, a bagful of folk-tales, individually and collectively beyond the bounds of credibility. The blithe way in which Peele has airily piled folk-tale on top of folk-tale quadruples the absurdity of the story.[8] The enchanter with his secret lamp, the old man at the cross who is really a youth, the abducted maiden, the heads in the well, the wandering knight, the grateful corpse – Peele's bland stitching together of these and the other folk narratives from which he has made his play has produced something unique in our literature, as amusing as it is beautiful, a great joke that derides nothing. It might seem that the braggart Huanebango is being used to debunk the world of romance and folk-tale as he assumes the role of questing knight, seeking his fortune 'among brazen gates, enchanted towers, fire and brimstone, thunder and lightning' (275–6), looking for precious beauty whom 'none must inherit but he that can monsters tame, labours achieve, riddles absolve, loose enchantments, murder magic, and kill conjuring' (280–3). But Huanebango is only at the extreme edge of an attitude to folk/romance material which is *never* serious but which never attempts to capsize or explode the subject.

When Huanebango, who has become deaf, is married off to the good-looking daughter with the shrewish tongue, and Corebus, who has become blind, is married off to the ugly daughter with the heart of gold, it is more than a good joke, and one is really quite perplexed and uncertain about one's response. There is something here which survives and outlasts the banter and the ridicule, and we feel this throughout the play.

Undoubtedly it is the language which in part at least gives the folk material its power to endure the treatment it is subjected to.

> *First Brother.* . . . . If I speed in my journey, I will give thee a palmer's staff of ivory and a scallop shell of beaten gold.
> *Erestus.* Was she fair?
> *Second Brother.* Ay, the fairest for white and the purest for red, as the blood of the deer or the driven snow. (156–60)

Erestus has not been told what the object of the journey is. (One scholar thought that his question was a sign of textual corruption.) The play is full of magical and evocative phrases, from the riddles of Erestus to the song of the three lost youths, the speeches of the Head in the well, and quite ordinary exchanges:

> – How now, fair Delia, where you have been?
> –At the foot of the rock for running water . . . (371–2)

'Gently dip, but not too deep', says the Head in the well where is the water of life. Peele is dipping with the utmost gentleness in the deepest waters.

If Madge is not in control of the story, who is? One of the remarkable features of this ingenious conglomeration of folk-tales is that although many people seem to be directing its progress, there is really no one in charge. Certainly not Sacrapant the sorcerer, who has the most uneasy control over his victims and who is overcome with staggering ease by Jack and Venelia. The Ghost of Jack is in charge some of the time, directing Eumenides to Delia, outwitting and killing Sacrapant, and also interpreting the action. There is then the strange figure of Erestus, the young man on whom Sacrapant has forced his own aged and ugly visage, and who becomes a bear at night. He stands at the cross roads, issuing his riddling prophecies to all who pass. He seems to know the future as well as he knows the past. When Eumenides the wandering Knight enters (452), he addresses the empty air:

> Tell me, Time; tell me, just Time,
> When shall I Delia see?

Catching sight of Erestus, he asks him to tell him his fortune, and Erestus gives him the riddling advice which eventually leads him to Delia.[9] And then there is also the Head in the well of life, who has the power to award good and bad fortunes.

Peele seems to organise his play on the principle of superfetation. There is an abundance of plots, an abundance of quests, an abundance of presenters – and an abundance of deliverances, in that the sorcerer is defeated twice (Jack kills him and Venelia blows out the magic light). Since its light-hearted irresponsibility is part of the secret of its enchantment, how can we possibly ask serious questions about it?

In an important lecture in 1975, Inga-Stina Ewbank spoke of the relation between *word* and *show*, or language and spectacle, in Peele's plays.[10] She was particularly interested in the arousing of wonder, and several times pointed to resemblances between Peele's work and Shakespeare's final romances in the counterpointing of word and vision to create wonder in the audience. She said: 'At the heart of all living theatrical experience there is a kind of mystery: a creation, through what we see and hear, of a world which we accept as possible.'[11] In the published lecture there is at this point a footnote: ' "Possible" seems to me a more adequate word in this context than "real", with its misleading associations of "suspension of disbelief" '. It seems to me that 'possible' is in fact a very dangerous word to use, and I would be happier with that always misleading word, real. For Peele in *The Old Wives Tale* has strongly urged not merely the improbability but the *impossibility* of his story, while at the same time using all his powers as a dramatist to give that impossible fiction a vitality, a *life*, which has the power to interrogate, though it cannot challenge, the more sober range of happenings which makes up our 'possible' life. The tale which the old woman starts to narrate is a poor thing indeed, but as the characters arrive unsummoned to *perform* it, the vagueness and casualness disappear in favour of something wonderfully bright and magical – though still an old wives tale so far as possibility goes. 'Gently dip, but not too deep.' There is no need to be portentous or apologetic about folk-tales. *The Old Wives Tale* is a brilliant success in achieving the lightest conceivable treatment of folk-tale without betraying or ridiculing those deeper things which folk-tale may be held to represent and incorporate. J. D. Cox is quite right to point to Peele's 'combination of *joie de vivre* with a celebration of great creating nature', and to say that Peele 'successfully preserves the fertility implications inherent in his folklore sources'. The end of the play, he wrote, gives us 'a vision familiar from Shakespearean comedy and romance'. There is a problem here, however, in that the familiar vision of Shakespearean romance is itself full of perplexity, at least so far as *The Winter's Tale* is concerned.

The text for our discussion of *The Winter's Tale* is Paulina's remark in the final scene, when the statue of Hermione is revealed to be Hermione herself.

> That she is living,
> Were it but told you, should be hooted at
> Like an old tale, but it appears she lives . . .   (V.iii. 115–17)

Seeing is believing. Narration would be hooted at, but it *appears* she lives.
There are three narrations in *The Winter's Tale* which are of outstanding
importance: the Clown's account of the shipwreck and of the bear devour-
ing Antigonus at the end of Act III; the words of Time as chorus at the
beginning of Act IV; and the account given by the Third Gentleman in Act V
of the meeting of the kings and the recognition of Perdita.

To begin with 'Time, the chorus'. *The Winter's Tale* has no frame, but
Time is the concealed presenter, and the play is his tale as *Pericles* is Gower's
tale. He does not appear until Act IV, but then he calls the play 'my tale' (14),
and 'my scene' (15). 'Remember well', he says 'I mentioned a son o' th'
king's, which Florizel / I now name to you.' It was Hermione, Leontes and
Polixenes who spoke of the son in Act I. Time is clearly the tale-teller. Or
rather, the tale-teller adopts the guise of Time; he says he will 'Now take
upon me, in the name of Time, / To use my wings' (3–4). This is his little
joke. As a tale-teller, he is proposing to miss out sixteen years altogether,
which is the one thing Time cannot possibly do, and he justifies it as the sort
of thing that Time *can* do, on the specious analogy that 'it is in my power / To
o'erthrow law' (7–8). This master tale-teller, masquerading as Time, does
not reappear. The entire story, however, is his contrivance. Things happen
as he wills them; the play is his tale. He has two subordinates who do some
tale-telling for him, the Clown and the Third Gentleman.

The narrations by the Clown and the Third Gentleman are always recognised as perplexing in their tone. There is in both cases a great incongruity
between the quality of the event and the manner in which it is narrated. The
Clown has to tell the story of a ship being wrecked with the loss of all
aboard, and of the death of Antigonus, attacked and eaten by a bear. The
Clown is distressed and shocked by what he has seen, but his account of it is
embarrassingly comic.

> – How the poor souls roared, and the sea mocked them; and how the poor
> gentleman roared, and the bear mocked him, both roaring louder than the sea or
> weather.
>
> – Name of mercy, when was this, boy?
>
> – Now, now; I have not winked since I saw these sights; the men are not yet cold
> under water, nor the bear half dined on the gentleman; he's at it now!
>
> (III.iii. 96–103)

The emotions of the Shepherd and the Clown are not made fun of. The
gravity of the deaths and the awe at discovering the baby come over to
everyone. And yet the coincidence of the bear and the shipwreck is really
preposterous, and is made to seem more so by the Clown's ludicrous
account. Not even the burial of Antigonus is free from black humour: 'If
there be any of him left, I'll bury it', says the Clown.

In the later narration, the assertion of the First Gentleman (who wasn't a
witness) that 'the dignity of this act was worth the audience of kings and

princes, for by such was it acted' (77–8) only emphasises the cheapness given
to the momentous events by the prattle of the Third Gentleman, who is
over-articulate as the Clown was inarticulate.

> One of the prettiest touches of all, and that which angled for mine eyes – caught
> the water though not the fish – was, when at the relation of the queen's death, with
> the manner how she came to 't bravely confessed and lamented by the king, how
> attentiveness wounded his daughter; till, from one sign of dolour to another, she
> did, with an 'Alas' – I would fain say – bleed tears; for I am sure my heart wept
> blood.   (V.ii. 79–86)

It is notable that the Third Gentleman re-tells the incidents of the bear and
the shipwreck related by the Clown (61–76). It is notable also that both the
bear–shipwreck episode and the meeting of the kings with the opening of the
fardel were not in Greene's *Pandosto*. The first episode is entirely new
material created by Shakespeare; the second a re-working of Greene. It is not
a question, that is, of Shakespeare hurrying over a necessary part of the story
as told in his source. To create these incidents and to have them related in a
particular way is a single act of free artistic choice.

The arresting coincidence of the bear and the shipwreck is required in
order to destroy all the evidence of witnesses to the abandoning of Perdita:
'so that all the instruments which aided to expose the child were even then
lost when it was found', as the Third Gentleman puts it (68–70). This
destruction of the witnesses is necessary only because Shakespeare has
provided the witnesses; in *Pandosto* the babe is set adrift in a boat which is
washed up on the shore for the shepherd to find and no one has to be
liquidated. Shakespeare seems to have set up the problem in order to
produce its far-fetched solution. Similarly, the pell-mell of greetings and
discoveries in V.ii is entirely Shakespeare's choice.

> There was casting up of eyes, holding up of hands, with countenance of such
> distraction that they were to be known by garment, not by favour. Our king, being
> ready to leap out of himself for his found daughter, as if that joy were now become
> a loss, cries, 'Oh, thy mother, thy mother'; then asks Bohemia forgiveness, then
> embraces his son-in-law; then again worries he his daughter with clipping her.
>   (V.ii. 45–52)

It is the Third Gentleman who says plainly that what he is relating is
incredible, and beggars *description*. Of the meeting of the kings, he says it
was 'a sight which was to be seen, cannot be spoken of'. It 'lames report to
follow it, and undoes description to do it' (41–2; 54–5). Of the bear and the
shipwreck he says, 'Like an old tale still, which will have matter to rehearse,
though credit be asleep and not an ear open'. These old wives tales maunder
on though the audience, and belief, have fallen asleep and are paying no
attention. It won't do to say that Shakespeare is using the old device in
fiction of disarming incredulity by saying it's so improbable you'd think it
were fiction. He has increased the improbabilities of his source, and then

further intensified them by the 'lame' reports, the 'broken delivery', of the Clown and the Third Gentleman.

Why should Shakespeare emphasise the absurdity of his story every time that it is narrated? In proposing an answer to this, I want to make an excursus to the sheep-shearing feast in IV.iv.

Perdita, we recognise, has a great passion for what is natural. There is not only her absolute refusal to grow 'streaked gillyvors', whatever Polixenes says, because in setting them human art has to assist 'great creating nature', but also her discomfort with the costume she is wearing, her 'unusual weeds', making her 'most goddess-like pranked up' with her 'borrowed flaunts'. She is afraid her character is changing because of the garments she is wearing.

> Methinks I play as I have seen them do
> In Whitsun pastorals: sure this robe of mine
> Does change my disposition. (IV.iv. 133–5)

Just as Polixenes' theory about the value of grafting is contradicted by his prejudices in the matter of Florizel marrying Perdita, so (on the other side of the argument) Perdita's commitment to naturalness in conduct and speech is contradicted by the fatal ease with which her unstudied talents translate her into another being. The sheep-shearing feast takes place (oddly enough) towards the end of summer, but, magnificently, Perdita creates spring in her words:

> Daffodils
> That come before the swallow dares, and take
> The winds of March with beauty – (IV.iv. 118–20)

ending with her vision of the flowered bank, with Florizel 'quick and in mine arms'. It is the vivid reality of her own imaginative recreation of spring which alarms her. But Florizel steps in to reassure her: 'What you do / Still betters what is done' (135–6). This phrase is often misunderstood to mean 'is an improvement on what you last did'. The ending of the speech explains the beginning:

> Each your doing,
> So singular in each particular,
> Crowns what you are doing in the present deeds,
> That all your acts are queens. (143–6)

As Dr Johnson put it, 'Your manner in each act crowns the act'. 'What you do / Still *betters* what is done.' That is to say, whatever you do always improves, or raises in value, the thing that is done. There is speaking, singing, buying, selling, giving alms, praying, ordering affairs, dancing. None of these is anything much in itself; everything depends on the way it is done. And everything that Perdita does finds its justification in the grace with which she does it. For Florizel, the acted presentation of the spring is as beautiful and real as anything else that Perdita has done; her role as 'no shepherdess, but Flora / Peering in April's front' as beautiful and real as anything else that Perdita has been.

By the brilliance of his art, and that of his boy actor, Shakespeare presents us Perdita, the princess-shepherdess who is all naturalness; and he emphasises the extent to which 'we are mocked by art'[12] by showing us how she, who is all naturalness, can bring alive by words and action a different being and a different season, making it real and convincing to her hearers in Bohemia, and in every theatre where the play is well acted.

'What the imagination seizes as beauty must be truth . . .' That is really the import of Florizel's speech, and is the underlying meaning not only of Perdita's impersonation of the spring-goddess but of the whole play.[13] The vividness of what is brought before us by speech and action in performance is its own certificate of credibility and acceptability. Shakespeare chooses to give emotional credence to particular scenes in *The Winter's Tale* by having them acted out in scenes which he has written with his full powers – particularly Leontes's jealousy, the springtime love of Perdita and Florizel, and the statue scene. But these scenes he so positions and illuminates that each is left with a very frail support in its before and after. Seeing is believing, and *only* seeing is believing. Those passages of the story which are not privileged with performance are relegated to the status of old wives tales.

It is not we who point to the fragility of the fiction in *The Winter's Tale*; it is Shakespeare. 'Such a deal of wonder is broken out within this hour that ballad-makers cannot be able to express it' (V.ii. 23–5). We have been told what colossal absurdities ballad-makers can get away with in Autolycus's description of the outrageous lies contained in the ballads he is selling at the feast. It is a mischievous stroke for Shakespeare to make Autolycus introduce the scene of the reunion of father and daughter as narrated by the various gentlemen. The reunion of Leontes and Perdita is narrated; the reunion of Leontes and Hermione is performed. Neither is likely; each is 'like an old tale still, which *will* have matter to rehearse, though credit be asleep and not an ear open'. But for some scenes credit is to be awakened, while for others it remains asleep. The most intriguing moment in this context is when Shakespeare suddenly materialises what is essentially narrated matter: 'Exit pursued by a bear'. Is credit here meant to be awake or asleep? It's a kind of after-dinner sleep, at the join between narration and action; a deliberate confusion of the two modes, and thus a pointer to their existence.

There is one very small piece of the story of *The Winter's Tale* which shows what by comparison seems a strange anxiety in Shakespeare to obtain credence for his story. The 'opening of the fardel' – the bundle in which the old shepherd had wrapped the clues to Perdita's identity – is a critical moment in the play. It happens when everyone is on Sicilian soil. I cannot think that any member of an audience has ever asked why the shepherd waited so long to open the fardel. If any question is asked, it is why the shepherd and his son consented to sail with Florizel, when their mission had been to Polixenes; in *Pandosto* it is described in detail how the shepherd is shanghaied aboard. On this matter, all that Autolycus says is that 'I brought the old man and his son aboard the prince'. (It is the audience he is giving this information to, at V.ii. 110, at the close of the Third Gentleman's narration.) He then enters into particulars about the fardel. He told the prince, he says, that 'I heard them talk of a fardel and I know not what'; but because both Perdita and Florizel *began to be sea-sick* 'this mystery remained unsolved'.

Why should Shakespeare be so concerned to give verisimilitude to his story just at this minor point when he has so ostentatiously refused it over much greater matters? It is curious that it is Autolycus who is so active here; he comes to look more and more like a surrogate of the tale-teller. Perhaps he is throwing dust in our eyes here: establishing the credibility of the tale just as we are being taken to the greatest improbability of all.

I refer of course to the sixteen-year concealment of Hermione. All that time, Paulina and Hermione have collaborated in pretending that Hermione has died.[14] After the revelation that the statue is in fact the living queen, only four lines of explanation or justification are given. Hermione says to Perdita:

> Thou shalt hear that I,
> Knowing by Paulina that the oracle
> Gave hope thou wast in being, have preserved
> Myself to see the issue. (V.iii. 125–8)

This explains nothing: the question is not why Hermione has preserved herself but why she has kept Leontes in ignorance of her existence all these years. But even this explanation is cut short by Paulina.

> There's time enough for that,
> Lest they desire upon the push *to trouble*
> *Your joys* with like relation. (V.iii. 128–30; my italics)

At the very end of the play, Leontes says:

> Good Paulina,
> Lead us from hence, where we may leisurely
> Each one demand and answer to his part
> Performed in this wide gap of time since first
> We were disseverd. Hastily lead away.

Those are the last words spoken. The emphasis in these extracts on explanations still to be given – but *not* in the play – is striking. How terrible this demand and answer would be! What Leontes had done came as near to the unforgivable as the mind can conceive. His contrition and penitence are complete and unquestioned. Even after all this time, however, he fears that recollection of his responsibility for the death of Mamilius might 'unfurnish me of reason' (V.i. 123). For sixteen years his wife goes on punishing him, punishing herself as she punishes him. Where in the last scene is the exchange of forgiveness – that most Shakespearean feature – between Hermione and Leontes? Shakespeare could not conceivably have put it in, because what it would have awakened would have destroyed the joy of the final scene. 'Hastily lead away!'

Shakespeare put everything into the intensely moving reunion between Leontes and Hermione. For the original audience, who might well have known Greene's *Pandosto*, in which the calumniated queen did indeed die, the surprise that she was still living would have been as great as that of Leontes. The surge of their pleasure would have mingled with the joy of the dramatis personae, and quite submerged the questions that might have been asked. Shakespeare placed the beauty of the statue scene over a void of questioning, and pointed to the void. Leontes saw Hermione 'as I thought, dead'. What was in her coffin at the double funeral with Mamilius (III.ii. 233) is anyone's guess. Never before in his career as a dramatist had Shakespeare kept secret from his audience a main element of the plot, as here in 1611 he kept secret from them the fact that Hermione had not died. It is an arresting innovation: it became absolutely commonplace in the tragicomedies of Fletcher and Massinger, and that is one reason why their plays are inferior to Shakespeare's.

Of course, it's only a play. But to accept the improbability of Oberon and his love-juice, or Portia's take-over of Venetian law, is very different from accepting the improbabilities and the plot manoeuvring of *The Winter's Tale*. What is so interesting is Shakespeare's keenness to impress on us that we have been cheated.

> That she is living,
> Were it but told you, should be hooted at
> Like an old tale, but it *appears* she lives . . .

The beauty of *The Winter's Tale* is its insubstantiality, to be compared with 'the uncertain glory of an April day', or the vanishing glory of the masque in *The Tempest*. The play consists basically of three extended actions: calumny and rejection; love in the younger generation; reunion and restoration. Each of these actions is brilliantly realised before us. But they are brought before us as make-believe, and their status insisted on by those parts of the story that are narrated rather than performed. They are moments in a most improbable tale, moments that a supreme dramatic artist has chosen to make real and convincing. It is not in any way a new thing for Shakespeare to demonstrate how 'we are mocked by art', and an ironical or quizzical presentation of the artist at work, in *The Winter's Tale* as elsewhere, serves to affirm rather than sabotage the power of art. Much of Shakespeare's greatness, it can be argued, derives from the balancing of what I have called elsewhere the epic and the burlesque visions of his own activity.[15] The opposed visions are remarkably demonstrated in the self-images of the artist in the last plays. Beside the heroic image of the brooding, careworn Prospero, we have the anti-heroic image of Autolycus, the man who depends for his living on his protean resourcefulness and the gullibility of the public.

In both Peele's *Old Wives Tale* and Shakespeare's *The Winter's Tale*, segments of a very tall story are snatched from the inadequacies of narration and realised before us in action. Each dramatist tells us in his own way that this realisation does not one whit alter the improbability of the fiction. Life is 'not like that', whether we are talking about heads in a well or the preservation of Hermione and Perdita. In spite of the dramatist's care, you will find critics inattentively referring to 'the miracle' at the end of *The Winter's Tale*. What miracle there is is just there: in our being so convinced by what the dramatist keeps assuring us is an old wives winter's tale. In the end, those who claim so little for their fictions turn out to be their best advocates.

NOTES

1 The general similarity is noted by J. D. Cox, 'Homely matter and multiple plots in Peele's *Old Wives Tale*', *Texas Studies in Literature and Language*, 20 (1978), p. 343.
2 Text (with minor modifications) and line references for *The Old Wives Tale* are from the Revels Plays edition by Patricia Binnie, 1980.
3 The parallel is pointed out by C. Frey in *Shakespeare's Vast Romance: A Study of 'The Winter's Tale'* (Missouri, 1980), p. 99.
4 On Shakespeare's responsibility for the design and shape of *Pericles*, see the introduction to the New Penguin edition of the play by Philip Edwards (1976), pp. 31–41.
5 E.g., J. D. Cox as cited in n. 1; Joan C. Marx, ' "Soft, who have we here?": the dramatic technique of *The Old Wives Tale*', *Renaissance Drama*, N.S. 12 (1981), pp. 117–43; Susan T. Viguers, 'The hearth and the cell: art in *The Old Wives Tale*', *Studies in English Literature*, 21 (1981), pp. 209–21.
6 Viguers, 'The hearth and the cell' (n. 5), pp. 219–20.
7 *Ibid.* (n. 5), p. 212.
8 For the folk-tale material in the play with reference to earlier studies, see F. S. Hook's introduction to his edition in Vol. 3 of the Yale Peele, 1970.
9 Erestus's assumption of the role of Time (which I suggest above provides a link with *The Winter's Tale*) is pointed out by Susan Viguers in the article cited in n. 5, p. 217.
10 ' "What words, what looks, what wonders?": language and spectacle in the theatre of George Peele', *The Elizabethan Theatre*, V, ed. G. R. Hibbard (Toronto, 1975), pp. 124–54.
11 p. 125.
12 Leontes' phrase (V.iii. 68) when he is marvelling at the 'motion' in the eye of what he thinks is Julio Romano's statue. This is a brilliant double-cross by Shakespeare, for Leontes is mistaken; it is not a triumph of art that Leontes is beholding, but Hermione herself. It is in that 'Hermione herself' that the mockery

lies, for Hermione is a boy-actor pretending to be Hermione pretending to be a statue.

13 Keats's phrase is quoted by E. A. J. Honigmann in his chapter on *The Winter's Tale* in *Shakespeare's Impact on his Contemporaries* (London 1982), pp. 111–20, in the footsteps of which the present article treads. Honigmann argues that the assertion of unlikelihood in the play is an answer to the crudity of Jonson's demand for fidelity to life in art. Shakespeare's conclusion is 'more complicated than Keats's famous compromise that Beauty is Truth' (p. 115).

14 The morality of the deception is discussed in the context of the 'good deceivers' in Shakespeare in Philip Edwards, 'Shakespeare and the healing power of deceit', *Shakespeare Survey*, 31 (1978), p. 117.

15 See *Shakespeare and the Confines of Art* (1968), chapter 1.

H. NEVILLE DAVIES

Pericles and the
Sherley brothers

❧◦❧

On the face of it there is good reason to compare *Pericles* with *The Travailes of the Three English Brothers*, a play printed in 1607 'As it is now play'd by her Maiesties Seruants', and written jointly by the three dramatists John Day, William Rowley and George Wilkins, who all put their names to a brief preface. *Pericles*, too, has been thought by some to be a collaborative work, and at one time or another Day and Wilkins (and, less plausibly, Rowley) have each been nominated as Shakespeare's possible collaborator. Probably not many would now claim that Wilkins had any sort of a hand in the composition, yet he was the author of a prose fiction substantially based on the play, *The Painfull Adventures of Pericles Prince of Tyre* (1608). The full title of his book boldly advertises the connection by making it clear that he is capitalising on 'the Play of *Pericles*, as it was lately presented' by the King's Men at the Globe towards the end of 1607 or early in 1608, that is, presented at much the same time as *The Three English Brothers* was being performed by the Queen's Men at the Red Bull or the Curtain, or even at both of those houses. But more importantly, one of these two plays that entertained London audiences in 1607–8 is apparently responding to the other.

Even discounting *Pericles*, *The Three English Brothers* looks to Shakespeare in a remarkably direct way, for it includes a couple of scenes set in Venice in which a Jewish money-lender, Zariph, maliciously seeks to ruin one of the English brothers merely because he is a Christian; and contrives to do this by invoking the full rigour of the law when his victim is unable to discharge a bond. Shylock is undoubtedly the inspiration for speeches like this:

> A hundreth thousand Duckats! sweete remembrance.
> Ile read it againe; a hundreth thousand Duckats!
> Sweeter still: who owes it? a Christian,
> *Canaans* brood. Honnie to my ioyfull soule:
> If this summe faile (my bond vnsatisfied)
> Hee's in the Iewes mercy; mercy! ha, ha!
> The Lice of *Ægipt* shall deuoure them all
> Ere I shew mercy to a Christian.
> Vnhallowed brats, seed of the bond-woman,

Swine deuourers, vncircumcised slaues
That scorne our Hebrew sanctimonious writte,
Despise our lawes, prophane our sinagogues,
Old *Moises* ceremonies, to whom was left -
The marble Decalogue twice registred
By high *Iehouahs* selfe. Lawlesse wretches!
One I shall gripe, breake he but his minute.
Heauen grant he may want money to defray:
Oh how Ile then imbrace my happinesse.
Sweet gold, sweete Iewell! but the sweetest part
Of a *Iewes* feast is a Christians heart.[1]

Crude though Zariph's soliloquy may be, the dramaturgy of *The Three English Brothers* is of a highly self-conscious kind, so that reference to Shylock and, through him, to the Venice to which he belongs is quite deliberate. Equally deliberate may be an allusion to the dramatist and theatrical company to which, in a proprietary sense, Shylock also belonged.

The degree of theatrical awareness emerges particularly in the bizarre and unexpected scene that separates those two Zariph scenes. Rather than advancing the action this interlude focuses and reflects, in a comic mode, the play's preoccupation with the nature of stage illusion. What happens is that the same English brother meets the actor Will Kempe who is, by chance, travelling in Italy (such a meeting actually occurred in Rome in 1601), asks him for news of the London theatres, and engages him to put on a performance with a local Harlequin. The news from London is of *England's Joy*, this being the advertised title of a non-existent play which had been used to lure an audience to the Swan, the perpetrator of the hoax then absconding with the takings: an extreme instance of drama as illusion! Kempe's encounter with the Harlequin that occupies most of the scene provides excellent scope for a lively comic routine, the English comedian repeatedly upstaging the Italian as play roles are amusingly confused with real-life relationships, while the two performers supposedly work out the basis of a *commedia dell'arte* improvisation. The performance, in which Harlequin's wife and Kempe's boy are also to play parts, is to be presented in the following scene at a banquet given by the English brother, but in the event this play within a play proves to be scarcely more substantial than *England's Joy*. The Prologue enters and manages to speak only a single conventional couplet,

Our act is short, your liking is our gaynes;
So we offend not, we are pay'd our paines,   (p. 376)

before Zariph intervenes and instructs officers to arrest the party giver.

This theatrical impersonation of Will Kempe, a famous and charismatic performer who had died only within the last few years and who must have been affectionately remembered by audiences, is an amazingly bold undertaking: an actor acts the role of a known actor who creates humour by confusing stage roles with actual reality in a performance of a performance that masquerades as a rehearsal. Furthermore, the combination of this reincarnation of Kempe with the brazen appropriation of Shakespeare's Jew of Venice, another actor's distinctive performance, raises intriguing questions. Could Zariph's sabotage of Kempe's play have been seen by experienced theatre-goers as Shylock's revenge upon Kempe's Lancelot Gobbo? What sort of rivalries were there between the King's Men and the Queen's Men; and where did Kempe's loyalties lie in the last years of his career when he had withdrawn from the Globe?

When it comes to the relationship between *The Three English Brothers* and *Pericles*, it is not known for certain which play has precedence. Just possibly Wilkins responded to performances of *Pericles* one way in *The Painfull Adventures* and, with his collaborators, another way in *The Three English Brothers*, one of the team (probably Rowley) widening that response by alluding to *The Merchant of Venice* in addition. But since *The Three English Brothers* was performed and published in 1607, and was entered in the Stationers' Register as early as 29 June, and since there is no clear evidence of *Pericles* on stage before 1608, it is more likely that the sequence after *The Merchant of Venice* was *The Three English Brothers*, then *Pericles*, and finally *The Painfull Adventures*, each of the first three items influencing the next in the series. That being so, *Pericles* would appear to be doubly distinguished by, on the one hand, having been influenced by an inferior play that was itself indebted to an earlier work of Shakespeare's, and, on the other hand, by having in its turn become the basis of a publication by one of the writers who collaborated in that inferior play. The degree of reciprocation is extraordinary, but Shakespeare's indebtedness includes nothing as crude as taking over, let alone debasing, a ready-made character in the way that his Shylock was appropriated, or simply exploiting a successful narrative in the way that Wilkins latched on to *Pericles*. While *The Three English Brothers* dramatised material that was strikingly up-to-date, Shakespeare, in sharp contrast, turned to the ancient story of Apollonius (whom he renamed Pericles), and deliberately emphasised the story's antiquity, having it presented by 'ancient Gower' who himself calls his narrative 'a song that old was sung'.[2]

In real life the brothers Thomas, Anthony, and Robert were the three remarkable sons of Sir Thomas Sherley, well-known adventurers of the day.[3] Their father lived until 1612, while Thomas, born in the same year as Shakespeare, and Anthony, one year his junior, both survived until 1633; Robert, the youngest, until 1628. Several publications helped to spread the family reputation. Of these, Anthony Nixon's commissioned pamphlet, *The Three English Brothers* (1607), was entered in the Stationers' Register only three weeks before the play itself was registered, while *A True Report of Sir Anthonie Sherlies Iourney* (1600), which had been suppressed shortly after publication, and William Parry's entertaining *New and Large Discourse of the Travels of Sir Anthony Shirley* (1601) were written before the later events dramatised in the play had actually happened.

The action of the play begins with the two younger Sherley brothers, Anthony and Robert, leaving England and arriving, in December 1598, at Casbin (Qazvin) where they are well received by the Persian Sophy, Shah Abbas, who has just defeated a Turkish army. He displays his military strength to the two Englishmen by having his troops reenact the recent victory, and the brothers return this compliment by staging an exemplary '*Christian battell*'. The Sophy, much to the chagrin of his Persian counsellors (especially one named Hallibeck or Husein Ali Beg), is impressed by their use of gunpowder and by the Christian practice, unknown in Persia, of taking prisoners. When intelligence arrives that the defeated Turks have regrouped and are now once more on the offensive, the brothers join forces with the Sophy. In the ensuing battle Anthony takes prisoner a Turkish Pasha and leaves him in young Robert's custody. The jealous counsellor Hallibeck fails in an attempt to bully Robert into handing over his charge, and when, thanks to Anthony's bravery, the Persians win the battle, the Sophy, to the further resentment of Hallibeck, releases the Pasha in the Christian manner, and agrees to the establishment of an anti-Turkish Perso-Christian league. Appointed as joint leaders of an embassy to negotiate such a treaty with Christian rulers are Anthony and the discontented Hallibeck. Robert replaces Anthony as General of the Persian army, and we discover that though the Persian counsellors resent the success of these foreign interlopers, the Sophy's niece greatly admires them.

Hallibeck and Anthony travel to Europe through the Russia of Tsar Boris Godunov where Anthony is imprisoned when Hallibeck dishonestly schemes against him. Fortunately, the English merchants trading there testify to Anthony's good name, and he is in the end restored to favour. The embassy subsequently reaches Rome, where Anthony and Hallibeck quarrel disastrously during their papal audience, but Anthony recoups the situation, eventually winning for himself the good opinion of the pontiff. The embassy then proceeds to Venice.

At this point Thomas, the eldest brother, arrives in Italy from England, and after various adventures around the Mediterranean raids Ieo (the island of Kea in the Cyclades), a Turkish possession. All but one of his men desert him, however, and he is taken prisoner. Prudently he takes care not to disclose to the Turks that he is the brother of the dreaded Englishman in command of the hostile Persian army.

Back on the Levantine mainland Robert and his Persian troops are fighting the Turks once more, and this time they capture a great number of the enemy commanders. Constrained by Persian military practice Robert orders their execution, but when another 'prisoner' reveals himself as Thomas's faithful servant bringing news of his master's incarceration in Constantinople, and a plea for help, the executions are halted. The lives of the remaining twenty or thirty captured Turkish commanders are used by Robert to bargain for Thomas's release, though without indicating that the prisoner in question is actually his own brother. Not surprisingly, the marked inequality of the proposed exchange arouses the Sultan's curiosity about the identity of this English prisoner, now revealed as a man of importance.

In Venice Anthony is in trouble again as Hallibeck continues to scheme against him. On behalf of the Sophy, Anthony has borrowed money to buy a jewel, but the reimbursement sent by the Sophy has been diverted by Hallibeck with the result that Anthony is imprisoned at the suit of Zariph the Jewish money lender. This is the low spot in the fortunes of the Sherley brothers. Two of them are now in prison, and in Persia Robert's enemies have turned the Sophy against him by misrepresenting his attempt to exchange prisoners with the Sultan, and by saying that he has presumed to court the Sophy's niece. However, Robert and the niece manage to prove their innocence, find that they are in love after all, and win the Sophy's approval for their marriage; and when a message from the Sultan then declines Robert's suggested exchange of prisoners the Sophy's anger is redirected against the intransigent Turks. In Constantinople Thomas is tortured to force him to reveal his identity. He holds out bravely, but when an unexpected letter from King James to the Sultan demands his release, and names him as a Sherley, his relationship to Robert is at once apparent. Fortunately, such is the prestige of James that the Sultan complies with the demand on condition that Thomas returns to England and does not join his brother in Persia.

Anthony, meanwhile, is still languishing in a Venetian jail when Hallibeck arrives home in Persia from Italy. He wickedly reports discreditable stories about Anthony to the Sophy, but Robert, who has had letters from Anthony, reveals the truth and Hallibeck is obliged to confess his treachery and dishonesty. Although Robert pardons him his malice, the Sophy condemns him to death for betraying a royal trust, and as Persian reparation to the Sherleys invites Robert to ask for whatever he wants. Prompted by a recent encounter with a missionary, Robert begs permission to have his baby daughter christened, to have a Christian church built, and a Christian school founded. The requests are graciously granted, and at the christening the Sophy himself stands godfather. The play ends with all three brothers simultaneously on stage, though geographically dispersed: Robert, favoured by the Sophy, remains in Persia; Anthony, now released from prison, is seen highly honoured as an admiral in Spain; while Thomas is shown with his father back in England, held there in great respect. Illusion and reality must have met even more strangely if the real Thomas was in the audience.

If one overlooks the distinction between particularly ancient and particularly up-to-date narrative, and the qualitative difference between a pot-boiler and a work of real imaginative power, significant similarities between

Pericles and *The Three English Brothers* are plain to see. The 'purchase' of both plays is 'to make men glorious' (I.Ch.9) by displaying the '*Idea and shape of honor*' (p. 318), but in both it is the strong feeling for family unity that is of paramount importance, though the members of the two families become widely separated during the course of each play. Pericles recovers his daughter Marina and his wife Thaisa in the final act of the play, and even though he unhesitatingly then gives his daughter away in marriage and decides to reign in Thaisa's Pentapolis while Lysimachus and Marina are to reign across the sea in Tyre, the play ends with a triumphant and serene sense of relationships restored. The Sherleys, on the other hand, are fully together *en famille* only in an opening dumbshow, when the two younger brothers '*take their leaues*' and set out from home (p. 320). At the end of the play, because

> Their destinies mutable commandresse
> Hath never suffer'd their regreeting eyes
> To kisse each other at an enteruiew,   (p. 403)

the complementary concluding dumbshow requires the stage to be divided into three distinct zones. Each of the brothers, isolated in a different country, is provided with '*a prospective glasse*', and thus equipped '*they seme to see one another and offer to embrace*' before they are parted by Fame, the chorus-presenter (p. 404). The play, with its own control of space and its science-fiction technology, momentarily transcends harsh reality and re-unites the brothers before recognising that the discipline of life imposes a stricter law. A modern dramatist would probably use telephones to make a comparable point.

Tyre, Antioch, Tharsus, Pentapolis, Ephesus, Mytilene – the locations of *Pericles* – lie dispersed around the eastern Mediterranean, and travel and the travails of travel, including the travails of childbirth, determine the progress of this play. Above all *Pericles* is a journey. The dramatisation of the Sherley adventures takes the form of a travel-travail play too, but though its geography extends on a hugely ambitious scale, and the brothers traverse its territory in a relentless quest for fame and honour, theirs are not journeys in anything like as full a sense as *Pericles* can offer. One needs only an atlas to chart the Sherley achievement: *Pericles* visits the extremities of human experience. Its mileage may be comparatively slight, but the sense of magnitude is infinitely greater. And always there is Shakespeare's sea, linking and separating, destroying and sustaining, a 'great vast' whose 'surges . . . wash both heaven and hell' (III.i. 1–2).

The two plays are related in minor respects as well. Tell-tale verbal and notional similarities too small to be commented on in this essay have been assembled by F. D. Hoeniger in his Arden edition.[4] Of larger interest, though, is the matter of technique, for the problems raised by embarrassingly copious plot material, dispersed locations, diverse incidents and the divided focus that occurs when no single protagonist predominates, have been tackled in basically similar ways. In particular, both plays depend heavily on a chorus figure to preside over the entertainment as a whole: Gower the poet in one case, and the female figure of Fame in the other. With his distinctive style, personality, and reputation, Gower is much the more interesting presenter. His appearances, not only because they are more numerous and better distributed, seem altogether more substantial. He is not just a device to solve a problem when one arises. He contributes to the variety of his play as well as presenting it, the hobbling versification of his lines sometimes setting off what he introduces by exaggerating the contrast between narration and drama, as when his quaint account of how a storm at sea

> Disgorges such a tempest forth
> That, as a duck for life that dives,
> So up and down the poor ship drives   (III. Ch. 48–50)

precedes the sublimity of Pericles's powerful speech on board this 'dancing boat' at the beginning of Act III; and sometimes sustaining through the same stylised versification independent effects of the greatest charm:

> The cat, with eyne of burning coal,
> Now couches fore the mouse's hole;
> And crickets sing at the oven's mouth,
> Aye the blither for their drouth.   (III. Ch. 5–8)

Ostensibly, the prime responsibility of both presenters is to supply economic narrative. They 'stand i' th' gaps', as Gower says, 'to teach . . . The stages of our story' (IV.iv. 8–9). But in addition, both of them encourage the audience, rather as the Chorus of *Henry V* had, to use their imagination, especially when rapid changes of place are encountered.

> Imagin now the gentle breath of heauen
> Hath on the liquid high-way of the waues
> Conuaid him many thousand leagues from vs:
> Thinke you haue seene him saile by many lands,
> And now at last, arriu'd in *Persia*,
> Within the confines of the great *Sophey*,
> Thinke you haue heard his curteous salute
> Speake in a peale of shot, the like till now
> Nere heard at *Casbin*, which townes gouernor
> Doth kindelie entertaine our English knight.   (p. 320)

That is Fame speaking, and here, without any of the poetic posturing of Fame's first two lines, is the more vigorous Gower making a similar appeal:

> Imagine Pericles arriv'd at Tyre,
> Welcom'd and settled to his own desire.
> His woeful queen we leave at Ephesus,
> Unto Diana there a votaress.
> Now to Marina bend your mind,

> Whom our fast-growing scene must find
> At Tharsus, and by Cleon train'd
> In music, letters.   (IV. Ch. 1–8)

Gower's liveliness includes a characteristically nervous and fussy didacticism that makes him all too ready to explain his function:

> Thus time we waste, and longest leagues make short;
> Sail seas in cockles, have an wish but for't;
> Making, to take our imagination,
> From bourn to bourn, region to region.   (IV.iv. 1–4)

Fame shares this willingness to comment on the need for abridgement, but is more tiresomely pompous than engagingly nervous. When she talks of 'restless' time she sounds dilatory, and she delays where she should hurry:

> Time [,] that vpon his wrestlesse wings Conueies
> Howers, daies and yeares [,] we must intreat you think
> By this hath borne our worthy Travailor
> Toward Christendom as far as Russia.   (p. 348)

The adequacy of what they have to offer is a matter that worries both presenters. In Gower's case the concern involves his responsibility to glad the ears and please the eyes of an audience 'born in those latter times, / When wit's more ripe' while he remains tied to the facts of the story, 'what mine authors say' (I.Ch. 11–12, 20). 'Please you sit and hark' he begs solicitously at one moment (V. Ch. 24); at another, with old-fashioned courtesy, asks his audience to consent to a 'last boon' (V.ii. 3), and elsewhere flatters us by acknowledging his dependence on our contribution:

> The unborn event
> I do commend to your content;
> Only I carry winged time
> Post on the lame feet of my rhyme;
> Which never could I so convey
> Unless your thoughts went on my way.   (IV. Ch. 45–50)

Fame's particular concern, appropriately enough, is over an even more inhibiting authenticity. The conditions of theatrical performance require her to reconcile the demands of 'poesie' with those of 'history', and this means that the play is accompanied by an argued justification of the act of dramatisation itself. The distinction between the raw and the cooked is one down-to-earth way the issue can be presented, though the stilted formality of the verse spoils the homely wit of the analogy:

> Who giues a foule unto his Cook to dresse
> Likewise expects to haue a foule againe;
> Though in the Cookes laborious workmanship

101

Much may be deminisht, som-what added,
(The losse of fethers and the gaine of sauce),
Yet in the back surrender of this dish
It is, and may be truelie cald, the same.
Such are our acts,   (p. 319)

acts that present the Sherley adventures drawn, plucked, and served with sauce. A sprawling documentary that could have lasted five days has been made to fit 'the stage and your attention'.

The outstanding method of vivid, rapid presentation in both plays is through the use of dumbshows. Gower is responsible for three that all reinforce his narrative by adding a visual dimension to the aural experience. In the first, a messenger from Tyre arrives in Tharsus with the news that Pericles is no longer safe there; in the second a messenger from Tyre arrives at Pentapolis with the news that Antiochus is dead and Pericles safe at last, and with an appeal for Pericles to return immediately to his kingdom (III. Ch.). The effect of both these interventions is to jolt the story forward to the next stage, and, by formal repetition, to mark the episodic nature of the dramatic structure. Gower's third dumbshow, though, is more elaborate and has no messenger. This time a complete episode – Pericles's third visit to Tharsus – is represented (IV.iv). Pericles arrives to fetch his daughter home, only to learn of her death and be shown her tomb. Once again his departure concludes the show and his narrative moves on to another stage as he re-embarks, but the following scene does not dramatise Pericles's next adventure. The tempest, associated with the loss of his child, that he must now endure is a tempest of the mind, not of the elements; and this internalised experience, that is to reduce him to a living corpse, exceeds the dramatised storm in which he lost his wife, as that had itself exceeded the narrated storm in which he lost only possessions and unspecified, unlamented travelling companions.

The Three English Brothers includes various sorts of dumbshow. One episode totally in mime is '*A show of the Christning*' (p. 403) that forms a spectacular climax to the action of the play, rather as the christening of Elizabeth was to conclude *Henry VIII*, but with the sacramental and festal here combined in a ceremonious ritual lacking the aid of speech. There is no presenter either. A different sort of spectacle in mime is provided by the two mock battles, one presented by the Sophy and the other by Anthony and Robert, in the first episode of the play (pp. 323–4). Different yet again are the dumbshow in the Prologue when the Shirleys separate, the dumbshow in the Epilogue when the Sherleys once more share the stage, and the two or three internal dumbshows; all these presented by Fame in something like the way that Gower presents the dumbshows in *Pericles*. The formal similarity with *Pericles* is most marked in the internal dumbshows. In the first of them the arrival of Anthony and Hallibeck in Russia is presented. Fame's narrative account introduces the dumbshow, but the show does not replicate the narrative, and the narrative does not stop to explain the show. A forward impetus is, therefore, constantly maintained:

> before their Ambassy
> Had time of hearing with the Emperor,
> Great *Haly* trayterously suggests against him
> Of his low birth, base manners and defects;
> Which being fastned in their credulous eares,
> How he was welcome by this show appeares.
> *Enter in state the Emperor of Russia, with three or foure Lordes[;] to him, Sir Anthonie and Haly. S[ir] Anthony offering to kisse his hand is disgrac'd and Haly accepted, the Emperor disposing theyr affayres to the Counsell, Exeunt.*
>
> (pp. 348–9)

And just as this dumbshow picks up the narrative at the point where explanation can be conveniently replaced by spectacle, so, as the Tsar leaves the stage, mime expands into dramatic speech.

'*Onely Sir Anthony at the going out of the rest speakes*' is how the stage direction misleadingly cues in the new section. In fact, although Anthony speaks first, Hallibeck and at least some of the Russian lords, probably all of them, have to remain on stage. In the space of 32 lines Anthony attempts to defend himself, is denigrated by Hallibeck, and taken prisoner by the Russians pending an investigation of the charges against him, while Hallibeck, in contrast, is honourably entertained, and briefly concludes the episode with a gloating aside. The Chorus-presenter now picks up the narrative once again to explain how Hallibeck's malice eventually came to light and how Anthony's good name was vindicated, before preparing the audience for a second Russian dumbshow:

> How he left the Court
> To please your eyes wee in this shew report.   [*A shew*. (p. 351)

This time the mimed action has no printed scenario, but the line that picks up the narrative, 'Thus grac'd by the *Muscouian* Emperor', indicates that its content is antithetical to the dumbshow in which the Tsar had received the embassy on its arrival. Fame's seven lines that then follow this second Russian dumbshow transport us peremptorily to Italy and, if we are to trust the printed text, introduce yet another dumbshow:

> Time now makes short their way, and they at Rome
> In state are brought before his holiness:
> Where what succeeded for the former grudge
> Giue you vs leaue to shew, take leaue to iudge.
>
> [*A shew*.
>
> *Enter the Pope and his Cardinals.*   (p. 351)

In all probability, though, the direction for this '*shew*' ought to be edited out of the play since the quarrel that flares up between Anthony and Hallibeck during the papal audience, referred to by Fame as the result of the 'former grudge', is to be performed in a fully-scripted dramatic scene. The only spectacle required to follow Fame's interlinking speech is the dignified entrance of the Pope and his entourage, and the entrance of the Persian embassy, not a dumbshow as such. The superfluous direction for '*A shew*' looks like a textual intrusion prompted by an over specific response to Fame's use of the verb 'to shew', and by a failure to take account of the action about to be presented in the subsequent scene.

It is, then, primarily the two Russian-dumbshows that invite comparison with Gower's three dumbshows, though the comparison is one that reveals important differences. The use of dumbshows to impel Pericles into a new phase of the story has no equivalent in *The Three English Brothers*, and although the antithetical Russian dumbshows of arrival and departure, like the two messenger dumbshows in *Pericles*, form pairs, there is no attempt in *The Three English Brothers* to stylise the play's episodic structure by introducing recurrent dumbshows at the punctuation points. Indeed, the authors do what they can to prevent such patterning, and their management of the story by allowing it to pass freely between narration, mime, and spoken drama is part of that endeavour. The trouble is that the opportunistic and unsystematic mixing of media is unsettling. Progress through the play becomes like a journey in which, without warning, the mode of transport keeps changing. Bus, bicycle, taxi, ferry – one never knows what will be next, or how long any stage will last.

The initial dumbshow presented by Fame in the Prologue has no mimed counterpart in the opening chorus of *Pericles*, but like all the dumbshows in Shakespeare's play it represents a leavetaking prior to embarkation on a voyage:

> Enter Sir Thomas [and] his three sonnes, Sir Thomas, Sir Anthony, Maister Robert[.] Sir Thomas goes back with his Father, the other take their leaues.
>
> (p. 320)

Rather as the internal messenger–dumbshows in *Pericles* restart the action when narrative progress peters out and the plot threatens to subside into a natural repose, so the initial dumbshow of *The Three English Brothers* sets the whole play going, though without any compelling reason being given for the sons to leave home. The strong documentary interest of the play is here combined with an archetypal folktale quality that dispenses with the need for explanation. The brothers go out to seek their fortune because that is what three brothers always do, and true to form it is 'Maister Robert' the youngest brother who marries the beautiful niece of the Sophy and acquits himself best of all.

The dumbshow presented by Fame in the Epilogue is a special case, utterly distinct in its staging from any mode of presentation in *Pericles*, for it manipulates conventions of theatre in a sophisticated way that allows representation to transcend reality. Compelled by the strength of family feeling, illusion takes precedence over life. But although the staging of *Pericles* provides no parallel with this extraordinary dumbshow – a device that momentarily makes the impossible possible by eliminating the great distances that separate Persia, England and Spain – the enlarged spirit of its brief transcendence is magically suffused through Shakespeare's last act. It is to be found in the wonder of the restoration of Marina 'not dead at Tharsus, as she should have been' (V.i. 213); it is there in Pericles's privilege of hearing the music of the spheres; and present in the miracle of his vision, the goddess Diana, almost like a presenter, then making possible the final fulfilling reunion, that with Thaisa:

> *Pericles*   The voice of dead Thaisa!
> *Thaisa*   That Thaisa am I, supposed dead
>   And drown'd.   (V.iii. 35–7)

The language of recognition that Inga-Stina Ewbank has analysed, and shown to be central to the experience of Shakespeare's last act, depends above all on this simple act of naming,

> As a mother names her child
> When sleep at last has come
> On limbs that had run wild.[5]

No attempt is made in *The Three English Brothers* to dramatise the wonder of recognition through language of any sort, let alone Shakespeare's language of strangely moving literalism. Mime and trick telescopes are all we are offered. But the importance of recognition and the value attached to Sherley family unity in the Epilogue of *The Three English Brothers* is necessarily limited anyway by the knowledge that it is essentially their own choice, not fate, that keeps the Sherleys apart. Besides, the concentration towards the end of the play on Robert virtually turns him belatedly into the play's protagonist, and his betrothal to the Sophy's niece and the christening of his daughter provide him with the full achievement of a settled family life. Like Pericles, Robert is blessed with a wife and daughter, and, like Pericles, he is favoured with the opportunity of a miraculous recognition that fleetingly unites him with his dispersed family; but, for Robert, these two experiences are totally unconnected, and the satisfactions of one detract from the need for the other. As for his new family, perhaps the most telling contrast with *Pericles* is that the dramatists do not trouble to give names to either wife or daughter. They have created a family in which even the most basic vocabulary for a language of recognition is lacking.

Both *Pericles* and *The Three English Brothers* can be accurately described as episodic plays, but while *The Three English Brothers* is undeniably something of a loose baggy monster, *Pericles* is much tighter in construction

than is usually acknowledged. It would be a mistake, though, to regard even
The Three English Brothers as a totally formless play, for the adventures of
the Sherleys have been organised by the dramatists in a distinctly symmetrical way. Besides the matching family dumbshows at either end of the play,
the symmetry of Hallibeck's departure from Persia and return there, the
concentric arrangement of scenes in Venice (Zariph/Kempe/Zariph), and
the way that Thomas's adventures start late in the play and finish early all
stand out. Other elements whose symmetrical placing is less obtrusive help
to substantiate the design (see Fig. 1).

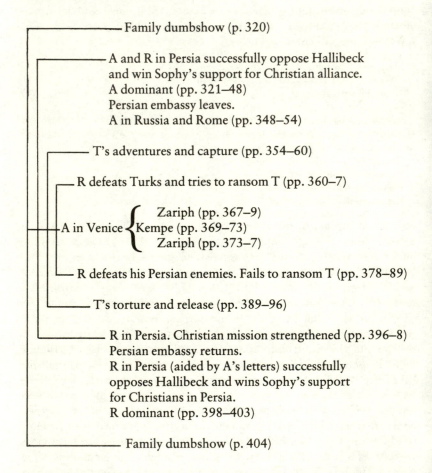

Family dumbshow (p. 320)

A and R in Persia successfully oppose Hallibeck
and win Sophy's support for Christian alliance.
A dominant (pp. 321–48)
Persian embassy leaves.
A in Russia and Rome (pp. 348–54)

T's adventures and capture (pp. 354–60)

R defeats Turks and tries to ransom T (pp. 360–7)

A in Venice { Zariph (pp. 367–9)
Kempe (pp. 369–73)
Zariph (pp. 373–7)

R defeats his Persian enemies. Fails to ransom T (pp. 378–89)

T's torture and release (pp. 389–96)

R in Persia. Christian mission strengthened (pp. 396–8)
Persian embassy returns.
R in Persia (aided by A's letters) successfully
opposes Hallibeck and wins Sophy's support
for Christians in Persia.
R dominant (pp. 398–403)

Family dumbshow (p. 404)

The symmetry is less strongly marked in the play itself than in Fig. 1,
partly because Fame as chorus does not, except in the matching Prologue
and Epilogue, control its use or exploit its possiblities; partly because the
first half of the play is disproportionately long; and partly because other

elements smudge the schematic sharpness. In particular, the two scenes involving the Sophy's niece, one in the first half (pp. 341–7) and one in the second (pp. 379–88) are asymmetrical; and there is one scene with Thomas in Turkey (pp. 365–7) that finds no place in the symmetry at all. Presumably the authors thought not in terms of precise diagrams but in terms of a rather general symmetrical shapeliness. Their concern must have been simply to impose some semblance of form on a body of inconclusive material that had, in the family leavetaking, an obvious point of departure, but no clear natural shape thereafter. A formal rounding off supplied the necessary sense of completion, and an overall symmetrical design that did not require rigid adherence to a detailed plan provided a neat way of working towards it.

When in 1647 William Cartwright praised Fletcher's skill as a dramatist he singled out the ability to control 'free fancy' and contrive plays that displayed the grace of symmetry:

> 'twas not chance that made them hit,
> Nor were thy playes the Lotteries of wit,
> But like to Durer's pencill, which first Knew;
> The laws of faces, and then faces drew;
> Thou knowest the air, the colour, and the place,
> The simetry, which gives a Poem grace:
> Parts are so fitted unto parts, as doe
> Shew thou hadst wit, and Mathematicks too;
> Knewst where by line to spare, where to dispence,
> And didst beget just Comedies from thence.[6]

Wit and mathematics in *The Three English Brothers* are of no great subtlety, but the qualities that Cartwright discerned in Fletcher are evidently ones that the authors of *The Three English Brothers* had some feeling for. Other dramatists too have shown a concern for 'The simetry, which gives a Poem grace', and also for the symmetry that can help to give meaning to dramatic action. Shakespeare is among them.[7]

The extreme unreliability of the corrupt 1609 text of *Pericles* makes close analysis of this play of Shakespeare's a dubious undertaking. However, a symmetrical structure, much more interesting than that of *The Three English Brothers*, is preserved in the 1609 text, and there is every reason to regard this structure as essentially undamaged, at least in general conception. It is a concentric design with Pericles's experiences at the court of 'the good Simonides', king of Pentapolis, as its centre-piece. In the Renaissance manner this centre is triumphal, showing Pericles victorious in arms, in arts, and in love.[8] His first success is in knightly contest in the lists (II.ii) and this triumph in arms leads to success in arts, when, in the feast that follows, he excels in dancing (II.iii). A nocturnal episode that is alluded to but not represented reveals him to be 'music's master' by enabling his skill in dancing to be matched by his skill in singing, and this demonstration of musical prowess leads to his third triumph, success in love; for Pericles outrivals the knights who have come to Pentapolis to woo Simonides's daughter just as surely when he wins Thaisa's affection as he had when he took the prize in the lists (II.v). And just as his triumph in arms provided the occasion for Pericles's excellent dancing, so his excellent singing provides the opportunity for his triumph in love.

Since the play begins with Pericles's quest for a wife, marriage to Thaisa brings the initial impulse to a romantically satisfactory conclusion, but Pericles's achievements in Pentapolis are only one aspect of his good fortune. At the middle of the play, in a pivotal scene that surprisingly takes us away from Pentapolis and replaces, as it were, the nocturnal scene in which we would have heard Pericles charming Thaisa with his singing, we learn that Antiochus and his incestuous daughter have been destroyed by fire from heaven, and that the threat against Pericles's life is thereby removed. Though he does not yet know it, Pericles is now free to retrace his journey and return to his native Tyre. Diagrammatically the centre of the play looks as in Fig. 2.

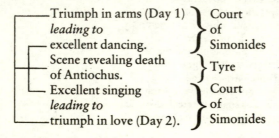

Either side of the triumphal centre are great storms at sea, one marking Pericles's arrival at Pentapolis and the other his departure. In the first, Pericles is shipwrecked, washed ashore, and helped by fishermen on the coast of Pentapolis; in the second, Thaisa, supposed dead in childbirth, is cast overboard, washed ashore, and tended by Cerimon and his helpers. In performance the doubling of parts by actors could well reinforce the relationship between the fishermen and Cerimon and his helpers, and similar groupings on stage would also tend to emphasise the structural connection.[9] The symmetry is further stressed by the dumbshows and choruses that initiate the two voyages.

From a straightforward narrative point of view it might seem excessive for two storms to be included in a single play, especially as they come so close together, but deliberate contravention of the literary decorum that calls for variation is the means of drawing attention to the pattern and making plain where the centre of the system lies. The repetition provided by the second storm at sea indicates that the route earlier taken towards the centre is now being retraced away from the centre. To meet the objection that repetition is uninventive and uninteresting Shakespeare offers a contrast in dramatic method. Rather as in the triumph of arts he chose to stage Pericles's dancing but was content with a mere account of Pericles's singing, he now has the first storm related, it being just the sort of unstageable episode that we might expect Gower to supply by narration, but then amazes his audience by having the second storm, in one of his most daring scenes, directly staged despite the limitation of having to use a fixed stage floor for the deck of a storm-tossed ship. It was only the second time in his career that Shakespeare had set a scene at sea, and on the last occasion, in *Antony and Cleopatra*, the ship had been at anchor.

Enclosing the middle span of the play that has just been described are paired episodes in Tharsus. In the first of them (I.iv), Pericles, coming *from* Tyre, relieves the city from famine and earns the gratitude of Cleon and Dionyza. In the second (III.iii), on his way *to* Tyre, Pericles gives Cleon and Dionyza the opportunity to repay their debt of gratitude and now relieve him by caring for his infant daughter. On neither occasion are the expectations of the distressed party borne out. When Cleon hears of Pericles's ships off the coast in the first Tharsus scene he is convinced that the purpose is hostile even though white flags are being flown. 'Who makes the fairest show means most deceit' (I.iv. 75), he comments, but he is wrong. In the second Tharsus scene, Pericles expects kindness and finds no lack of 'fairest show', but this time it is Pericles who is mistaken. Cleon and Dionyza will deceitfully fail to fulfil their promises, and after fourteen years Dionyza will attempt to have Marina murdered by Leonine. The murder attempt itself (IV.i) forms a neat symmetrical pair with Antiochus's attempt to have Pericles murdered by Thaliard (I. iii).

The symmetry of the play is sufficiently relaxed for there not to be a tight scene-by-scene relationship between the first half and the second half, and so, though the pattern as a whole is strongly marked and strongly felt, not every single element in the play rigorously serves that pattern. Narrative considerations and the need for the fourteen years of Marina's childhood to elapse account for the interpolation of the very brief scene (III.iv) in which we witness Thaisa's resolution to enter Diana's temple at Ephesus, but, conversely, structural reasons probably lie behind the decision to relegate to dumbshow Pericles's third visit to Tharsus (IV.iv), and so prevent it from unbalancing the symmetry as it would were it presented as a fully drama-tised episode. There is, none the less, a problem about judging how far to go in the recognition of symmetrical pairs. Although it is possible to see a link between Act I, scene ii, in which after discovering the evil at Antioch Pericles loses his peace of mind, and Act IV, scene iii, in which Cleon, after discover-ing that Dionyza has arranged for Marina to be murdered, also loses his peace of mind, the connection is strained, and the realisation that the text of I.ii is badly corrupt makes one reluctant to pursue the parallel closely. All that is indisputable is that IV.iii, like Gower's IV.iv, heightens suspense about Marina's fate by interrupting the sequence of brothel scenes.

The outermost pairing of the play's symmetry is provided by the contrast between the opening scene of Act I, in which the sexually impure life of a king's daughter is revealed in a royal court where we would expect to find purity, and the three brothel scenes of Act IV, in which the chaste life of a king's daughter is shown in a place where we would expect to find impurity. In production, the actress who plays Marina may well be the same actress who plays the unnamed daughter of Antiochus. Julie Peasgood played both in Ron Daniels's intelligent RSC production at The Other Place, Stratford-upon-Avon, in 1979. For the incestuous daughter she wore a distinctive black dress, and for Marina a white dress of identical design.

The cardinal points of any symmetrical system – the centre and the two extremities – are emphasised in *Pericles* by the way the extremities are linked to the centre. The beginning is linked to the middle by contrasting father-daughter relationships: Antiochus pretends to offer his daughter in marriage but in fact retains her for himself, while Simonides pretends to be angry and to oppose his daughter's love for Pericles but in fact applauds it. The end is linked to the middle by the contrasting ways in which Thaisa and Marina meet their future husbands. The distinction between Simonides's genial last line, 'And then, with what haste you can, get you to bed', and the determined attempts to persuade Marina to do likewise in the brothel, and 'go her ways', is particularly striking.

The whole symmetrical design is a pattern that Shakespeare has skilfully imposed on his material. It has no basis in either Book VIII of the *Confessio Amantis* or in Twine's *The Patterne of Painefull Adventures*, the play's two narrative sources. Indeed, Twine's romance is so lacking in any sense of pattern that the disparity between the title and the work might well have stimulated Shakespeare to envisage how the ramshackle adventures could be reworked in a truly patterned way. But the full pattern of Shakespeare's play is more than just a resourceful exercise in symmetry, for free from and extending beyond the closed concentric design of the four acts of painful adventures are the unconstrained revelations of Act V. Unhampered by adherence to pattern or probability these discoveries establish an overwhelming and self-sufficient climax to the narrative that wonderfully transcends all that has gone before. In effect, the structure of the whole play articulates a vision of life formulated in story by ancient wisdom and transmitted by the moral Gower to a new generation, a vision that teaches that only after the pattern of endeavour and endurance is completed do the joys that outweigh all sorrows become available, and only with the final awakening into felicity do the travails of embattled existence become tolerable. Describing the slow process of conversion, Kierkegaard noted in his journal the need to 'tread the same path backward which one has previously trodden forwards'.[10] *Pericles* is no allegory and a process of conversion is not what it records, but its progress involves a strategy and discipline similar to Kierkegaard's, and the happy certainties and stabilities of its miraculous conclusion carry with them the unmistakable quality of religious beatitude.

Pico della Mirandola's neoplatonic definition of felicity, 'the return of each thing to its beginning', has found here both a human reality and a dramatic form.[11]

The revelations and resolutions that conclude *Pericles* look back comprehensively to every aspect of the foregoing narrative. Rather than being paired in a limited symmetrical relationship with a structurally determined counterpart, Act V is the consummation of everything that has preceded it, and as part of that rich rapport it develops its own distinctive way of using the pattern that shaped the painful adventures of Acts I–IV. The principle of concentric symmetry reappears in the last act, but transmuted and powerfully concentrated in the rhetorical figure that above all patterns the play's language of recognition. 'Shades of Tully and Erasmus / Teach us to use the strange chiasmus' declares a schoolroom rhyme, and the patterned strangeness of chiasmus does indeed provide an appropriate form in which to record miraculous truths that are stranger than fiction. The way the reflexive AB/BA pattern returns on itself allows experience to be held suspended in contemplation, allows wonder to be lingered over, savoured, possessed, while the weight of the repetition affirms and reassures. 'Where were you born? / And wherefore call'd Marina?' (V.i. 153–4), asks Pericles urgently, and Marina's chiastic response 'Call'd Marina / For I was born at sea' (V.i. 154–5) matches the question's sequence of 'born . . . fore . . . call'd Marina' with her own answering sequence of 'Call'd Marina . . . For . . . born'. She completes a pattern, and by so doing demonstrates the instinctive bond that unites a daughter and her father.

The pattern sounds again when Marina herself wonderingly poses the question,

> Is it no more to be your daughter than
> To say my mother's name was Thaisa?
> Thaisa was my mother, who did end
> The minute I began,   (V.i. 207–10)

where the chiasmus of 'my mother's . . . was Thaisa' / 'Thaisa was my mother' is extended by framing references to Marina ('your daughter' / 'I'), and by the chiming of echoed sounds ('be . . . than' / 'began'; 'Is it' / 'minute') that all accord with the notion of ends in beginnings and beginnings in ends, of Marina's birth and Thaisa's supposed death. When Pericles recognises Thaisa's voice at Ephesus a chiastic response combines certainty with strangeness, ritual with emotion ('dead Thaisa' / 'Thaisa . . . dead'):

> *Pericles*   The voice of dead Thaisa!
> *Thaisa*   That Thaisa am I, supposed dead
>   And drown'd.   (V.iii. 35–7)

The strongest chiastic patterns are to be found in the play's most lastingly resonant lines, Pericles's

> Thou that beget'st him that did thee beget;
> Thou that wast born at sea, buried at Tharsus,
> And found at sea again! (V.i. 194–96)

The first statement pivots its heavily accented and antithetical 'beget'st him' / 'thee beget' around the line's caesura, while the second balances an 'at sea' either side of a pivotal 'at Tharsus'. But the two statements, anaphorically paired by their parallel openings ('Thou that . . .'), also form the double centre of a speech with its own concentric disposition. Either side of the double centre are similar sounding appeals, 'O, come hither', that introduces the central lines of the speech addressed to Marina, and 'O Helicanus', that repeats the speech's opening words, so reverting to the person originally addressed. Enclosing the symmetrical appeals are half lines less securely linked to each other as the attenuated pattern begins to dissolve, the rhyme of 'drown' and 'down', and the matching assonance of 'me . . . sweetness' and 'knees' (see Fig. 3).

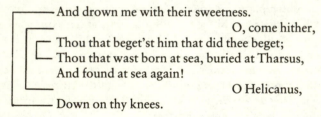

> And drown me with their sweetness.
> O, come hither,
> Thou that beget'st him that did thee beget;
> Thou that wast born at sea, buried at Tharsus,
> And found at sea again!
> O Helicanus,
> Down on thy knees.

Pericles's strange chiasmus is, of course, also Polonius's 'foolish figure' (*Hamlet*, II.ii 96–7), and it is well to remember that the worth of any rhetorical device depends on the use to which it is put. To observe that the authors of *Pericles* and *The Three English Brothers* share a sense of symmetrical form is true enough, but the distinction between a symmetry that lends grace to an otherwise rambling plot and a symmetry that is an indispensable and integral part of a whole complex poetic conception is a distinction that eclipses the original comparison. The relationship between *Pericles* and *The Three English Brothers* is one with many superficial connections, and it is right to be aware of them. They help to measure Shakespeare's achievement, and they provide an entry into the milieu in which Shakespeare worked, with its rival theatrical companies and dramatists who took cognisance of each other's productions. But what matters most is that the two plays are worlds apart. Although in this essay, like the Sherleys at the end of *The Three English Brothers*, they offer to embrace, Fame will inevitably part them.

NOTES

1 *The Works of John Day Reprinted from the Collected Edition by A. H. Bullen (1881)*, introduced by Robin Jeffs (London, 1963), pp. 373–4. All references to *The Travailes of the Three English Brothers* are to this makeshift edition.

2 *Pericles*, I.Ch. 1–2.
3 D. W. Davies's *Elizabethans Errant: The Strange Fortunes of Sir Thomas Sherley and His Three Sons As Well in the Dutch Wars As in Muscovy, Morocco, Persia, Spain, and the Indies* (Ithaca, NY, 1967) is the best account of the brothers, but Samuel C. Chew includes an account of them and of the play in *The Crescent and the Rose: Islam and England during the Renaissance* (New York, 1937).
4 (London, 1963), pp. xxii–iii and 178–9.
5 W. B. Yeats, *Collected Poems* (London, 1958), p. 204; Inga-Stina Ewbank, ' "My name is Marina": the language of recognition' in *Shakespeare's Styles: Essays in Honour of Kenneth Muir*, eds Philip Edwards, Inga-Stina Ewbank and G. K. Hunter (Cambridge, 1980), pp. 111–30.
6 'Another on the Same', 33–42, in *The Life and Poems of William Cartwright*, ed. R. Cullis Goffin (Cambridge, 1918), pp. 90–1.
7 See, for example, Mark Rose, *Shakespearean Design* (Cambridge, Mass., 1972). For strict concentric symmetry in later drama see, for instance, Tom Stoppard's *Artist Descending a Staircase* and Strindberg's *To Damascus, Part 1*. Both Stoppard and Strindberg have commented on their structural patterns.
8 See especially Alastair Fowler, *Triumphal Forms: Structural Patterns in Elizabethan Poetry* (Cambridge, 1970).
9 For the way this worked in one strikingly successful production see J. R. Mulryne, 'To Glad Your Ear and Please Your Eyes: *Pericles* at The Other Place', *Critical Quarterly*, 21 (1979), 35–6. Significant doubling was a strong production point in the 1984 *Pericles* at the Theatre Royal, Stratford East, also.
10 *The Journals of Søren Kierkegaard*, edited by A. Dru (Oxford, 1938), item 61.
11 *Heptaplus*, translated by Douglas Carmichael, in Pico della Mirandola, *'On the Dignity of Man', 'On Being and the One', 'Heptaplus'*, introduced by Paul J. W. Miller (Indianapolis, 1965), p. 148.

DIETER MEHL

Corruption, retribution and justice in *Measure for Measure* and *The Revenger's Tragedy*

⟨⟩◦⟨⟩

Shakespeare's *Measure for Measure* and *The Revenger's Tragedy* are not often considered as in any way closely related plays. Many critics have, of course, noticed that the author of *The Revenger's Tragedy* is demonstrably indebted to Shakespeare and must have been familiar with several of his plays.[1] The dependence of *The Revenger's Tragedy* on *Hamlet* is obvious enough and has been studied in sufficient detail.[2] There are also close links with *King Lear* and, perhaps, other tragedies, but *Measure for Measure*, too, though not usually thought of in this connection, seems to have been very much in Tourneur's mind at the time of writing *The Revenger's Tragedy*. It belongs to the same period and must have been written no more than one or two years before *The Revenger's Tragedy*; both plays were, in all probability, acted by the King's Men between 1604 and 1606, although in both cases there is some uncertainty as to whether the play was designed for the public theatre or for more exclusive audiences.[3]

Apart from these more technical links, the two plays share a number of themes and concerns central to their design and they are also connected by several verbal and situational echoes, none of them, perhaps, very startling in itself (or else they would not have escaped earlier readers) but, taken together, close enough to suggest that the author of *The Revenger's Tragedy* was familiar with the text and possibly with the theatrical impact of *Measure for Measure* and may have been provoked by it to make some of his surprising adaptations of the revenge theme. Many of the parallels between the two plays may be commonplaces of the period and it would be very difficult to prove direct dependence of one play on the other, but these parallels are more often than not related to issues the two plays have in common and they support the impression of a close thematic affinity, although it is evident that they belong to very different dramatic genres. This may well be the reason why they have not been studied side by side and even the more glaring parallels have hardly been noticed. The only two critics who, as far as I know, have made more than passing remarks on the connection disagree totally about *Measure for Measure* and, in consequence, about their relationship.

For Una Ellis-Fermor, *Measure for Measure* represents 'the very nadir of disgust and cynicism . . . It is indeed the lowest point', and she comes to the rather surprising conclusion: 'The all-comprehending doubt, the dead disgust of *Measure for Measure* sounds a lower note than does the burning satanism of *The Revenger's Tragedy*'.[4]

Rosalind Miles, on the other hand, points to the differences in genre, in the treatment of disguise and the trial of chastity, but does not otherwise recognise any direct connection between the two plays.[5] Yet they both express not only the worried obsession of two dramatists with the concepts of divine order, justice, mercy and retribution, but also the longing for a community in which corruption is exterminated by whatever might be the most efficient measure.

We have all, I assume, become rather diffident about the concept of literary influence and about simple source-studies. The indebtedness of one author to another is such a complex phenomenon and even in cases where it seems to stare one in the face, as with *Hamlet* and *The Revenger's Tragedy*, it is impossible to measure it, to count the echoes or even to agree what really constitutes an echo.[6] How much less can one define the precise influence of *Measure for Measure* on *The Revenger's Tragedy*! Shakespeare's play is evidently not a 'source', but the plays have enough in common to make comparison fruitful and interesting. It is by no means my main purpose to prove that Tourneur was decisively influenced by *Measure for Measure*, but rather to compare the treatment of certain fundamental themes and situations in the two plays. Such comparative reading should help to a better understanding of the plays, their real differences as well as their common basis.

The first and perhaps least debatable common denominator is the fact that both plays deal with a thoroughly corrupt society, a society without effective authority, where evil has been allowed free rein without fear of just punishment. In both plays, corruption is described mainly in terms of sexual indulgence and its concomitant diseases. In both plays, the human body, eaten away by infectious poison, is a powerful image of moral perversion and decay. Such parallels may, of course, simply mean that certain ideas and commonplaces were 'in the air' during the first decade of the seventeenth century, but even this is worth closer investigation and helps to a clearer view of the two plays and their environment. But it is more than a matter of a few commonplaces.

What in *Hamlet* was 'leperous distilment', poisoning the blood and disintegrating the skin, has, in *Measure for Measure*, become a polluting disease, hollowing the bones and peeling off hair and all. The second scene of Shakespeare's play is full of nasty puns about hollow bones, 'sound'-ness, 'three-piled' bodies, French velvet, infectious breath and baldness produced by venereal disease. This state of society is marked by the absence of 'Grace' in any form and by a flagrant disregard of the seventh commandment.

All these ideas and some of the puns recur in *The Revenger's Tragedy* where Vindice comments on 'hollow bones' (I.i. 6), 'three-piled flesh' (I.i. 46) and the 'French mole' (I.i. 101), as well as on the 'unsound'-ness of lust (I.i. 89). Like Lucio, he finds that 'Grace' has become rare (I.iii. 16), it has become a bawd (a word very frequent in both plays). Here, too, the seventh commandment is picked out (I.ii. 162) and 'Madam Mitigation' recurs as 'that bald Madam, Opportunity' (I.i. 55).

In *Measure for Measure*, sexual corruption is still, to a large extent, a matter of the 'low' characters, of prose comedy and deliberate contrast to the more complex and dignified conflicts of the protagonists. *The Revenger's Tragedy* makes a far more radical statement by satirical generalising, not only through personifying names, but by extending the theme of corruption to all the characters of the play. There is no difference between low life and high life except that sexual perversion seems an aristocratic vice, concentrated in the Duke's family, and there is hardly any of the saving humour and disarming commonsense of Pompey or the almost endearing incompetence of Elbow. Shakespeare, *pace* Una Ellis-Fermor, makes vice far less uniformly repulsive. It is so common, so much a mark of natural inclination and appears in so many different forms that neither wholesale revulsion nor 'but heading and hanging' are adequate responses.

In *The Revenger's Tragedy*, too, we find in places this cheerful acceptance of the seamy facts of life, but usually in a much more sinister context. Pompey, the 'Clown' as the Folio calls him, defies Escalus to exterminate vice and will let 'flesh and fortune' determine his conduct. Junior Brother, in Tourneur's play, asserts his amoral disregard of civilised morals in a similar spirit:

> 2. *Judge.* . . . Confess, my lord,
>   What mov'd you to 't?
> *Junior Bro.* Why, flesh and blood, my lord;
>   What should move men unto a woman else? (I.ii. 46–8)

This exchange is part of a court scene that curiously conflates the comic trial of Froth and Pompey and the discussion about justice and mercy in Isabella's plea for her brother. Pity, in this nastier situation, is begged for by a corrupt woman and on behalf of a crime far worse than Claudio's:

> *Duchess.* My gracious lord, I pray be merciful.
>   Although his trespass far exceed his years,
>   Think him to be your own, as I am yours;
>   Call him not son-in-law. The law, I fear,
>   Will fall too soon upon his name and him.
>   Temper his fault with pity!
> *Luss.* Good my lord,
>   Then 'twill not taste so bitter and unpleasant
>   Upon the judges' palate, for offences
>   Gilt o'er with mercy show like fairest women,
>   Good only for their beauties, which wash'd off,
>   No sin is uglier. (I.ii. 21–31)

The vague reminiscences of Shakespeare's play are obvious here, as is the far more cynical spirit of the whole scene. 'The justice of the law' (I.ii. 71) is even more ambiguous here than in *Measure for Measure* ('The law is a wise serpent', 50) and it is administered by one who is himself by no means untainted. This idea is spelt out in a soliloquy with a sententiousness very similar to some of the Duke's speeches in Shakespeare's play and in terms that might also describe Angelo:

> *Duke.* It well becomes that judge to nod at crimes,
>   That does commit greater himself and lives;
>   I may forgive a disobedient error,
>   That expect pardon for adultery,
>   And in my old days am a youth in lust!   (II.iii. 124–8)

The whole episode (I.ii; II.iii; III.i–iv) is full of vague echoes of *Measure for Measure*: there is the idea of a trial by dissembling; the Duke wants to test his sons who hypocritically plead for their brother's life: and there is the scene in prison when the warrant from the Duke has arrived and Junior Brother is asked to 'prepare to die' though he had reason to expect his release. The execution is ordered earlier than even the officers expected and Junior Brother's description of his own crime reminds one of Lucio's attitude towards Claudio's trespass:

> My fault was sweet sport, which the world approves;
> I die for that which every woman loves.   (III.iv. 80–1)

Earlier in the play he had taken his verdict rather in the spirit of Lucio:

> Her beauty was ordain'd to be my scaffold,
> And yet methinks I might be easier 'sess'd;
> My fault being sport, let me but die in jest.   (I.ii. 64–6)[7]

Although the impression of general corruption looms large in both plays there is a significant difference in the characters. The world of Vienna may be a fallen world; it is peopled by all sorts of depraved, weak and even unredeemable characters, but among the main actors in the drama, none is so thoroughly corrupt that he cannot be reclaimed and made to see his imperfections. Even Angelo is not a villain in the conventional sense – he is neither a Iago nor a Shylock nor even Don John; he is as alive to the corruption around him as Vindice and as eager to punish it. Unlike Vindice, he tries to know himself and has a keen awareness of his own sinfulness, more so than Isabella who is never beset by any real doubt about herself and who seems to take much less note of the disturbing state of society; she is more concerned with individual failing and salvation than with any political issues, as her moving but, in political terms, irrelevant plea for mercy shows.

Tourneur's play seems rather more preoccupied with the social and moral conditions of a specific time and culture. Corruption here is not simply the result of human weakness or of too much public indulgence, but certain changes in society have made sin fashionable. The moral decline is closely associated with the contrast between Court and country and with the passage of time.[8] The Court and the present are inherently evil:

Let blushes dwell i' th' country.   (I.iii. 5)

That maid in the old time, whose flush of grace
Would never suffer her to get good clothes.   (I.iii. 13–14)

Live wealthy, rightly understand the world,
And chide away that foolish country-girl
Keeps company with your daughter, chastity.   (II.i. 81–3)

Come, you shall leave those childish haviours,
And understand your time.   (II.i. 170–1)

. . . what woman is
So foolish to keep honesty,
And be not able to keep herself? No,
Times are grown wiser . . .   (II.i. 183–6)

That nobleman
Has been i'th' country, for he does not lie.   (V.i. 111–12)

Virtue is unfashionable, is a thing of the past and of the backward rural culture. This is more like the tone of *Timon of Athens* than of *Measure for Measure*.

Measure for Measure and *The Revenger's Tragedy* are not only deeply concerned with a corrupt society, they are both unusually explicit in their references to Christian and biblical concepts. Shakespeare's play has often been read in relation to the Gospels, and *The Revenger's Tragedy* has been called a dramatisation of 'the traditional Christian doctrine of fallen man and the traditional pattern of sin and redemption'.[9] Man's relation to God and, in particular, the nature of human and divine justice, is one of the central concerns of both plays. Human justice demands 'death for death!' (*MM*, V.i. 407) and this is what even divine justice seems to do in Tourneur's play:

Vind.   The rape of your good lady has been quited
            With death on death.
Ant.   Just is the law above!   (V.iii. 90–1)

Thunder is Heaven's answer to human crimes (IV.ii. 199) and a sign of divine approval whereas in *Measure for Measure* it becomes, at least in Isabella's plea, an image of the difference between God's prerogative and human presumption. The answer to the disruption of society is very different in the two plays. The Heaven that delights in the carnage of Tourneur's revenge is not the same as the Heaven that Isabella and Vincentio look up to (the word 'Heaven' occurs thirty eight times in Shakespeare's play) although Isabella comes perhaps near it when 'she seems to imagine God as a kind of Angelo';[10] she knows, however, that 'He that might the vantage best have took/Found out the remedy'' (II.ii. 74–5). In the oppressive Calvinist world of Tourneur's play there is little sign that the remedy has been found. Yet there is a character in whom the principle of grace is personified, Gratiana, and her daughter who stands out as a singular instance of uncorruptible virtue.

In a society poisoned by lust and sexual indulgence, chastity becomes of very rare value; it is as exceptional as it is precious and it is (after the father has died) a brother's particular responsibility to watch over it. Claudio is himself tainted by the vice his sister abhors and he is certainly no reliable protector of her chastity. Castiza, 'the symbol of a heavenly order whose mark is chastity',[11] could well, like Castabella in *The Atheist's Tragedy*, be modelled on Isabella. In both cases, the brother represents a potential threat to chastity and Castiza would certainly not hesitate to proclaim, like Isabella, 'More than our brother is our chastity'. But, as Foakes says, 'Castiza cannot be a tragic figure because she is incorruptible'.[12] Tragedy is not, however, excluded by her being incorruptible, but by the nature of her 'temptation', if Vindice's trial of her chastity can be called a temptation. Isabella, about whom critics have been violently divided, is a far more tragic character. She may be as incorruptible as Castiza and as little wavering in her firm chastity, but Shakespeare presents her trial as a genuinely tragic dilemma and her breakdown when she feels betrayed by Claudio is a personal crisis more pitiful than anything Castiza has to go through, although she has reason to feel equally let down by her own mother.

For Castiza, strangely called 'a pure novice' by her brother (I.iii. 144) – another link with Isabella? – there is no real temptation, no rival claims are set before her, only the transparent seduction of the court. Her choice is not a problem, neither for herself nor for the audience. She is Chastity personified, the daughter of Grace and 'a glass for maids' (IV.iv. 157), which very few critics would claim for Isabella. Gratiana's fall on the other hand, introduces an element of choice and shows that different decisions are possible. Castiza's own pretence in IV.iv, like that of Isabella in the last act of *Measure for Measure*, presents the alternative choice as reality on the stage, even though it is only an act put on for a certain purpose. In Isabella's case, we know that she is lying, yet it is a very significant moment when she claims to have come to the same decision as Whetstone's Cassandra:

> the vile conclusion
> I now begin with grief and shame to utter:
> He would not, but by gift of my chaste body
> To his concupiscible intemperate lust,

Dieter Mehl

> Release my brother; and, after much debatement,
> My sisterly remorse confutes mine honour,
> And I did yield to him.   (V.i. 95–101)

Castiza's feigned compliance serves a similar purpose as moral trial and it is in a way more effective because the audience does not know for certain that her 'fall' is only a piece of didactic play-acting: 'I did but this to try you' (IV.iv. 148). Chastity and Grace are triumphantly vindicated.

Chastity and Honour are, in both plays, very closely related. For Isabella, her virginity is practically identical with her honour and that of Claudio, and Lussurioso makes a similar point, even though he is mocking at the idea:

> Bewitch her ears, and cozen her of all grace;
> Enter upon the portion of her soul,
> Her honour, which she calls her chastity,   (I.iii. 112–14)

Both Isabella and Castiza would prefer death to the sacrifice of their honour and it has been noticed that death is envisaged in strangely sensual if not sexual terms. Isabella and Claudio talk of death in images that suggest an erotic encounter (cf. II.iv. 100–4; III.1. 84–6) and the idea recurs, up to Lucio's comic complaint: 'Marrying a punk, my lord, is pressing to death, whipping and hanging' (V.i. 520–1).

The Revenger's Tragedy is clearly influenced by the same tradition. Antonio's wife is an explicit emblem of the choice Isabella did not have to make in earnest:

> She, her honour forc'd,
> Deem'd it a nobler dowry for her name
> To die with poison than to live with shame.   (I.iv. 45–7)[13]

The play's opening image of Gloriana's skull is another powerful statement about pure love and death. The theme of revenge itself is, in Vindice's mind, closely allied to the thought of sexual indulgence; indeed, revenge is for him, as Stilling suggests, a kind of 'sexual pleasure'[14] and chastity is the highest form of virtue; it is perhaps the only positive value acknowledged and respected by him, but, like Lucio, he can never think of chastity and holiness for long without mentioning their opposites. Even Gloriana's former beauty is remembered in a way that associates it with sinful lusting, provoked desire and irresistible temptation. Saintliness is more sexually exciting than lasciviousness. Junior Brother refers to his victim ('that religious lady', I.i. 111) as 'goddess' (I.ii. 61) and the lecherous Duke knows by experience: 'Give me that sin that's rob'd in holiness' (III.v. 141). This clearly recalls Angelo's more intensely felt moral conflict:

> Most dangerous
> Is that temptation that doth goad us on
> To sin in loving virtue. (II.ii. 181–3)

Chastity, in Shakespeare's play, is, however, presented as only one of several possible attitudes in answer to a corrupt society, not as an absolute value and certainly not without troubled questioning. Isabella's 'temptation' not only raises the fundamental problem of the relative value of chastity and charity, it also demonstrates the way in which lust and sexual licence pervert the course of justice and corrupt 'of government the properties'. Isabella's cry for 'justice, justice, justice, justice' (V.i. 25) is a powerful expression of this breakdown in public order and it is echoed in many revenge tragedies, from *The Spanish Tragedy* to Tourneur.[15] In *The Revenger's Tragedy*, it is very clear that 'the perversion of love (the most basic disorder in the individual) becomes the pervading cause of the perversion of justice (the root source of disorder in the state)'.[16] The effects of lust are the same as in Vincentio's Vienna and the desire for justice is one of the central issues in both plays.

Where Shakespeare's comedy and Tourneur's tragedy differ radically is in the solution they offer. The impact of *Measure for Measure* on *The Revenger's Tragedy* is clearly confined to certain themes and motifs; it does not extend to the play's structure or the development of plot and character, a point to which I shall return.

There is, however, another close link between the two plays in the continuous presence of the disguised manipulator. As far as *The Revenger's Tragedy* is concerned, this probably derives from Marston's *The Malcontent*, as several critics have pointed out, but *Measure for Measure* certainly belongs in the same group.[17] Its precise connection with *The Malcontent* is not clear: both plays were probably performed by the King's Men around 1604 and they both seem to have been tried on the Globe's public stage as well as in private performance, at the Court or the Blackfriars. The prominent part of the disguiser is common to all three plays and in some ways both *Measure for Measure* and *The Revenger's Tragedy* are closer to *The Malcontent* than they are to each other. And yet, in the energy of his moral commitment and his disturbing intensity Tourneur appears to have been more deeply influenced by Shakespeare than by Marston.

The chief difference lies, of course, in the disguiser's intention, or rather in his idea of himself. Both plays are variations on the Jacobean theme of the exiled discontent: Vincentio chooses to leave his court in order to give law and severity a new chance as well as to try his deputy, whereas Vindice believes in revenge as the most effective means of setting right the time out of joint. The omnipresence of the disguised observer, in consequence, has a very different effect in the two plays. Though it is generally true that 'Disguise is most often used to comfort an audience,'[18] this is not quite the case in *Measure for Measure*. The impression of surprising discoveries, unexpected developments, of the disguiser being nearly shocked into help-less impotence is, at least in one or two scenes, as pronounced as any comforting certainty of eventual justice. We know, of course, that all the time, the Duke, 'like power divine', observes his failing subjects, but – and recent productions often emphasise this – he does not always seem to be in complete control of the events and he is genuinely unsettled by what he sees. Besides, he has evidently been rather ineffectual for the last nineteen years and there is, for the spectator, no guarantee that he will change the state of Viennese society at one stroke.[19]

Vindice, who has waited for nine years, is in a somewhat similar position although, of course, he has no public responsibility and none of Vincentio's desire for self-knowledge, only a very strong sense of right and wrong and of his duty to do something about the evil around him. Naturally, the audience will react very differently to this kind of disguiser though I would not agree that 'Such disguises are used to unsettle the spectators, to bring them to the fearful, dislocated emotional state which tragedy demands'.[20] Vindice lays open the corruption of the court and his presence serves, to some extent at least, to reassure the audience that the villains will meet their deserved punishment. We, the spectators, know that we are not the only ones who recognise and are morally shocked by the perversions of the Duke's family. If Vindice 'sounds an increasingly urgent note of doom every time he appears',[21] he does this in the context of a society that richly deserves its doom and there is a similar element of providential watchfulness in both plays. No sinner escapes his judgement and in this sense the ending of *The Revenger's Tragedy* is as poetically just as that of *Measure for Measure* or, indeed, *Volpone*.[22]

Where Vincentio differs fundamentally from Vindice (and Volpone) is in his attitude towards his disguise. Observing the corruption around him he neither becomes actively implicated in it nor does he fall in love with his new role. Vindice and Volpone come to be so enamoured of their play-acting that they are unable to leave off when there is still time and thus become the instruments of their own undoing. In *Measure for Measure*, disguise does not appear as 'a wickedness', but remains beneficial throughout the play. All the ingenuity in planning and intriguing is directed towards the thwarting of evil intentions. In *The Revenger's Tragedy* evil is allowed to run its course and retribution cannot, therefore, take the form of forgiveness. There is at least no doubt about the play's concept of justice, whereas critics have found the ending of *Measure for Measure* unsatisfactory precisely because 'The conflict between divine commandment and human frailty, between the high ethic of the Gospel and the necessity of punitive law, is brushed aside, not resolved'.[23] It may have been a similar kind of dissatisfaction that induced Tourneur to treat the theme of corruption in such a different way. 'Tourneur's borrowings are creative',[24] in the sense that even clear echoes and parallels are transformed into something completely different from the original. Tourneur was not attempting to rewrite any particular play by Shakespeare, but he was inspired or provoked by several of them and the new synthesis is unlike any of his models.

Measure for Measure is, technically, a comedy with a happy ending (four more or less happy couples) and it was, perhaps, only the first part of the play that really interested Tourneur, but Shakespeare has incorporated in this new version of *Promos and Cassandra* a surprising amount of tragic and satirical material and the laughter is never very far from disgust or an apprehensive uneasiness. Whatever we choose to call the play, it is not a comedy pure and simple, like *The Comedy of Errors* or *Much Ado About Nothing*. Nor is *The Revenger's Tragedy* a tragedy in the unmistakable sense of *The Spanish Tragedy* or *Hamlet*. It has been called a farce or melodrama and it flaunts the name of tragedy in a way that seems to put it in quotation marks: 'When the bad bleeds, then is the tragedy good' (III.v. 205) and 'No power is angry when the lustful die; / When thunder claps, heaven likes the tragedy' (V.iii. 46–7). It is, however, worth emphasising the 'ironically comic energies of the text'[25] which might well be brought out with more force and clarity in a lively production. Of course, the play could not be turned into a simple comedy, without distorting its thematic drive and moral earnestness, but it has not always been sufficiently noted how many comic devices Tourneur employs and how self-consciously many tragic conventions are used.

Yet the difference in the mood of the two plays is obvious. Some of the worst criticism of society is placed by Shakespeare in a context that takes some of the venom out of the attack. An instance is Vincentio's devastating verdict:

> My business in this state
> Made me a looker-on here in Vienna,
> Where I have seen corruption boil and bubble
> Till it o'errun the stew: laws for all faults,
> But faults so countenanc'd that the strong statutes
> Stand like the forfeits in a barber's shop,
> As much in mock as mark. (V.i. 314–20)

Vindice's diagnosis could not be worse; but we know that this is the Duke speaking who 'like power divine' has not only witnessed all this corruption, but has already prevented some of its worst consequences and will soon reveal himself as the comic *deus ex machina*. In *The Revenger's Tragedy*, the disguised moralist is as deeply implicated in the general corruption as any of the villains and nobody sees to it that bad intents are not overtaken by acts as in Shakespeare's comedy, where the intent was hardly less bad than anything in Tourneur's play.

The Revenger's Tragedy carries the self-destructive 'justice' of the traditional revenge morality to its extreme limit while *Measure for Measure* explores very different ways of establishing justice. The titles of the two plays point to the almost opposite approaches pursued by them: the word 'revenge' does not occur in *Measure for Measure* at all. There are proper institutions for the administering of justice though there are moments in the play when lawlessness seems to reign supreme, as in Isabella's cry: 'To whom should I complain?' (II.iv. 171), or some of the Duke's own experiences. But *Measure for Measure* is concerned less with retribution and with private grudges than with the nature of government and the enforcing of general justice. Law and justice are understood as forms of protection and education rather than instruments of retaliation and chastisement. Throughout the play, there is in the person of the Duke, of Escalus, and even in the incompetent officer Elbow a clear standard of what is just and right. Like Dogberry, though with less of Dogberry's luck, Elbow knows a villain and a bawd when he sees them and his sense of what makes an ordered commonwealth is as sure as the Duke's, if we may discount his malapropisms. The comic trial of Pompey is not just a demonstration of lawless chaos; there is a prevailing impression of a well-meaning authority, even though the varlets are told to continue and Escalus may well wonder 'Which is the wiser here, Justice or Iniquity?' (II.i. 163).

In *The Revenger's Tragedy*, the revenger feels that he is the lone individual to whom justice has been denied and who therefore tries to be judge and executioner in one person. The ruler is as corrupt as the rest of society, but the revenger who, for large stretches of the play, is our only standard of justice, falls under his own verdict. When Vindice, near the end of the play, draws Antonio's attention to the neat working out of justice, 'death on death' (V.iii. 91), he indirectly passes sentence on himself. He never afterwards sues for grace; all his actions were based on the principle of 'measure for measure' and he is more interested in the ingenuity of his revenge than in repentance. The whole play delights in grotesque forms of 'measure for measure', especially in the emblematic murder of the Duke, an ingeniously literal application of 'poison for poison'. The 'quaintness' of Vindice's stratagems (III.v. 109), applauded by his brother, consists chiefly in their fittingness, in their clever adaptations of 'Like doth quit like' (*MM*, V.i. 409).

In *Measure for Measure*, this law of 'Like doth quit like' is overruled by Isabella's discovery of mercy, and by comic reconciliation and beneficent counterstratagem, 'craft against vice' (III.ii. 259); corruption is reduced to amusing harmlessness. Under the firm rule of Vincentio and Isabella, Vienna may yet become a more orderly community although, to many readers and audiences, the conventional neatness of the ending does not carry the same conviction as the disillusioned analysis of society earlier in the play. The final prospects in *The Revenger's Tragedy* are even less reassuring. Old Antonio who, to his great surprise, finds himself in charge, has not, so far, actively promoted justice; he has kept aloof from intrigue and has let others do the dirty work of retribution. There is no clear indication in the text that he is against revenge in principle as long as others taint themselves. The most explicit prophesy comes, characteristically, from Vindice:

> Your hair will make the silver age again,
> When there was fewer but more honest men.   (V.iii. 86–7)

It is a feeble hope, not supported by the rest of the play.

Critics have commented on the general shift from the tragedy of individuals to a more societal perspective during the first years of the Jacobean era.[26] Shakespeare's tragedies seem only marginally affected by this; his most devastating comments on society as a whole (after *Hamlet*, which is at the same time very much the tragedy of an individual) occur in *Troilus and Cressida*, *Measure for Measure* and *Timon of Athens*, all plays that seem to experiment with traditional patterns and conventions of genre and to explore different relationships between the protagonists and society. *Measure for Measure* begins in some ways as uncompromisingly and bitterly as *Troilus* and *Timon*, but suddenly abandons its near-tragic intensity in favour of a comic solution. In *The Revenger's Tragedy*, too, the emphasis is on the corruption in society rather than on the tragic dilemma of the individual. As spokesman of an individual consciousness, Vindice is not particularly moving and does not much appeal to our sympathy. His sensitive awareness of injustice does not seem to cause any deep personal pain, as it does in Hamlet's case. Tragedy in the Bradleyan or indeed Shakespearean sense is no longer possible when drama ceases to be concerned with the existential dilemma of a single human being, with the agony of moral choice. Shakespeare always encourages 'moral involvement with the character'[27], not only in tragedy, but also in comedy of the kind of *Measure for Measure*. There is a far more disturbing tragic dilemma in the 'total psychic impasse' of Isabella, Angelo and Claudio[28] than in any of the 'tragic' tantrums of Vindice although 'tragedy' seems to be constantly on the actors' lips. It is, however, tragedy in the vulgar sense of dead bodies, 'tragic bodies', as the villains' corpses are theatrically called in the last lines of the play, or 'A piteous tragedy', Antonio's description of the wholesale slaughter (V.iii. 60). There is no sense of tragic waste, rather an indiscriminate triumph of poetic justice. The audience is presumably meant to agree with Antonio's 'Just is the law above!' (V.iii. 91) and Antonio himself may indeed feel, as Ambitioso did a minute earlier, 'Here's a labour saved' (V.iii. 51). There is no 'great ruin', as in *The Duchess of Malfi*: none have died except corrupt criminals and villains. (The death of Antonio's wife is only reported; we have never seen her alive, just as we have not seen Gloriana, or Ragozine). It is, on the other hand, significant that Castiza and Gratiana are absent from the holocaust of the last act. Unlike Isabella, they are not able to influence society and the administering of justice. They remain isolated and, in the last resort, ineffectual instances of constant virtue, like Antonio's wife and

Gloriana. There is no explicit hint to the effect that their example will in any
way influence Antonio's government.

With two plays as different from each other as *Measure for Measure* and
The Revenger's Tragedy, a comparison can only point to certain common
preoccupations of both authors and, due to apparently very different tem-
pers, to divergent ways of dramatising fundamental conflicts in society. The
plays have to be understood as responses to a particular theatrical, political
and moral *milieu*. They show a very similar concern with the disruption of
society, the poisoning effects of lust and the collapse of punitive justice. *The
Revenger's Tragedy* might well have been entitled *Measure for Measure*, in
which case the title would have repeated and endorsed the play's message,
whereas Shakespeare qualifies and partly refutes the title by the comic
solution, although in its analysis of society and corrupt authority, *Measure
for Measure* seems to me closer to *The Revenger's Tragedy* than any other
play by Shakespeare, except perhaps *Timon of Athens*. The comic solution,
however, takes the sting out of the satire and turns even corruption into 'a
physic / That's bitter to sweet end' (IV.v. 7–8).

Readers and spectators will, finally, differ as to which is the more optimistic play. Is 'speedy execution' or 'apt remission' the more efficient physic
for the perversions of a decadent society? Neither of the two plays provides a
confident answer, both are, in a way, utopian phantasies, provocative games
that cannot be literally applied to the reality they respond to. They both have
been described by some critics as gloomy, cynical and disillusioned, by
others as funny or as informed by a simple, orthodox faith. They definitely
belong to the same period and express some of its most disturbing concerns.

NOTES

1 See the excellent edition by R. A. Foakes, The Revels Plays (London, 1966), pp.
   lxviii–lxix. All quotations are from this edition.
2 See, for instance, David L. Frost, *The School of Shakespeare* (Cambridge, 1968),
   pp. 36–47 and 188–90; R. A. Foakes, 'The art of cruelty: Hamlet and Vindice',
   ShS, 26 (1973), 21–31; Richard T. Brucher, 'Fantasies of violence: *Hamlet* and
   The Revenger's Tragedy', *Studies in English Literature 1500–1900*, 21 (1981),
   257–70.
3 For *Measure for Measure*, see the editions by J. W. Lever, The Arden Shakespeare
   (London, 1965) and by Mark Eccles, A New Variorum Edition of Shakespeare
   (New York, 1980), also Alice Walker, 'The text of *Measure for Measure*', *RES*,
   NS 34 (1983), 1–20, esp. pp. 19–20.
      It is not really relevant to my purpose who wrote *The Revenger's Tragedy*
   although I may as well state my conviction, shared by the majority of the most
   sensitive critics of the play, that in spirit and dramatic technique, it is closer to *The
   Atheist's Tragedy* than to any other play of the period, certainly any play by
   Middleton. It is for this reason (and for the sake of convenience) that I shall refer
   to the author as Tourneur.
4 See Una Ellis-Fermor, *The Jacobean Drama*, repr. 1965 (London, 1965), p. 263
   and 259. Her book, though many would disagree with some of her

interpretations, is by no means as out of date as some other books on the subject written very much later.

5 See Rosalind Miles, *The Problem of Measure for Measure. A Historical Investigation* (London, 1976), *passim*. There are some fine observations, more on the problems of Shakespeare's play than on Miles's book in the review by Philip Brockbank, *TLS*, 26 November 1976.

6 See E. A. J. Honigmann, *Shakespeare's Impact on His Contemporaries* (London, 1982), p. 31, with particular reference to *Hamlet* and *The Revenger's Tragedy*.

7 This may be an echo of Gloucester's reminiscence (with reference to Edmund): 'there was good sport at his making' (*King Lear*, I.i. 20). The bastard Spurio has been linked with Edmund by several critics.

8 See Leo Salingar's influential essay '*The Revenger's Tragedy* and the morality tradition', *Scrutiny*, 6 (1937–8), 402–22.

9 See Peter B. Murray, *A Study of Cyril Tourneur* (Philadelphia, 1964), p. 247.

10 Ernest Schanzer, *The Problem Plays of Shakespeare* (London, 1963), p. 100.

11 Irving Ribner, *Jacobean Tragedy: The Quest for Moral Order* (London, 1962), p. 83. Castabella is linked with Isabella by Una Ellis-Fermor who remarks pertinently: 'even the inhumanity of her chastity, which has not escaped Tourneur's notice, is akin to Isabella's' (Ellis-Fermor, p. 165). There are other clear echoes of *Measure for Measure* in *The Atheist's Tragedy*; one obvious case is pointed out in Irving Ribner's edition, The Revels Plays (London, 1964), pp. 70–1.

12 Foakes's edition, p. xxxi.

13 The Latin tag, '*Melius virtute mori, quam per dedecus vivere*' emphasises that this is, of course, a classic dilemma, the situation of Lucrece and of Virginia; Tourneur did not need Shakespeare for this idea, but the whole context suggests that the two characters are related.

14 See Roger Stilling, *Love and Death in Renaissance Tragedy* (Baton Rouge, La. 1976), p. 212.

15 See, for instance, G. K. Hunter, 'Ironies of justice in *The Spanish Tragedy*', *Renaissance Drama*, 8 (1965), 89–104, and in *Dramatic Identities and Cultural Tradition* (Liverpool, 1978), pp. 214–29.

16 Charles A. Hallett and Elaine S. Hallett, *The Revenger's Madness: A Study of Revenge Tragedy Motifs* (Lincoln, Nebr., 1980), p. 228.

17 See Ribner, *Jacobean Tragedy*, p. 13, and Miles, *The Problem of Measure for Measure*, pp. 125–60.

18 Miles, *The Problem of Measure for Measure*, p. 131.

19 Adrian Noble's Stratford production of 1983 made it fairly clear that this duke was deeply worried about his subjects and by no means cheerfully confident of success. This made excellent sense of the play and seemed to remove some of its traditional difficulties very convincingly.

20 Miles, *The Problem of Measure for Measure*, pp. 130–1.

21 *Ibid.*, p. 130.

22 *Volpone* is another play that is closely related to *The Revenger's Tragedy*, as several critics have pointed out. It was performed by the King's Men at the Globe, probably in 1606. The similarities between the two plays support the impression that the difference between comedy and tragedy need not be all important and appears to have narrowed considerably by 1605, mainly, perhaps, due to the increasing element of satire and invective in both genres.

23 See Robert Ornstein, *The Moral Vision of Jacobean Tragedy* (Madison, 1965), p. 258.

24 Ibid., p. 124.
25 Stanley Wells, 'The Revenger's Tragedy revived', The Elizabethan Theatre, VI (1978), 105–33; the quotation comes from p. 128. On the comic elements see also: Nicholas Brooke, Horrid Laughter in Jacobean Tragedy (London, 1979), pp. 10–27, and Jonathan Dollimore, Radical Tragedy: Religion, Ideology and Power in the Drama of Shakespeare and his Contemporaries (Brighton, 1984), pp. 139–50 ('The Revenger's Tragedy (c. 1606): providence, parody and black camp'). T. B. Tomlinson comments, 'In the last analysis, few I think would want to call this play a tragedy'; see A Study of Elizabethan and Jacobean Tragedy (Cambridge, 1964), p. 126.
26 See Larry S. Champion, 'Tourneur's The Revenger's Tragedy and the Jacobean tragic perspective', SP, 72 (1975), 299–321, and his Tragic Patterns in Jacobean and Caroline Drama (Knoxville, 1977), pp. 89–118 (most of the article is incorporated in this chapter).
27 Champion's article, p. 319.
28 See Lever's edition, p. lxxv; Lever also speaks of 'this terrible encounter of absolutes' (p. lxix); his introduction is still one of the best accounts of the play I have seen.

ALEXANDER LEGGATT

A double reign: *Richard II* and *Perkin Warbeck*

⟐○⟐

At the battle of Shrewsbury, which forms the climax of *Henry IV Part One*, King Henry dresses a number of followers as himself, confusing his opponents with a proliferation of imitation kings. The result is that when one 'king' is killed another appears; to the rebels it must look at first like an image of the immortality of kingship. But as the trick becomes apparent the effect is rather to devalue the office: Henry is, as it were, producing inflation by debasing the coinage. When Douglas finally confronts the real Henry Bolingbroke and declares, 'I fear thou art another counterfeit' (V.iv. 35), his words have a distinct edge. In the same battle two possible heirs to the throne confront each other, as Hal tells Hotspur,

> Two stars keep not their motion in one sphere,
> Nor can one England brook a double reign
> Of Harry Percy and the Prince of Wales. (V.iv. 65–7)

Though the lineal claim belongs to Mortimer, Henry has warned Hal that Hotspur has shown himself a true contender for the crown by his skill at raising an army (III.ii. 97–105). A kingship that can be thus imitated, fought over, or simply earned is a kingship that has lost its unique, sanctified character and become a role or an office like any other. In the preceding play, *Richard II*, Shakespeare had shown how this happened. A generation later, on the eve of a revolution in which the monarchy was not just challenged but – for the only time in England's history – abolished, John Ford was to return to the theme in *Perkin Warbeck*, a play that consciously echoes *Richard II* at several points[1] and takes its argument a stage further.

When, during the deposition scene, Richard poses himself and Bolingbroke on either side of the crown, each with a hand on it, he is deliberately calling attention to the absurdity, even the impossibility, of what is happening. The rule is, one king at a time. Yet here we are forced to contemplate two living kings on stage together, with the crown between them.[2] The brutal flippancy of Richard's 'Here, cousin, seize the crown' (IV.i. 181) emphasises that the crown is trivialised by being passed from hand to hand. Richard then repeats his invitation, suggesting that Bolingbroke himself has hesitated for a moment, nonplussed. For the rest of the

129

play Richard's position is paradoxical and so, by extension, is Boling-broke's. Richard is deposed and not deposed: he has gone through the forms, given away the crown, but he cannot cease to be king. Henry is called king, and the crown is on his head, but the reality of kingship is never quite his. We see the difficulty this produces in the recurring problem of what to call Richard after his deposition. The groom who visits him in prison says, 'I was a poor groom of thy stable, King, / When thou wert king' (V.v. 71–2). Exton, presenting the corpse to Henry in the final scene, has just enough tact to call it 'Richard of Bordeaux' (V.vi. 33), but earlier and more revealingly he has said, 'This dead king to the living king I'll bear' (V.v. 117). Richard exploits the difficulty with his ironic greeting, 'God save King Henry, unking'd Richard says' (IV.i. 220). With deliberate impudence he narrowly avoids calling himself 'King Richard'.

The fact that the kingship cannot simply be removed from one man and given to another without creating this sort of difficulty suggests that its sanctity is still a live idea. During his decoronation Richard himself stresses the full meaning of the office:

I give this heavy weight from off my head,
And this unwieldy sceptre from my hand,
The pride of kingly sway from out my heart;
With mine own tears I wash away my balm,
With mine own hands I give away my crown,
With mine own tongue deny my sacred state,
With mine own breath release all duteous oaths;
All pomp and majesty I do forswear;
My manors, rents, revenues, I forgo;
My acts, decrees, and statutes, I deny.
God pardon all oaths that are broke to me!
God keep all vows unbroke are made to thee!   (IV.i. 204–15)

What radiates outward from the sacred office, what its symbols stand for, is a whole structure of oath and obligation, property and law. The deposition is not just a change at the top but a blow struck at the centre of society. Yet the king deals the blow himself in a series of dramatically self-destructive gestures. Again we confront the paradox of the deposition: I, the King, declare I am no longer the King; and only I have the right to do this because I am the King. It is as though the Pope in his last infallible pronouncement were to declare himself fallible.[3]

The coronation ceremony is doubly violated: in being reversed, and in having this reversal conducted by the king himself. (We remember that in the coronation proper the king does not crown himself but receives his crown from a representative of the Church.) Here, as throughout the play, Richard shows his flair for the theatrical.[4] But theatre and ceremony, analogous up to a point, are fundamentally different in the last analysis. For believers at any rate, a High Mass is not just a grand show, the principles it operates on are not just aesthetic, and it requires for its full effect belief of a literal kind that the theatre never expects. The same applies to a coronation. Richard, challenging his on-stage audience to feel their own complicity, hovers between the ceremonial and the theatrical: 'God save the King! Will no man say amen? / Am I both priest and clerk? Well then, amen' (IV.i. 172–3). He initiates a ceremonial action in which he knows his hearers will not participate; this leaves them feeling that they have spoiled the ceremony themselves. But in using ceremony this way he himself has turned it into a theatrical trick to make his audience feel uncomfortable. The powerful effect he makes through the long sequence of his fall depends not just on the sacredness of his office but more obviously – and, in a way, more dangerously – on his sheer skill in upstaging everyone else. As Northrop Frye puts it, 'Bolingbroke can steal his crown but not his show'. But while Frye calls Richard's acting talent 'one of the essential characteristics of royalty',[5] theatrical skill is strictly speaking as irrelevant as political skill if kingship is regarded as a sacred office. The Lord's anointed is the Lord's anointed, and while lack of skill in politics, administration or showmanship may make him an incompetent king he is still a king. Richard is, from a theatrical point of view, masterful. From the mischievous 'To do what service am I sent for hither?' (IV.i. 176) to the commanding 'Now mark me how I will undo myself' (IV.i. 203) he keeps all attention focused on himself. If he cannot save his kingship by such means he can at least blight Bolingbroke's. But in doing it this way he is, as it were, playing in Bolingbroke's court, matching skill against skill.

In his own fashion he knows the brute realities of politics as well as Bolingbroke does:

> For every man that Bolingbroke hath press'd
> To lift shrewd steel against our golden crown,
> God for his Richard hath in heavenly pay
> A glorious angel. Then, if angels fight,
> Weak men must fall; for heaven still guards the right.
> *Enter* SALISBURY.
> Welcome, my lord. How far off lies your power?   (III.ii. 58–63)

He talks brilliantly of his sacred office but he knows the relative practical value of angels and soldiers. If the sanctity of kingship remains a live idea throughout the play it is as much in spite of Richard as because of him. It lives in some of his speeches, to be sure; but it lives also in the stubborn quietism of Gaunt, the protests of York, the apocalyptic vision of Carlisle and the humble confusion of the nameless groom. It is not Richard's property in particular, and in so far as it *is* his property he abuses it as he abuses the land of England. Strictly speaking he and Bolingbroke are not to be compared. But he is led by his aesthetic sense into comparing them, as critics have been doing ever since. He is the sun, Bolingbroke a thief in the night (III.ii. 36–53); then their positions are reversed, as Richard urges his followers to flee 'From Richard's night to Bolingbroke's fair day' (III.ii. 218). They are two buckets in a well, one up and the other down. York picks up this habit of thought, comparing the two kings to two actors, one popular and the other jeered at. In passages like these the relative fates of the two men seem arbitrary. They are equal components of the same system, complementary opposites balanced against each other. Their positions could easily be reversed. The picture Richard contrives of the two kings each with a hand on the crown suggests, I have argued, the absurdity of the deposition. But it may be more deeply subversive than that, suggesting that neither man has a claim that finally outweighs the other's. Each has a hand on the crown, neither is wearing it, and the crown itself is empty.

That is not the overall effect of the play. The dramatic attention is heavily weighted in favour of Richard[6] and so, finally, is the regal claim. But the possibility that there could be equal and opposite claims is in the air; and when we come to *Perkin Warbeck* one of the first things we notice is that this time the attention, theatrically, is evenly divided between the two claimants. Shakespeare's pattern has been reversed: the established king has the practical skill and the rebel the imagination. When York says of Richard, 'Yet looks he like a king' and laments 'That any harm should stain so fair a show' (III.iii. 68, 71) he reveals both the strength and the weakness of the claim Richard exerts theatrically (as opposed to the claim he actually has). Warbeck's claim is described by King James of Scotland in similar terms: 'He must be more than subject who can utter / The language of a king, and such is thine' (II.i. 103–4).[7] Later, more defensively perhaps, he exclaims,

> How like a king a' looks! Lords, but observe
> The confidence of his aspect! Dross cannot
> Cleave to so pure a metal. . . .   (II.iii. 73–5)

He may or may not be Richard IV, but he is good casting. The validity of his claim, and the extent of his own belief in it, are enigmatic; but even to say that shows the power of his performance: we might have expected the story of a simple impostor. If he is indeed a player king, he is one who 'fires our imaginations in response'.[8]

But the aesthetic claim cannot carry the day for him any more than it does for Richard. Richard's army melts away before battle can be joined; at Taunton it is Warbeck himself who deserts. Katherine's shocked reaction, 'Fled without battle given?' (V.i. 58) puts the matter with brutal clarity, and Dalyell's explanation that this was 'foresight' (V.i. 66), as Perkin had word he was going to be betrayed, follows lamely after it. Peter Ure chides Ford for not contriving 'a more impressive and more strategically disposed justification of his hero's behaviour'[9] but the embarrassment is surely deliberate. Foresight is one of the skills of the less romantic King Henry; we feel that in exercising it Perkin has in some way let us down. Similarly, the greatest challenge Ford presents to Warbeck is not his regal adversary but his ridiculous followers. They spoil the dignity of his first entrance, and they lumber every scene they appear in with their painfully mechanical comedy. When we compare them with Richard's ineffectual but sympathetic and dignified supporters we see the care Ford has taken to ensure that even Perkin's aesthetic appeal is compromised.

But it is not compromised, we note, by anything in Perkin's own manner. He never becomes as self-conscious or self-indulgent in his language as Richard does. Perkin is no fool, and he senses the coming desertion of both James and Frion – though like Richard he is better at seeing trouble coming than at preventing it. But his farewell to the treacherous James is remarkably gracious, particularly when compared with Richard's hysterical outburst against the mere thought, based on misunderstanding, of the treachery of Bushy, Greene and the Earl of Wiltshire (III.ii. 129–34). He treats Frion with similar courtesy, undeserved but attractive. Richard dictates the terms of his own disaster, as part of the aesthetic control he claims all through the play: 'Down, down I come, like glist'ring Phaethon' (III.iii. 178). In Ford's play it is Crawford who, in a simpler and more perfunctory line, calls Perkin 'this young Phaëthon' (II.ii. 16). The hero himself shows nothing like Richard's rage for self-destruction. For all his weaknesses he is an altogether steadier and more dignified character than Shakespeare's brilliant, infuriating king. This may be the reason why, if the play is to stay in balance, our sympathy for him needs the heavy counterweight provided by his followers and by his own behaviour in the Taunton débâcle. Richard provides his own counterweights.

Another reason is the characterisation of Henry. His managerial efficiency is beyond question, and gets less and less attractive as the play progresses. He too is a kingly actor, but one whose performance as the gentle and gracious father of his people wears thin very fast.[10] While the pretender is seen in public, courtly settings or in the open air, Henry operates from a candlelit room in the Tower.[11] The tone of his administration is set by the stage direction '*Enter* King HENRY *and* URSWICK, *whispering*' (IV.iv. 23). He invests even the promotion of a bishop with an air of cynical conspiracy:

> Should reverend Morton our Archbishop move
> To a translation higher yet, I tell thee,
> My Durham owns a brain deserves that see.
> He's nimble in his industry, and mounting:
> Thou hear'st me?
> *Urs.*   And conceive your highness fitly.   (IV.iv. 71–5)

He addresses the captured Katherine with fulsome affection until she touches on a forbidden subject:

> *Kath.*   But my husband?
> *Hen.*   By all descriptions, you are noble Dalyell . . .   (V.ii. 162–3)

Having promised his soldiers 'A largesse free amongst them, which shall hearten / And cherish up their loyalties' he adds, 'O, happy kings, / Whose thrones are raisèd in their subjects' hearts!' (III.i. 111–13, 117–18). There may be a rueful admission that if he has his subjects' loyalty he has paid good money for it.

In war and politics he is the effective king of England, and Perkin is helpless against him. But in their theatrical confrontation in V.ii Perkin upstages him as decisively as Richard upstages Bolingbroke. In the very first speech of the play Henry anticipates what will happen:

> Still to be haunted, still to be pursued,
> Still to be frighted with false apparitions
> Of pageant majesty and new-coined greatness,
> As if we were a mockery-king in state,
> Only ordained to lavish sweat and blood
> In scorn and laughter to the ghosts of York,
> Is all below our merits . . .   (I.i. 1–7)

The last line turns the speech around, but not before Henry has sounded the depths of a real fear. Against the shadow-kings who haunt him he appears to be not the real thing but another shadow. There is a distant echo of the exhausted, defensive speech with which Bolingbroke opens *Henry IV Part One*, and a clear echo of Richard's view of himself as 'a mockery king of snow' (IV.i. 260) melting in the sun of Bolingbroke.[12] Irving Ribner applies the analogy one way: 'In the tragedy of Perkin Warbeck we see the appearance of kingship melting and crumbling before the reality of kingship, just as the king of snow, Richard II, had melted before the sun of Bolingbroke.'[13] But that is not quite how Ford applies it. If we seek for 'the reality of kingship' in *Perkin Warbeck* we find ourselves chasing shadows.

The military action, and some of the political action, are offstage. Here Henry is master. But when the two men are brought together it is onstage and here Perkin, like Richard, is master. Henry goes on the attack quickly:

> We observe no wonder; I behold, 'tis true,
> An ornament of nature, fine and polished,
> A handsome youth indeed, but not admire him.   (V.ii. 37–9)

Condescension and contempt are nicely balanced, the limits of Warbeck's appeal carefully staked out. In reply Perkin reminds Henry how he himself came to be king:

> Sir, remember
> There was a shooting in of light when Richmond,
> Not aiming at a crown, retired, and gladly,
> For comfort to the duke of Bretagne's court.
> Richard, who swayed the sceptre, was reputed
> A tyrant then; yet then a dawning glimmered

To some few wand'ring remnants, promising day
When first they ventured on a frightful shore
At Milford Haven —
Dau.   Whither speeds his boldness?
Check his rude tongue, great sir!
Hen.   O, let him range:
The player's on the stage still, 'tis his part,
A' does but act. What followed?
War.   Bosworth field:
Where, at an instant, to the world's amazement,
A morn to Richmond and a night to Richard
Appeared at once. The tale is soon applied:
Fate, which crowned these attempts when least assured,
Might have befriended others like resolved.   (V.ii. 58–74)

To Henry's charge that he is just an actor, Warbeck can reply that Henry is
king only because he happened to win the battle of Bosworth. Henry's
earlier reference to 'our own royal birthright' (I.iv. 9) is misleading. The
Tudor dynastic claim was somewhat devious, and Shakespeare at the end of
Richard III tactfully avoided going into it. Ford does not go into it either;
but the glamour with which Perkin invests Richmond's victory (the images
of light recall *Richard II*) is not so much that of a saviour as that of a
successful rebel who won against the odds, as Perkin himself might have
done. The curtness of 'Bosworth field' suggests the blunt realism of which
Warbeck is occasionally capable; and the contrast of Richmond's morning
and Richard's night suggests, as in *Richard II*, a pattern that could easily
have been reversed. In the lines that follow all Henry can do is reiterate his
charge that Perkin is an actor reciting a part. The effect is that he has no real
counter-argument, and has run out of ideas; in the rest of the scene we see
him increasingly nettled. With this in mind, we listen with new attention to
the normally ridiculous John-a-Water, who, ordered to cry 'heaven save
King Henry!', will not do as he is told: 'For mine own part, I believe it is true,
if I be not deceived, that kings must be kings and subjects subjects. But which
is which – you shall pardon me for that' (V.ii. 112–16).[14]

There is no longer such a thing as an absolute claim to the English crown.
When the Epilogue tells us that the play has shown

                    all
What can to theatres of greatness fall,
Proving their weak foundations.   (3–5)

– the plural suggests that this principle applies equally to Warbeck and to
Henry. Historically, the play shows the end of a long period of confusion in
which old certainties have been lost (I.i. 16–21) just as on a smaller scale
Dalyell's pedigree has been lost through time (I.ii. 29–38). The play itself,
the Prologue tells us, is an attempt to revive a dead form (1–5). The old idea
of kingship and the old idea of the history play are gone; as Tennyson put it,

allowing reservations about the Arthurian material, 'nature brings not back the mastodon'.[15] But these admissions clear the ground for a new way of using the history play, and for a different concept of kingship; the key to both lies in the character of Katherine and her relations with Warbeck. She avoids any commitment about his claim to the English throne, and when he uses the word 'counterfeit' she asks him not to (III.ii. 171–3). But she declares, 'your right / In me is without question' (III.ii. 163–4) and later, 'You must be king of me' (III.ii. 168). When Oxford, separating them, calls Warbeck an impostor, she takes it that he is questioning his marriage, not his dynastic claim; she replies,

> You abuse us:
> For when the holy churchman joined our hands,
> Our vows were real then; the ceremony
> Was not in apparition, but in act.   (V.iii. 112–15)

We have moved from a literal kingship that seems, increasingly, a dead idea, to the sort of figurative kingship, the royalty of nature, that any person with integrity can claim.[16]

For all the talk of Perkin's fine language in the early scenes, his words really catch fire for the first time when he is alone with Katherine –

> Swift as the morning
> Must I break from the down of thy embraces
> To put on steel. . . .   (III.ii. 143–4)

– as though to signal that this is indeed the sphere in which his royalty is beyond question. And this is the royalty that comforts him as he goes to his death: 'Spite of tyranny, / We reign in our affections, blessed woman!' (V.iii. 121–2); 'Even when I fell, I stood enthroned a monarch / Of one chaste wife's troth pure and uncorrupted' (V.iii. 126–7). Figurative kingship of this kind can be bestowed widely, and not always deservedly. When Perkin tells James, 'Two empires firmly / You're lord of – Scotland and duke Richard's heart' (IV.iii. 92–3) we may consider that this reflects his courtesy more than James's merit. We will certainly be uneasy when Perkin addresses his loutish followers, in his final moments, as 'peers of England' (V.iii. 186). But there are no reservations about his words to Huntly, 'A crown of peace renew thy age, / Most honourable Huntly' (V.iii. 175–6). And Perkin's own courage earns him the figurative kingship he claims at the very end. Building on a hint from Surrey, who has come with the order for execution – 'Prepare your journey / To a new kingdom, then' (V.iii. 156–7) – Perkin declares, 'So illustrious mention / Shall blaze our names, and style us Kings o'er Death' (V.iii. 206–7). The fact that he includes his followers, those unlikely 'peers of England', in his final vision keeps the effect from being simple, reminding us of an element of make-believe in this figurative kingship. But Perkin's courage, dignity and courtesy have earned him the right to claim this crown for himself, and the plural suggests it is a crown any man can claim.

Perkin Warbeck is a post-Jacobean play, moving from the solipsism of Flamineo's 'at myself I will begin and end' to a redefinition of that self using an image of dignity that may have lost its reality in society but retains the power of metaphor. It may no longer be possible to be unquestioned king of England, but it is possible to be king in one's own mind. As Anne Barton points out, Ford may have taken the hint from the figurative kingship Richard II intermittently claims: 'You may my glories and my state depose, / But not my griefs; still am I king of those' (IV.i. 192–3).[17] But figurative kingship never has the power for Richard that it has for Perkin and Katherine. For one thing, the private sphere is less fully developed in Shakespeare. Richard and his Queen have virtually no onstage relationship until their last scene together (V.i), and that is mostly a somewhat artificial exercise in pathos. Instead of looking inward to private lives, Shakespeare looks outward to the fate of England, a matter in which Ford has virtually no interest. More important, Richard is so committed to the literal kingship he is losing, and so dependent on it for his identity, that when it goes he feels he has nothing left:

> I have no name, no title –
> No, not that name was given me at the font –
> But 'tis usurp'd. Alack the heavy day,
> That I have worn so many winters out,
> And know not now what name to call myself! (IV.i. 255–9)

When he smashes the mirror the gesture is, among other things, a symbol of the breaking of his identity. As long as he has an audience, he can play on their pity and outrage 'For the deposing of a rightful king' (V.i. 50). But he cannot, like Warbeck, claim a new kind of kingship; and in his last scene, as he explores 'the nothingness of his existence',[18] he imagines himself alternately kinged and unkinged but for all his restlessness he never tries to make the word 'king' mean something new.

When Perkin addresses his followers as 'peers of England' we are aware of the irony but it is not certain he himself intends it. There is no question about the equivalent moment in *Richard II*:

> Groom.   Hail, royal Prince!
> K. Richard.   Thanks, noble peer!
> The cheapest of us is ten groats too dear. (V.v. 67–8)

We are all made of the same dust. When Perkin makes such an admission it is with serious reservations: 'Princes are but men / Distinguished by the fineness of their frailty' (IV.v. 59–60). Some grains of dust are more precious than others. And as he develops the idea the admission of a king's mortality starts to fade: 'Herein stands the odds: / Subjects are men on earth, kings men and gods' (IV.v. 63–4). Richard's end is also quite different from

Alexander Leggatt

Warbeck's:

> Exton, thy fierce hand
> Hath with the King's blood stain'd the King's own land.
> Mount, mount, my soul! thy seat is up on high;
> Whilst my gross flesh sinks downward, here to die. (V.v. 109–12)

The kingship he claims is literal. His death is like any man's, a parting of soul and body; he claims no kingship over that. He even addresses his triumphant soul as though it were something other than himself. Earlier he had recognised that, if anything, death was king over him rather than the other way round. Arguably the one moment when figurative kingship (as opposed to the literal kingship of England) has real power in this play is Richard's recognition that

> within the hollow crown
> That rounds the mortal temples of a king
> Keeps Death his court. . . . (III.ii. 160–2)[19]

Death has no such royalty over Perkin, and the moment of parting (which in this case we do not see) is not the wrenching climax it is for Richard:

> Death? pish, 'tis but a sound, a name of air,
> A minute's storm, or not so much; to tumble
> From bed to bed, be massacred alive
> By some physicians for a month or two,
> In hope of freedom from a fever's torments,
> Might stagger manhood; here, the pain is passed
> Ere sensibly 'tis felt. (V.iii. 199–205)

Richard II recognises both the sanctity of kingship and the final authority of death. *Perkin Warbeck* removes the power of both ideas to concentrate on the will and imagination of the individual. If that suggests a contraction of vision, there is some compensation in the freeing of the idea of kingship for other uses. *Richard II* finally implies that a double reign is impossible: kingship is unique; there cannot be two kings at once. *Perkin Warbeck* asserts that there can, since the word 'king' no longer has a single meaning. It is a view that can easily lapse into fantasy and cliché, and readers unsympathetic to Ford will find both in *Perkin Warbeck*. For some of us the experiment works, if only just, and part of the excitement lies in the risk. But it has to be admitted that no one made the English history play work quite this way again, and that Ford's revival of it proved to be not a new spring but an Indian summer. In the end, the form did not lend itself naturally to a drama centred on private integrity. But if *Perkin Warbeck* is a fascinating oddity among English history plays, it takes its place with other works of seventeenth-century literature that turn inward – of which the most conspicuous is *Paradise Lost*, where an old form is also adopted to a new use as the battles that count are the battles of the mind and the true paradise is the paradise within.

NOTES

1 The similarity most commonly noticed is the characterisation of the two central figures as complementary opposites, one imaginative and the other pragmatic. See, for example, Jonas A. Barish, '*Perkin Warbeck* as anti-history', *Essays in Criticism*, 20 (1970), 168. Richard's return from Ireland and Warbeck's landing in Cornwall are compared by Donald K. Anderson, Jr, '*Richard II* and *Perkin Warbeck*', *Shakespeare Quarterly*, 13 (1962), 260–3.

2 The scene in which Hal takes the crown from his still living father may be, among other things, an echo of this moment.

3 We may also think of the Cretan liar paradox: 'All Cretans are liars; I am a Cretan'.

4 Criticism has frequently called attention to this aspect of his character: see, for example, Georges A. Bonnard, 'The actor in *Richard II*', *Shakespeare Jahrbuch*, 87 (1951), 87–101.

5 *Fools of Time* (Toronto, 1967), p. 36.

6 Bonnard, p. 90, speculates that this happened during the writing of the play and was contrary to Shakespeare's original intention.

7 All references to *Perkin Warbeck* are to the Revels edition, ed. Peter Ure (London, 1968).

8 Barish, p. 167. See also Ronald Huebert, *John Ford: Baroque English Dramatist* (Montreal and London, 1977), p. 71.

9 Revels introduction, p. lxxv.

10 See Anne Barton, 'He that plays the king: Ford's *Perkin Warbeck* and the Stuart history play', *English Drama: Forms and Development (Essays in Honour of Muriel Clara Bradbrook)*, ed. Marie Axton and Raymond Williams (Cambridge, 1977), p. 85.

11 See Ure, p. lvii.

12 See the commentary on this passage in the Revels edition.

13 *The English History Play in the Age of Shakespeare* (second edition, revised, London, 1965), p. 303.

14 See Barton, p. 86.

15 'The epic', 36.

16 See Barish, p. 160; and Dorothy M. Farr, *John Ford and the Caroline Theatre* (London, 1979), p. 117. The idea is hardly a novel one, as witness Sir Edward Dyer's 'My mind to me a kingdom is' and countless other examples, but *Perkin Warbeck* is unusual for the power and consistency with which the idea is developed.

17 Barton, p. 82.

18 Robert Ornstein, *A Kingdom for a Stage* (Cambridge, Mass., 1972), p. 121.

19 The final image of John Barton's 1973 Royal Shakespeare Company production was of the figure of Death, robed and crowned. See Stanley Wells, *Royal Shakespeare: Four Major Productions at Stratford-upon-Avon* (Manchester, 1977), p. 80.

INDEX